America's Culture Wars And Its Idiotic Clichés

36 Destructive Clichés that Undermine our Culture, Values, and Security

By
Charles A. Pulsipher

Providential Publishing

ISBN 978-0-9817042-3-4

Printed in the U.S.A.

Dedicated to a:
Mission President,
professor,
intellectual and spiritual inspiration,
mentor,
and selfless friend;

Russell N. Horiuchi

Table of Contents

Section 3 - Culture

Section 4 - Personal Responsibility

Introduction

This book was principally motivated by frustration; I got tired of yelling at television, radio, newspaper, and magazines. Frankly, they were not responsive to my rants (yes, I know; I'm a little psycho about this). As I grew up and became politically and culturally conscious, I started venting while watching or listening to programming that I recognized as irrational and dangerous. For the most part, this was a common occurrence when catching up on the news, but it also would occur during entertainment programming as well. I was frustrated not only because of the mindless unthinking drivel that was being passed off as commonly accepted truth, but because even those who had the opportunity and intent to set the record straight often did not seem to know how.

My frustration led me to make my arguments here, which are responses to ideas that have been repeated so often that many, if not most, accept them as fact. Most of these clichés are not just idiotic, but also deceptive and dangerous. Now, many of them are being used in a cultural offensive against traditional values. If we continue to think like this, our culture and nation will suffer. Under a worse case scenario, enemies that desire to destroy our liberty and society could overcome us.

The United States of America was founded on July 4, 1776 with the Declaration of Independence. This document asserted that the Creator had endowed all men with certain inalienable rights, that governments existed by the consent of those governed, and that those governed had the right to replace any government that denied its citizens the rights they had been granted by God. For the signers of that Declaration, the most basic rights were life, liberty, and the pursuit of happiness. These have become the core values of our culture. Anything that undermines these values is a threat to our culture. Unfortunately, many of the our most common sayings have this effect. I have tried to emphasize the preservation of these values in the essays that follow.

I will admit that some of the clichés are not idiotic, although the net effect is that while honest and thoughtful people may disagree, I still believe the net effect of perpetuating the cliché to be destructive to our culture. I will also admit that I have written a chapter that I have mixed emotions about; it took me some time to convince myself to keep it in the book. However, in the end, even though the performance of Congress is much less than adequate, I still believe that the cliché "Do nothing Congress" has a corrosive effect on confidence in government. To those who argue that the Congress could dispel this perception by acting responsibly, I have no rebuttal.

I have tried to use logic and reason to draw conclusions rather than emotion (by the way, I thought the antipathy that Dr. McCoy had for Spock on Star Trek because he was logical was obsessively irrational, so you know my attitude about logic). I describe the result as I understand it; readers may choose to agree or disagree. I go where logic takes me. This reasoning seems sound to me and at a minimum it is internally consistent; I have never heard anyone successfully refute the logic contained in these commentaries. I recognize that the logic I use is a product of my cultural conditioning; however, I am unaware of any other acceptable mechanism to critically evaluate ideas. If someone has a valid argument which could undermine any of these theses, I would be interested in hearing about it.

I have used examples throughout the work that are extreme. This is deliberate; I have tried to make a special point of emphasizing where illogical arguments can lead when taken to the extreme. Mushy logic that does not consider all the ramifications of its results needs to be exposed to show its potential effect. By the way, to say that some of these results could never occur is not true; indeed most of these extreme examples are pulled from current events or history.

I have a Bachelor of Science degree in geography, which is a holistic science, so I know a little about a lot. Geography includes almost every other academic discipline, especially the physical sciences, because almost all events occur in space and geography concerns spatial relationships. While this background does not provide specialized competency in one specific field, it is useful in integrating knowledge between various fields. I do not have an advanced degree.

I say this to let you know that, while I have assembled a large number of essays on topics that I care and feel very strongly about, I am by no means an expert on any one particular subject. What I do bring to a discussion is basic competency in a variety of subjects which can be integrated to form a consistent whole. I like to think I am informed; indeed my government requires me to be aware of my obligations under the law. In addition to my educational background, I strive to keep up with current events. It is possible that I know just enough about most topics to be dangerous; I am sure many will argue this to be true after reading this book.

Many of the topics I address can be or have been the subject of volumes in their own right. My purpose is to get right to the point and make my specific argument as succinctly as possible. To do that, I present information that the reader can easily verify with basic research. I have deliberately not documented most of the information presented; if I did the book would have become hopelessly unwieldy. The internet has revolutionized information management, and anyone with a computer can research these topics with ease. Those who wish to corroborate the information I present need only to type a few words into a search engine and they will be rewarded.

In many of the chapters, I have been somewhat uncivil in my tone. I apologize, especially because one of my pet peeves is the lack of civility in public discourse; however, I felt it necessary to use this approach to communicate the depth of my concern about these critical ideas. I also seek to challenge and shock the reader into using his or her head for something besides a hat rack. Too much mushy thinking passes for intellect. I realize that many will react adversely, but I would encourage those offended by the tone to look beyond it to the rationale behind the argument, and honestly examine whether these ideas are well reasoned or not.

Some may need to occasionally refer to a dictionary to understand what I am saying. I have deliberately avoided dumbing down my vocabulary for three reasons. First, I am trying to communicate precise ideas and those ideas are best communicated by precise language. Second, I would make the book substantially longer by trying to communicate complex topics using four letter words. Last, I am philosophically opposed to using the language of a third grade elementary student to reward those who refuse to improve their verbal skills; as a society we should be encouraging people to improve their ability to communicate rather than assuming that the decline in language skills is irreversible.

I have tried to arrange the chapters in as logical a sequence as I can; however, given the range of topics and the interrelationship between many of them that is difficult. However, each chapter is independent of the others and when read separately the points related to the subject will either be covered or referenced in a different chapter. As a result, you will read the same argument in more than one chapter. While this is a bit redundant, it is better than leaving the argument unaddressed in the immediate chapter and require the reader to read another chapter to get that point. The book need not be read consecutively. The reader should look at the topics and pick the subjects of most interest to him or her.

Introduction

For organizational purposes I have separated chapters into four sections, one each dealing with political, religious, cultural, and personal responsibility issues. These categories are arbitrary; it is difficult to separate the issues by subject matter, again because most of them are hopelessly interrelated. That is the nature of knowledge, we have such a mass of it that we must organize it to make sense, but by doing so we tend to compartmentalize information and then think that it exists independent of other interrelated facts.

With respect to religion, I have used one particular source critical of religion and God, which you will find cited throughout the book. In 2006 Mr. Richard Dawkins[1] wrote a book entitled The God Delusion. Plausible though his arguments are, I believe they are fatally flawed and I rebut them throughout the book as the occasion arises.

I can pretty much guarantee that everyone reading this book is going to disagree with some of the arguments I make. Even though I am generally conservative, I have my own distinctive philosophy which will differ to some degree with the philosophy of everyone else. I would hope that when the reader comes across something they deem objectionable that they look beyond the specific and consider the big picture and how the logic of the argument works. Of course, I am always willing to listen to constructive criticism.

Some will say "who asked you?" or "who cares?" Of course, the answer is nobody asked me. So what? I am putting my two cents worth into the public debate anyway. Those who do not want to hear my opinion can put the book down (or burn it for that matter). As to "who cares", I am confident that there are many. To those who care enough to read on, if nothing else I hope you are intellectually stimulated. And for those who must deal with the irrationality of these clichés, I hope that you will be better armed to refute them as the occasion arises.

---

[1] The God Delusion, Richard Dawkins, Houghton Mifflin Company, A Mariner Book, 2006,

Section 1

Political

Chapter 1

"You Can't Legislate Morality"

I wish I had a nickel for every time I have heard the term "you can't legislate morality". It has been repeated so often that it has become a widely accepted axiom. No one, even those who decry the coarsening of our culture, seems to disagree. Well, you can put me down in the "no" column on this one. This one single cliché is perhaps one of the most destructive to our culture, and is being used in an attempt to transform moral values.

At this point it is important to define terms. This should minimize miscommunication and misunderstanding. "Moral" is defined at Dictionary.com as

–adjective

1. of, pertaining to, or concerned with the principles or rules of right conduct or the distinction between right and wrong; ethical: moral attitudes.

2. expressing or conveying truths or counsel as to right conduct, as a speaker or a literary work; moralizing: a moral novel.

3. founded on the fundamental principles of right conduct rather than on legalities, enactment, or custom: moral obligations.

4. capable of conforming to the rules of right conduct: a moral being.

5. conforming to the rules of right conduct (opposed to IMMORAL): a moral man.

6. virtuous in sexual matters; chaste.

7. of, pertaining to, or acting on the mind, feelings, will, or character: moral support.

8. resting upon convincing grounds of probability; virtual: a moral certainty.

–noun

9. the moral teaching or practical lesson contained in a fable, tale, experience, etc.

10. the embodiment or type of something.

11. morals, principles or habits with respect to right or wrong conduct.[2]

and "Morality" is defined as

1. conformity to the rules of right conduct; moral or virtuous conduct.

2. moral quality or character.

3. virtue in sexual matters; chastity.

4. a doctrine or system of morals.

5. moral instruction; a moral lesson, precept, discourse, or utterance.[3]

A clear pattern emerges from these definitions. Morals are defined by what is right and wrong. Someone who is moral will make right choices and someone who is immoral will make wrong choices. Of course, we all are moral and immoral to one extent or the other; no one always makes all right or wrong choices. This concept is not limited to what is right or wrong from a sexual standpoint; it applies to all of life's activities.

However, what is right and wrong? Here, we have a simple choice to make. We can say there is no such thing as right or wrong, only individual choices made by people living according to their individual concept of morality, which may or may not be immoral or illegal from a historical or legal standpoint. Alternatively, we can say there is right and wrong, either because we 1) believe in or assume the existence of God who has established moral standards of behavior, 2) think that right and wrong are principles that are universally accepted and understood by humans, or 3) believe that society has the authority to determine and enforce what is right and wrong.

If someone concludes there is no such thing as right or wrong, he/she has essentially said there is no such thing as morality. In this case, the statement "you can't legislate morality" seems to be true for that person, or at least he or she perceives it to be. If there is no right or wrong, there is no

---

[2] *Dictionary.com Unabridged (v 1.1)*. Random House, Inc. 16 May. 2007.
<Dictionary.com http://dictionary.reference.com>.
[3] Ibid.

basis upon which to judge a decision as right or wrong, so all decisions are equally acceptable regardless of their impact on others.

We saw this reflected to a minor degree in the "I'm okay, you're okay" attitude of the seventies, but it has become increasingly prevalent at least partially because of the widespread notion that we should not judge others (see Chapter 35). This conclusion ignores the impact that individual decisions have on others, including on society as a whole, and regardless of whether an individual believes that a destructive decision is not wrong, it does not negate the effect of the decision. More important, it is irrelevant, because whether we like it or not society will not accept behavior that the majority has deemed to be immoral, and will take punitive action to ensure such behavior is discouraged (see below). Those who believe in God will also say that it is irrelevant from an eternal perspective because God will judge those whose behavior is inconsistent with prescribed behavior.

For one who believes in God, it is impossible to escape the conclusion that there is right and wrong. By definition, if there is a God there is truth, which also means that human actions can be measured against that truth. Of course, this still leaves us wondering what is true, and therefore, what is right or wrong, and accordingly what is moral. However, I am getting ahead of myself. There is much more on that subject in Chapter 16. The important thing to understand at this point is that all the decisions we make are made in a moral environment, and those decisions can be judged against what truth we know. Indeed, if truth exists and we know what that truth is, the decisions we make must be measured against what we know to be true.

There are some who believe that what is right and wrong originates from sublime concepts that underlie all human activity and culture, which results in a universal system of belief, or at least will if humans are left to themselves to come to the realization of what is right and wrong. They point to beliefs that are commonly held throughout the world today as evidence, citing principles of love, respect for life, and tolerance for others. This is, as abundantly demonstrated by reality, ridiculous. The reason we have common values is because of the predominance of Judeo-Christian beliefs which have been disseminated and accepted throughout the world, especially in western culture. Other cultures and religions have been affected by the steady influence of this branch of religious thought over the centuries to a point where there is much universally held belief in what is right and wrong. However, history, anthropology, and current events teach us that there is no such thing as a universally accepted belief system of right and wrong. Slavery persists to this day. Tolerance for the beliefs of others

15

is expressly prohibited in some cultures and countries to the point that the execution of non-believers is justified. Margaret Mead demonstrated long ago there is not one value that is universally held by all human cultures. Cannibalism, human sacrifice, slavery, incest, polygamy, and any other practice abhorrent to our culture can be found to be acceptable in one culture or another, which either exists or has existed in the past. It is safe to say that right and wrong is defined either by religious belief or by society.

If we do not believe in God, but accept that society has the authority to determine what is right and wrong, we still have a moral environment against which decisions can be measured, and these decisions can be rewarded or penalized depending on a given society's values. For instance, if a society has decided to enforce a prohibition on the taking of innocent life, anyone discovered violating that norm would be punished. If the society does not prohibit the practice, such as a culture that practiced cannibalism, ritual human sacrifice, or honor killing, a person could kill without constraint within the boundaries set by the culture.

It is important to note that as I indicated before, even someone who does not accept the norms of a culture are expected to abide by them regardless of whether they feel they are subject to someone else's notion of what is right or wrong. For instance, serial killers in the United States who are caught are punished whether they think their actions are morally justified or not. Therefore, even if an individual does not perceive himself to be subject to moral judgment, he or she is. Because of this, the argument that there is no right or wrong becomes immaterial, because society will not let an individual be a law unto himself. Therefore, there is right and wrong if for no other reason than it is culturally imposed.

There have been some notable exceptions in history of those who imposed their personal morals on a culture; Adolph Hitler immediately comes to mind. However, most people are required to conform to cultural norms, or the morals of their society, or suffer the consequences when caught.

So what is the purpose of legislation? Let us look at the definition, which is as follows:

-verb (used without object)

1. to exercise the function of legislation; make or enact laws.

-verb (used with object)

2. to create, provide, or control by legislation: attempts to legislate

16

morality.[4]

As stated, the purpose of legislation is to make laws. This sounds simple enough. However, what are laws? Again, we look at the part of the definition of law relevant to this discussion, which is as follows:

> The body of rules and principles governing the affairs of a community and enforced by a political authority; a legal system.

Therefore, to legislate is to make laws, to make laws is to establish rules and principles that are binding on the community, and those customs and practices establish the norms for the culture or community. Because these norms are enforced, they become right and wrong choices for the members of the community, and right and wrong determines the morals of the group. It sounds to me that the whole point of making any law is to legislate morality.

I am convinced that an examination of law, both present and historical, will reveal that there has never been a law adopted by any governing authority at any place in the world or in any period since the dawn of civilization that has not been rooted in the morality of the culture. **In effect, morality is the only thing that has been, is, or ever will be legislated. If morality cannot be legislated, there will be no legislation.**

I occasionally meet people who disagree with this premise, and cite laws rooted in modern technology as justification. In these discussions, it is a very short chain of logic from a detailed regulation and the moral root of the regulation, most of the time not more than two degrees of separation. For instance, we require drivers to stop vehicles at stop signs, and the reason is that we place a high moral value on the protection of life and property and therefore establish laws and use traffic control devices to minimize the loss of life and property.

The next argument to support the continued use of this idiotic notion will be to insist that it is relevant to sexual practices only. When someone says, "You can't legislate morality" they are really saying you cannot regulate sexual morality. This is also patently untrue. Only a few counties in the United States allow prostitution, and offenders routinely face

---

[4] *The American Heritage® Dictionary of the English Language, Fourth Edition.* Houghton Mifflin Company, 2004. 16 May. 2007. <Dictionary.com

prosecution in spite of a long campaign by COYOTE[5] to decriminalize the practice. Sexual contact between consenting partners is prohibited when one of the partners is a minor child and the other is an adult. With the exception of NAMBLA[6], very few have argued that we cannot, or even should not legislate against this sexual practice. Unwelcome sexual contact is also expressly prohibited, and there are very few who will defend this practice. Rape and sexual assault are proscribed sexual practices. No thinking person should argue with a straight face that we cannot legislate against deviant sexual practices. After that conclusion is reached the only other thing to discuss is what constitutes a deviant sexual practice.

Next comes the assertion that we cannot use the law (legislation) to force our beliefs on others. However, if the purpose of legislation is to enforce cultural norms, is that not the point of the exercise? We as a society believe that murder is unacceptable, and we force that moral value on everyone living here. It does not matter if the person violating the law does not believe in that value. For that matter, it does not even matter if the person is unaware of the law. If a person emigrates from one country to another with a different culture and breaks a law unknowingly (such as performing an honor killing), he or she will still be prosecuted because "Ignorance of the law is no excuse".

In addition, we are told that we cannot legislate morality because to do so is an exercise in futility. Since the first legislative act there have been those who have rebelled against the tyranny of the majority or the ruling class and acted in defiance of them. Disobedience to established law also results because of greed, passion, and anger, among other reasons. If that is the case, why try? So the reasoning goes.

This is perhaps the most ridiculous argument against legislating morality. Using this logic, we would immediately abolish all laws and allow anyone to do whatever they are moved upon to do regardless of the impact on others, because there certainly is no law that has never been broken. That is anarchy, which is not a state that very many people will tolerate. In spite of widespread non-compliance with laws, we continue to make and enforce laws that restrict behavior without even daring to hope that they will be universally obeyed. We do not allow people to murder just because people have been murdering others since the advent of recorded history. In some cases, we re-evaluate restrictions that result in widespread

---

[5] "Call Off Your Old Tired Ethics"
[6] "North American Man-Boy Love Association"

revolt against them and often change them in response to pressure, including cultural and technological changes. However, even in doing that, we are still consistently legislating morality, because our morals are changing along with the legislation.

I am willing to bet that most thinking people will agree with me on this. The problem is that too many simply do not bother to think. They have heard so many people tell them that morality cannot be legislated so many times that they accept it without question. If this were simply an exercise in logic, it would not matter; however, there are important ramifications for our society if this notion is not challenged and debunked.

If the point of legislation is to establish behavioral norms, what is the point of the argument made by those who insist that we cannot legislate morality? While many unthinkingly accept the statement as fact, others are less than honest in their rationalization. For many, the purpose is to obfuscate the debate about what is right and wrong, and more importantly, what should be prescribed and proscribed by the legislative process. The real issue is not whether we legislate morality, that is a given. The question is what, or more to the point, *whose* morality is to be legislated. In my lifetime, I have seen society make a one hundred and eighty degree turn on human behaviors that have traditionally been prohibited by legislation. There is constant pressure brought to bear on legislators to continue this trend. In effect, what is often legislated today is not morality, but what we have historically called immorality.

This process is fine, so long as it occurs in an open society where the marketplace of ideas decide what moral value is imposed, it is acceptable. If morals did not change over time, slavery would be common (and not just for minorities), women would be second-class citizens, and we would be hiding our virgin daughters to protect them from ritual sacrifice. Everyone thinks his or her moral beliefs are superior, and tries to persuade others to believe the same. Some will even attempt to impose their beliefs on others. This includes those whose moral position is that all morals are equal and that those who try to impose their morals on others are harsh and judgmental. Ironically enough, by doing so they impose their morals upon and harshly judge those with whom they disagree. If they can persuade a majority to agree, I have no problem with the imposition of restrictions on behavior, even those that I disagree with.

Enshrined in the Constitution of the United States are express protections against discrimination for protected classes of people, and protections for religious and political speech. Protected classes are determined by either genetic characteristics over which no one has a choice in determining, or because of physical disabilities, which are for the most part not a result of the decisions we make. I say for the most part, because some engage in self-destructive behavior and reap the adverse consequences of their decisions in the form of physical disabilities. However, even those with self-imposed physical disabilities are protected, and properly so.

Nowhere in the Constitution is there a protection in favor of behavior, with the exception of a few specifically enumerated ones. These include freedom of speech, religion, assembly, and bearing arms, all of which were included with the purpose of furthering the population's ability to pursue life, liberty, and happiness. However, the purpose of the founders was not to allow general behavioral decisions to be used as a basis for establishing a protected class of people, especially for those engaged in self-destructive behavior.

The use of law to protect those engaged in self-destructive behavior has become increasingly common. The most obvious example of this is the protections for gay and lesbian relationships that are sweeping the country. In spite of the demonstrable fact that those engaged in such relationships are at severe risk of incurring diseases which will end their lives, and that as a result the lifespan of those who practice this lifestyle is well below the average for the country, this minority group has managed to brainwash a majority of Americans into believing that the practice is just another lifestyle choice equal in value to any other lifestyle choice, including the choice to marry and establish a traditional family. For more on this issue see Chapter 30.

Those who advocate in favor of these expansions of rights seek to do so legislatively, or lacking the support of the majority, seek to have the right imposed judicially, circumventing the legislative process. Generally, they tell us in one breath that we cannot legislate morality, and in the next breath tell us the new moral edict that has been imposed on the majority by a judge anxious to legislate morality. Those who disagree are "Neanderthals" or "homophobic", or some other term designed to focus attention away from the imposition of an objectionable morality on the majority, denigrate anyone so backward as to object, and ignore the overthrow of a traditional moral value that has served society well for centuries or millennia.

The result is that we are witnessing a revolution against traditional values that are still held by the majority. The family is derided as an institution for the enslavement of women and propagandization of children. Sex outside the institution of marriage is not only commonly accepted, but expected. In response to Supreme Court action, most states have repealed sodomy laws designed to restrict unsafe sexual practices. I could go on, but I think you get the picture. The goal of many is to remove traditional barriers against certain behaviors by trying to legitimize them, or even to go further and establish those who practice a behavior as a protected class.

History is being rewritten with a viewpoint sympathetic to these values. This is important because knowledge is generally transmitted from one generation to another, through families, friends, schools, community organizations, and, with an increasingly more prominent role, media. If cultural changes from one generation to another occur, only historians will know the old cultural norm, and if history is rewritten it may be entirely lost. In the electronic libraries of the future, it would be easy to have a search engine systematically purge historical records of offensive content. The transmission of cultural values is also from generation to generation, and if the generational link is broken, mass cultural change can result and values can change dramatically.

The same is true for religious and political speech. It staggers the mind to read the constant news releases describing the censorship of speech, particularly on college campuses. Gone are the days when the cliché "I disagree with what you say but I will fight to the death to protect your right to say it." applied. Now anyone with a view not in conformance with those who seek to redefine our culture is shouted down in group settings, and their ability to distribute printed opinion is stymied, either by heavy handed censorship or the confiscation of their printed material. They are also ridiculed and marginalized to teach a lesson to anyone else who would have the temerity to advocate in favor of traditional values.

In summary, we can and must legislate morality. In doing so, we should be tolerant of changes to our moral values if the change is a result of conscious decisions made by legislatures who represent the people who elected them. We should beware the shrill and loud voices of the minority who obfuscate with flawed logic and shout down the voices of reason. They have persuaded many to their position because they ridicule those who believe otherwise. The majority have not taken their position, so they seek to enforce it by judicial fiat. If the majority does not assert itself, they will win.

Chapter 2

"Separation of Church and State"

There is a widely held perception in the United States that the Constitution requires the separation of church and state. This is not, nor has it ever been, the case. The Constitution prohibits laws that have the effect of establishing a religion, which while close, is not the same thing. Even so, the term seems to describe a worthy goal, and on one level it is; however, the expression has been so abused over the last fifty years that the original intent and meaning has been turned on its head. The effect has been an attempt to significantly reduce the influence of religious belief on legislation.

The term originates with a letter that Thomas Jefferson wrote in 1802 to a religious sect in Connecticut in an attempt to clarify the Establishment Clause in the First Amendment. In the letter, he describes the Establishment Clause as "building a wall of separation between church and state" the purpose of which is to inhibit federal acts regarding religion. Because the letter was addressed to a specific sect, and also included the Free Exercise clause that followed, the intent was to clarify that federal action could not be taken to advance one religious sect above another.

The term as Jefferson used it was a accurate description of the principal purpose of the First Amendment clauses dealing with religion. The recent ancestors of the former colonists were all too painfully aware of the abuse that religious separatists had to endure, many of which fled to America to escape religious persecution. Ostensibly, the First Amendment was the guarantee to all religious organizations that the Federal government would not sponsor or oppose religious denominations, thereby theoretically ensuring that people could freely follow their conscience after choosing their faith without governmental pressure to join another group.

The term as interpreted today is profoundly different from Jefferson's meaning. Proponents of eliminating religious speech from public discourse have twisted the meaning of the term to include Federal acts that have nothing to do with the establishment or support of religious denominations. Even worse, they have twisted the statement to set the First Amendment against itself, the Constitution as a whole, and all the laws that govern our nation and states, including common law inherited from English precedent.

The first chapter of this book is a persuasive (if I do say so myself) argument that all legislation is based upon morality, or in other words that legislation is the collective enforcement of morals on all the members of a society. Legislation enforces moral conduct as determined by the majority. The next rational question is how the majority determines what is moral conduct and what is immoral conduct. The simple answer is religion.

Morality and mores are largely determined by the historically predominant religion of the society. In most Western societies, Judeo-Christian values forms the basis for law and the principles they advance. In most Middle Eastern countries, Islam is the dominant religion, and forms the basis for their law. Historical societies have also based law on religion, from the Romans and their polytheistic beliefs to the Aztecs whose religion was particularly intolerant of other cultures and peoples. Aztec practices seem extraordinarily barbaric to us, who are steeped in Christian theology, including the respect for life, tolerance and freedom. Historically we can find across the vast number of cultures those whose religious practices are alien and offensive to us, but we are looking at those beliefs through the lens of our religious heritage and culture. In any case, each current or historical culture's laws have been substantially affected by the religious thought prevalent in the culture.

In Asia there are a number of religions, some of which conflict with each other, which has lead to longstanding social conflict and instability in some areas just as there is conflict in the West. These include Islam, Confucianism, Buddhism, Hinduism, Taoism, and Shinto to name some of the major religions. However, religious conflict is not always the norm. Some countries have incorporated other religions into the fabric of their society with little conflict, such as the Japanese who have successfully melded various aspects of Shinto, Buddhism, and Christianity into their cultural practices and law (full disclosure, I spent two years in Japan where I gained a deep appreciation for the people and culture of that nation).

In the case of the United States, there is a very strong Judeo-Christian tradition that forms the basis for all of the laws that we have adopted. This runs the gamut from respect for life and the abhorrence of murder to a stewardship of the environment. In evaluating the effect of religion on law, it is easy to overlook the profound effect that it has. Many people grow up in this culture and are thoroughly indoctrinated in it, so much so that they perceive that all the world shares the same values, or at least if they don't, they should. As is the case with every other culture in the world, we tend to be ethnocentric in our view. This leads to conflict with other cultures, the

23

root of which stem from different religious traditions. Not all other cultures share the same values, and resist when we attempt to impose our values on them. Even more ridiculous are attempts to impose the same values on historic cultures or leaders and judge them according to current values. But I digress.

This same myopia with respect to other cultures extends to our own. Those that perceive their values to be universal because everyone they have met has shared those same values fail to recognize that every single belief that they believe to be true has at one time or another, or by one culture or another, been held to be untrue. Margaret Mead demonstrated decades ago that there is no natural universal taboo. What is taboo in one culture or time may be common practice in another. In fact, over the last two centuries these differences are becoming increasingly rare; we do not see many societies these days that routinely kill humans for food or practice incest. That is because the major religions have been transmitting their religious beliefs to cultures that formerly practiced these behaviors, and have largely convinced them that these practices are not moral. This in turn led to changes to the legal systems and practices of those cultures.

Most of those in western societies have been so acculturated to these beliefs that they no longer recognize nor accept the historical antecedents of the beliefs. They think that principles that are used as the basis for law are a universal norm that will be independently reached no matter what the religious foundation of the culture is. For instance, it is common to assume that the taking of innocent life is a universal truth that all people and cultures accept, and that truth has somehow been arrived at and accepted independent of religious beliefs.

It is easy to see the problem with that argument. We do not even need to go back to evaluate ancient cultures that pillaged, plundered, raped, and murdered for the sole purpose of acquiring goods or power, or small isolated groups limited to small geographic regions that practiced cannibalism, to disprove this notion, although that would do it. We have very large numbers of people on the planet as we speak who believe that the murder of innocents is justified, either as the means of achieving a political or cultural end or if the person will not accept their belief system. The "universal truth" in western culture that the killing of innocents is bad can be traced directly to Judeo-Christian belief, particularly the belief that all people are the children of God and that no one is more important in His eyes than anyone else.

24

The same can be said of our antipathy to slavery, discrimination, the treatment of women or children as chattel, forced conversion, or just about any other practice abhorrent to us. The reason values contrary to these practices are so widely held now (although by no means universally held) is that religious doctrine hostile to those practices has been spread across the earth by the major religions of the world, particularly Christianity. That many adherents to these religions did not practice what they ostensibly believed does not change the fact that over time those practices have become so abhorrent to the majority that they have largely been eliminated from western cultures.

Atheists like to think that morality has evolved independent of religion. While I might accept an argument that some moral shifts have occurred in the recent past that can be linked to humanistic and atheistic thought, to argue that historical morality evolved independent of religion is ridiculous. It is no accident that the laws of each culture have been affected by the dominant religion of the culture. Those arguing that morality is the result of shared values is not paying attention to history or geography.

For example, Richard Dawkins argues that "we do not - even the religious among us – ground our morality in holy books, no matter what we may fondly imagine."[7] If we accept this argument at face value, none of the precepts taught by Jesus Christ in the New Testament have had an impact on the evolution of western morality over the past two thousand years. Further, our current moral climate is not affected by the teaching of Christ. In addition, Islamic countries have not been affected by the Qur'an, India has not been affected by the Bhagavad Gita, and so on. The reasoning he uses is remarkably uninformed. This is a prime example of a person looking at human history through a western cultural lens and imagining all the world thinks as he does, even though a simple examination of morals within different cultures will clearly show his thesis to be incorrect.

Mr. Dawkins goes on to insist that our morals have evolved and are evolving (again independent of religious influence) by means of a collective consensus, which he calls the "moral zeitgeist", which he speculates as having a Darwinian origin.[8] He does so without explaining how, in spite of all the possible world views that could have prevailed over time, including not just current philosophies such as Islam, but historical cultures such as Aztec under Montezuma or Mongolian under Genghis Khan, the morality

---

[7] Dawkins, p. 298
[8] Ibid, pp. 245-254, 298-308

that has evolved can be directly linked to the teachings of Christ. For some strange reason, western society has the values enumerated in the New Testament, but according to Mr. Dawkins, our morality is unconnected to scripture and religious belief. Incredibly, he even has the temerity to suggest that some of Dr. Martin Luther King's moral stances were not affected by his Christian faith.

All it would have taken for the "moral zeitgeist" that Dawkins describes to be dramatically different was for western culture to be conquered by a different culture with dramatically different religious values. Those who prevail in war not only write history, but they historically have imposed their values on the conquered. If the Islamic or Mongolian invasions of Europe had been successful, I doubt that I would be writing this book. Even recent challenges to our culture would have dramatically affected our morality if they had prevailed. If the Axis powers had succeeded in World War II, or if Khrushchev's communism had buried capitalism our "moral zeitgeist" would be considerably different than it is today. Morality is inseparably connected to the religious beliefs of the culture and will be profoundly affected by the replacement of one religious tradition with another.

While Mr. Dawkins is right about the consensus, he is completely off the mark on the impetus for the consensus. In fact, the teachings of Christ in the New Testament have profoundly affected all western societies and subsequently the world as a result of the wide dissemination of those values since the time of Columbus. It is no accident that the former colonies of various European countries still have many cultural and legal traditions established under colonial rule. Even Japan has the McArthur Constitution that was heavily influenced by American thought, and they were only defeated in World War II. To argue that the common values that have independently evolved over the centuries are a result of non-religious thought is to ignore one of the simplest lessons that history has to offer.

Mr. Dawkins also argues that morality is shifting (outside religious influence) to be more tolerant of others. He does not explain how the pressure to eliminate slavery and the ownership of women, grant civil rights to women and minorities, and basic human rights to homosexuals has been affected by a simple but profound teaching found in the New Testament, which is that we are all creations of God and that all human beings have dignity and are entitled to certain rights. To be sure, it has taken two millennia for us to begin to realize those rights because of human greed and ignorance. But over time we have learned the implications of that teaching, and are getting close to almost fully incorporating it into our morality.

Actually, Mr. Dawkins seems to be a little schizophrenic about religious influence on morality. He steadfastly claims that the morality of the Old Testament is immoral based on selective readings and interpretations and that our morality is unconnected to that scripture. However, he then goes on to praise Jesus Christ because He ostensibly contradicted this immoral morality with revolutionary new precepts, precepts that (strangely enough for a morality that ostensibly evolved independent of religion) mirror the values we cherish today. He then goes on to dismiss the entire New Testament as a completely fabricated collection of books, and thereby throws out the precepts that he has just praised. Which is it? Is the New Testament a work to be dismissed as myth, or are the precepts taught by Christ as recorded in the various books of the New Testament revolutionary precepts that ostensibly undermine the morality of the Old Testament?

If we conclude that religious belief forms the basis for our morals, and that morals are the basis for our law, it is a short jump to the conclusion that separating church, the term used to describe religious belief according to the twisted interpretation of Jefferson's comment we constantly hear now, from the State is impossible. In order to do so we would need to construct a completely new value system based on ideas not grounded in religious doctrine. I would not want to be the person responsible for trying to develop such a system. There is no moral belief, and therefore no legislation, that is not founded on religious belief, and it is no more possible to separate religious belief from morality as it is to separate morality from legislation.

For that matter, why would we want to replace what we have with law that is based on values that we clearly do not value? Jefferson, in the Declaration of Independence, makes an impassioned assertion that "all men are created equal and that they are endowed by their Creator with life, liberty, and the pursuit of happiness". These core religious beliefs have served the United States (and all of humanity for that matter) well in the intervening two centuries, and have resulted in a system of government in this country that is designed to preserve those values. As a result, we have an open society that has served as an inspiration to the world. To deliberately subvert the underlying beliefs that form the foundation of our law is profoundly stupid.

No one can consider the assertions in the Declaration of Independence and still believe that the founders of this nation did not rely on religion as essential to good government and the maintenance of a moral society. The relevant clause in the document "that they are endowed by their creator with certain unalienable rights" clearly shows an intention to sever the colonial relationship with Great Britain because the founders believed that the British government was not governing according to principles consistent with God's desires, and that any future government to be established should.

Some may argue that those who signed the Declaration of Independence did not know what they were talking about, or that they were misguided or delusional with respect to God and religion. That is an argument that, while it seems to ignore historic fact, is at least logical. What cannot be argued is that the founders intentionally created a government that was designed to exclude religious belief, particularly Judeo-Christian belief. There was no intent to exclude religion from being a factor in making public decisions; indeed, it is clear that the expectation was that good government could only be accomplished with deference to and adherence to religious beliefs.

To be sure, our government is not without problems; however, it could be far worse. Those who are in power have a tendency to ignore core principles when faced with emergencies or political pressure. In the nineteenth century, this country went so far as to send an army against a religious denomination within its borders with the intent of finding a "final solution" in spite of the First Amendment (Johnston's Army did not succeed in this mission; the Mormon Church is with us still). However, in spite of human nature and the bumbling and egregious behavior of all branches of government and people who exercise power in conflict with our values, over time our system and values have prevailed. We live in conditions that the majority of the people who have ever lived on this planet over time could only wistfully imagine. The values described in the Declaration of Independence have won all the major challenges to it in the past, and continues to do so today because they are consistent with the core religious values we share.

So why is there such a campaign to completely disassociate religion from law (and from all public venues for that matter, but that is a different discussion)? I believe there are two kinds of people advocating this. One group is merely uninformed and are unconscious of the effect the mindless attempts to separate religion from the law has, and the other is willing to sacrifice the underlying basis for our peace, prosperity, and social justice system in order justify and ultimately impose values that the majority do not share. I am convinced that this is just another example of a continued campaign to replace traditional morals with convenient replacements that condone traditionally bad and destructive behavior. Ironically, the

28

foundations in law secularists attempt to subvert are the underpinnings for the freedoms that allow the secularists to flourish. If they are successful in removing religious influence from law, over the long term they will only undermine their own continued existence.

Those who do not believe in God and actively seek to undermine the influence of religion on society are functionally a religious group, even though the beliefs of their religion are against traditional religion. Call them the Church of Science if you will. They have a set of beliefs and moral positions that they represent to be true to the world. They seek to convert others to their cause, thereby increasing their influence and power. Most important, they lobby for changes to law they feel are a result of religious influence, but only when the law inconveniently proscribes behavior they want to perform. In our system of government, they are properly protected in their beliefs and attempts to influence legislation.

However, in addition to actively seeking to gain power and influence, secularists are also attempting to silence the voices of those who believe in God, using the argument that there should be a hard separation of church and state as the vehicle. They have been successful in removing many religious symbols from the public square, even though those symbols represent the foundation of our society and law. They claim they are not advocating for religion even though the results they seek are to persuade people and legislatures to take positions against law based on religious principles, particularly the dominant religion. They shut off the microphones of those who would speak in public about their religious beliefs.

Their arguments are self-serving in that they want to dominate the discourse to the extent possible. They are willing to concede that believers can express their views, but only in private, which is designed to ensure such discussion is marginalized when it comes to competing for the minds of those who have not yet determined what they believe. They are afraid of an honest exchange of ideas in the public square because they know their distortions will be evident, so they make the argument about separating church and state instead of an honest debate about the value of their own religious beliefs. Amazingly enough, they seek to deny the introduction and discussion of empirical evidence supporting the validity of religious beliefs. This is simply because they are afraid that the open discussion of this evidence may have the effect of someone believing in religious principles in conflict with their own.

Political

The actions taken to restrict the speech of individuals are evidence that the goal is not just to keep religious organizations from participating in public discourse. While that alone is a blatant misrepresentation of religion's role with respect to government, the attempts to silence individuals is stark testimony of the blatant attempts to deliberately take away the freedom of speech and religion guaranteed by the First Amendment to all individuals. It is amazing to me that these people argue that silencing an individual's religious expression in public represents adherence to a constitutionally imposed separation of church and state. If individuals are not free to speak their mind, whether at a public hearing before a governmental body or as a valedictory speaker before a graduating class, such an individual's rights are being trampled upon by those who seek to silence religious speech. Fortunately, legal groups such as the Thomas More Law Center have been active and successful in litigating against these blatant abuses in violation of First Amendment rights.

Not all religious beliefs are equal. The majority in this country routinely restricts the religious practices of minority religions. Few would argue that we should tolerate the practice of polygamy on the part of fundamentalist Mormon apostates. That practice was legislated against in the late nineteenth century, and court appeals upheld the prohibition of the practice. That has established a clear precedent that enables the majority to legislate against practices and behavior that it views as outside the mainstream. This makes it easy for us to tell Aztec wannabes that they cannot practice ritual human sacrifice. The same can be said of Islamic fundamentalists who advocate honor killing or forced conversion. For that matter, it also allows us to prohibit the use of peyote in Native American religious rituals if we want to do so. Laws preventing abhorrent religious practices, in spite of the fact that they are based on religious beliefs, are appropriate and illustrate the inseparable link between law and religion. No rational person claims that we should allow human sacrifice just because preventing it would be a violation of the First Amendment for a group that wanted to perform the practice.

That said, there is a natural tension between the First Amendment and proper regulation of religious practices. It is easy to conclude that ritual human sacrifice should be prohibited regardless of how sincerely a group believes that their crops will fail in the absence of the sacrifice. It is also easy to conclude that quiet and peaceful worship that has at its core a respect for the norms of civilized society should clearly be protected by the First Amendment no matter how unusual the beliefs may be to others. As with

30

any other right, the question is where to draw the line between the extreme of religious anarchy and totalitarian repression.

Religious regulation is also a double edged sword. If we allow native Americans to use prohibited drugs in their cultural practices, it is difficult to justify prohibiting another church, say the Church of the Leaf, from the use of marijuana in their services. (I thought I had just invented a cool name for a new church for potheads, but an internet search turned up the name. Oh well.) Likewise, if we prohibit Mormon apostate groups from practicing polygamy, we must also accept that other forms of marriage can be prohibited if they are outside the cultural norm. For more on the marriage debate see Chapter 30.

As previously mentioned, the United States was founded on moral principles with Judeo-Christian origins. We have adopted laws based on those religious principles and we enforce adherence to those laws. Fortunately, our religious heritage includes precepts that have resulted in the freedoms we have today. That includes the ethic of tolerance, which means we are much more willing to accommodate the religious views of others when not in direct conflict with the health, safety and welfare of our citizens. We can and do restrict religious practices, including when the predominant religious tradition forces the conformity of minority religions. It is in our interest to do so in order to maintain our cultural identity for the sake of unity and survival.

Many would like to see our culture destroyed. In particular, extreme religious jihadists would love to establish a dictatorial religious empire across the world. If we are to eventually prevail in the conflict with these extremists, we must recognize the value of our cultural traditions and defend them. Common religious values help preserve cultural cohesiveness. Evidence of the undesirability of the fragmentation of values is evident in the conflict and intimidation of public policy that can be seen today in European societies that allow Muslim extremists to dictate what is published or broadcast, including the murder of those who challenge their extreme views.

In the long term, our cultural, political, and perhaps even our physical survival depends on maintaining the link between religion and law. If we do not continue to value what the religious separatists brought with them from Europe when seeking religious freedom, we will forget the lessons they learned and will likely find ourselves being overwhelmed by the loudest voices in the public square. Those who seek to replace our values know the only way to accomplish that is to shout down the opposition and keep voices of reason from being heard. If they are successful, eventually we will be transformed into a cultural dictatorship similar to those we fled nearly four and one half centuries ago. If that cultural dictatorship happens to mirror the Taliban leadership that formerly ruled in Afghanistan, many of us would not survive.

Chapter 3

"All Politicians are Crooks"

How often do you hear this expression? Probably every time you listen to a news report that details political corruption, compromise, or even conflict over policy. We certainly love to be cynical about our political leadership. However, what price do we pay for this? I believe it is much higher than most people realize.

What happens when a person declares himself or herself a candidate for political office? The vast majority of the time, this will be an individual who, when the declaration is made, is successful in his or her private and professional life. He or she will have good people skills, is well educated, will have a good grasp of the issues that face the community, state, or nation, depending on the office sought, and will run for office because of desire to effect positive change in the community. In short, he or she will be an upstanding and well thought of leader in the community who is regarded as a role model to be emulated.

Upon announcing his or her candidacy, this person is immediately transformed into a politician. Instantly, he or she becomes a cheating, corrupt, crafty, crooked, cunning, and conniving charlatan whose only objective is to enrich him or herself at the public trough, or to obtain power at the expense of the downtrodden. It is truly remarkable how quickly this transformation occurs. All it takes is a simple announcement or registration with the government official responsible for elections. Just that quickly, in the eyes of many he or she is transformed from an upstanding member of the community to a crook.

It would not be so bad if it were a minority of the population who expressed these sentiments. There will always be a dissatisfied minority no matter how well government functions. However, it is not just a minority that equates politicians with corruption; it is the vast majority. Even worse, the media fuels the sentiment. Indeed, the media sees any announcement to run for office as the equivalent of the candidate posting a huge bull's-eye on his or her back.

Are there corrupt politicians? Of course there are. There are some who desire to enrich themselves at the expense of the public interest or who seek power for its own sake. These truly dishonest and dangerous people have

Political

no place in public office. Unfortunately, there will always be a small minority of candidates with ulterior motives who will fool enough voters to be elected. As with any profession, this small minority within it gives the majority a bad name.

However, what about the candidate whose motive is to act in the public interest to solve problems, meet economic and social challenges, and protect the public? What has the candidate done to warrant this treatment? The answer is nothing. He or she is tarred by a stereotype that he or she had neither a part in making nor any motivation to emulate. Their desire to help and serve is met with cynicism and derision.

Candidates risk much when they stand for election. One such risk is personal destruction, both by opposing candidates and the media who react like sharks at a feeding frenzy when any hint of a flaw in a candidate is exposed. In some cases, the media goes out of its way to manufacture flaws if they cannot find one. Their goal is to sell newspapers or airtime, and boring elections in which honest candidates have rational and civil debates about policy differences do not sell as well as corruption and scandal. Media and opposing candidates start digging through the candidate's past, seeking through opposition research to uncover anything that hints of unethical behavior for the sole purpose of discrediting him or her. Unfortunately, very few can withstand that kind of scrutiny, so we have elections dominated by a focus on candidate's mistakes no matter how trivial the infraction, which of course perpetuates the stereotype of the politician as a crook.

Many candidates are treated with none of the respect accorded to normal contributing members of society, especially by the press. Why would they when they are dealing with people they perceive to be crooks? The press routinely prints anything they can to denigrate a candidate, especially if the candidate represents conservative interests. Vicious personal attacks are common. They design interview questions to ensure that no matter how the question is answered the candidate will look bad. A very recent example is when Charles Gibson of ABC News interviewed Sarah Palin. Mr. Gibson asked the candidate if she thought she was qualified to become President if something were to happen to the President. If Palin had answered "no", the headlines for months would have told the electorate that the Vice-Presidential nominee did not think she was qualified. Because she answered yes, Mr. Gibson looked down at her and in as condescending a voice as possible asked if her answer constituted hubris on her part. Mr. Gibson's

34

attitude was breathtakingly arrogant, but is a good example of the campaign of the press to denigrate candidates.

Perhaps even worse than the politics of personal destruction of the candidate is the potential for destructive attacks on the candidate's family. While media outlets routinely claim that a candidate's family is off limits, the opposite is true, particularly in national campaigns. Many made President Clinton's brother the butt of jokes simply because he was the brother of the President. Even worse are attacks on the children of candidates and elected officials. Recent examples are President Clinton's and President Bush's daughters, who were held up for public ridicule early in both these President's tenures. Even more recent are the vicious attacks on the family of the Vice-Presidential nominee in the 2008 election even though (or is it because?) the daughter of the candidate chose to not abort the child. What this means is that in deciding to run for political office, a candidate must make a decision to bring ridicule and derision on those they care most about simply because they seek what they perceive is in the best interest of their community or country.

The political climate has been so poisoned against politicians that political witch-hunts are the norm. Politicians are being systematically attacked as liars, power mongers, and criminals because of honest policy differences. Ethical complaints are constantly filed, especially prior to an election, alleging unethical and criminal conduct on the part of the candidate because the person or group filing the complaint know that there is no chance of resolution of the complaint until after the election. The person or group that files the complaint then goes on to accuse the candidate of unethical behavior, and point to the unresolved complaint as evidence. Years later, the finding that the complaint had no evidentiary support is quietly announced when the complaint is dismissed, but by then the politician has long since been discredited and defeated. Even if a politician survives the attack, he or she will still have the dismissed complaint thrown against them in future elections and when debating policy issues unrelated to the original complaint. In spite of the evidentiary finding, many voters will believe that the politician pulled strings to get the complaint dismissed.

The latest trend is to attack candidates with civil lawsuits alleging impropriety or corruption. As with the ethics complaint process noted in the previous paragraph, the lawsuit is unresolved for an extended period of time, giving the opposition the opportunity to convict the candidate without a trial with media attacks. Even worse is the financial cost the candidate must bear to defend themselves against these often frivolous lawsuits.

Political

My perception is that many of the people and groups that frequently file these complaints and vociferously denounce the opposition as corrupt do so because of their own propensity for corrupt behavior. There are multiple reasons for this. First, the best defense against the media paying attention to their own unethical behavior is a good offense against the opposition's behavior whether it is supported by facts or not. Second, they perceive that because they have ethical lapses that their opposition surely must have them too. Third, they seek to excuse their behavior through the alleged behavioral problems of their opposition.

It is so bad that even appointed executives are being demonized and railroaded. In one notable case, Scooter Libby was convicted of perjury even though the prosecutor had full knowledge that there was no underlying crime about which Mr. Libby would have reason to lie. Sadly, the Bush Administration chose to appease the opposition, and let many embattled executives twist in the legal wind or requested their resignation. This only whets the appetite of the opposition, which begins a new campaign to smear another official knowing that they can get away with it. Many people see this and become disgusted with all involved parties, including those maliciously attacking for political gain and those who will not back up their most valuable supporters. Who would want to serve the public in an environment where jail could be in the offing because of honest policy differences?

Then there is the predilection to denigrate an individual who can weather opposition research because he or she has no significant scandal with which they can be attacked. After concluding that the person is squeaky clean, the next accusation is the person is not a normal human being because of the lack of scandal, and we cannot empathize with or support such a candidate. In other words, the candidate is damned if they have skeletons hidden for the opposition researchers to find, or they are damned if they do not.

The candidate also risks financial security or stability; elected positions do not pay anywhere near what other public positions or equivalent private positions pay. As an example, I as an un-elected bureaucrat personally earned more than double what the elected officials that I answered to earned. Is this beyond ridiculous or what? Any attempt to bring the remuneration for these positions in line with the responsibility they carry is always met with the standard response, which is that they are crooks. As a result, the pay for most elected political offices is stuck in a time warp that is consistently two decades behind what the position should pay. Most cannot

36

survive on these meager wages, which makes the positions possible only to those who are wealthy enough not to need the pay. That locks many worthy candidates out of any political office. Those that are not wealthy either suffer economically, work outside the elected office, or they abuse their position for economic gain because they think they are entitled to adequate compensation. In this case, we have a crook of our own making.

The candidate also must risk either their own personal funds to attain the office, or subject himself or herself to raising funds to mount a viable campaign. If he or she is independently wealthy, they can finance their own campaign. Of course, if they do they will be vilified for trying to buy the election. Imagine spending vast sums of your own hard-earned accumulated wealth solely for the purpose of trying to make a constructive difference in your community or nation, and you are vilified; not just for being a crooked politician, but also for trying to buy the election. If the candidate is not wealthy, he or she will need to raise funds from like-minded individuals. Much of the time needed for campaigning is instead devoted to fundraising rather than interacting with the electorate.

Because of campaign contribution limits, the candidate must raise small amounts from many people, which, because it is time consuming and difficult for someone who is not well known, strongly favors incumbents. Whoever is raising the money, because only those with significant interests will be motivated to contribute to political candidates, the money collected will be used as a hammer to demonstrate the candidate is corrupt because he or she accepts money from special interests. In other words, if the candidate uses money from any source he or she will be accused of corruption. Sounds like a catch 22 situation to me.

As a side argument, the practice of limiting campaign contributions is abominable. In spite of the warped decision of the Supreme Court, such limits are a clear unconstitutional restriction on free speech, and should be repealed. Anyone should be allowed to contribute any amount they desire to further their beliefs and values, and the candidate should be able to accept any amount so long as there is full public disclosure and transparency as to where the money originated.

All of these risks are taken with the full knowledge that the candidacy may be unsuccessful and the effort will wind up being a complete waste of time, effort, and money, often due to malicious and unjustified attacks by opponents or those seeking to sell a few more newspapers. It is truly amazing that anyone would voluntarily subject himself or herself to this process. Why would any sane and rational person do this? The true miracle is that there are enough wonderful people in this country whose desire to serve the public is stronger than their survival instinct.

Maybe I am exaggerating (I kinda doubt it!), but it is possible that there are some outstanding individuals who would be excellent choices as leaders to address the many significant problems we face who may decide that standing for office is not worth the risk when the threat to their personal, family, financial, and professional lives is factored into the decision. How many bright, resourceful leaders have weighed the risk and potential for failure and decided not to run? We will never know, but I believe there are many who choose not to run simply because the stereotype of the politician as a crook, when added to the other risks of the candidacy, makes the cost too high.

This is not to say that those who run for office should not be closely scrutinized and evaluated. Indeed, the only way to weed out the amoral from the altruistic is to assess carefully the candidate and his or her strengths and weaknesses. However, we need not start with the premise that the candidate is corrupt simply because of the candidacy. Indeed, what harm is there in giving a candidate the benefit of any doubt?

All honest and capable candidates will welcome a fair and objective evaluation of their abilities. Frankly, the electorate whose responsibility it is to elect honest, wise, and good candidates will also benefit from a fair and objective evaluation.

The same logic applies to those who have been elected. While careful scrutiny of an official's actions is warranted to educate the voters as to the actions of the politician and the effect of those actions, neither the public nor the media is justified in branding the politician as dishonest because a decision is made that reasonable people disagree about. It is impossible to make decisions that will please everyone. Elected officials are chosen to make hard choices that best advance the public interest, and denigrating as corrupt reasonable decisions is destructive to all, including the politician, the political system, and the population in general. No one is served by this mindless cynicism.

What are the effects of making all politicians the objects of ridicule? There are many, including discouraging good candidates, encouraging bad candidates, cynicism on the part of the general population, low participation in the political process, apathy that leads to ignorance of the problems we face and potential solutions to them, and the difficulty in reaching the political compromises needed to make government work.

As indicated above, cynicism about the ethics of politicians has the effect of discouraging good people from seeking political office. The risk simply becomes too great when all the risks, challenges, and work is factored into the decision. The result is that many good leaders choose to use their talents in pursuits that provide alternative personal or professional satisfaction, but which are not necessarily in the best interest of the public.

In addition, some unethical people, hearing the constant barrage of political vilification, conclude that if all politicians are crooks that they may as well get in on the action, and seek office motivated by reasons other than a desire to serve the public. Unfortunately, some succeed in fooling enough people to obtain the office, at which point they are most often eventually exposed as charlatans and the stereotype is perpetuated even further.

The highly visible prosecution of dishonest politicians leads to increased cynicism on the part of the electorate, further deepening the crooked politician stereotype. The general population, hearing the constant barrage of attacks on the character of all politicians, concludes that if all politicians are corrupt no matter who is chosen, then it does not make any difference who is chosen. These people drop out of political life, essentially putting their political well being in the hands of others who may not share their interests or values. Many cynics, in addition to adding their voices to the chorus of condemnation, divorce themselves from politics, and refuse to participate in elections or inform themselves about issues. They become apathetic about decisions that directly affect them and their communities, do not contribute to solutions to the problems of the community, and have only a destructive effect on civil discourse. Voter participation drops, with the result that a corrupt politician needs to fool fewer voters to be elected. All of these effects combine to make the stereotype self-fulfilling to a degree. All too often, we wind up with crooked politicians because we expect politicians to be crooked.

This apathy breeds ignorance. Having concluded that political participation is a fruitless endeavor, apathetic citizens also conclude that ignorance is bliss. They reason it is better to be uninformed about current events and issues because being informed and unable to have any impact on the issues is more stressful and frustrating than being ignorant.

This is a recipe for disaster. The foundation of a democratic society is an informed and educated electorate. Apathetic and ignorant citizens in effect undermine our democratic institutions and our ability to address the challenges that our society must face. All these consequences are partially because of our insistence in maintaining the stereotype that all politicians are crooks.

Even though the politician may belong to a specific political party, he or she has an obligation to represent the entire electorate to the best of his or her ability. If there are five hundred thousand people in a constituency, a majority of which elects an individual to represent them, there will be somewhere close to five hundred thousand different specialized philosophies about how problems should be addressed. To be sure, many of these are grouped into general categories that are represented by specific political parties; however, these are only general groupings and there is a vast range of ideas on a wide series of issues within these general categories. This means the politician, as a representative of the population that elected him or her, must find a way to best represent a multitude of differing and even conflicting opinions. Of course, this further alienates those on the losing side of a policy decision, and accusations of weakness or corruption inevitably result.

Because of the negative image of politicians, it is more difficult to reach the compromises that are an essential part of governing. Governing, or solving the problems facing the community, state, or nation depending on the political office held, can only be accomplished through compromise, which itself has a very negative connotation. Compromise, in spite of the fact that it is an essential component of governing, is seen as additional evidence of betrayal and dishonesty on the part of politicians, which makes compromise in the public interest that much more difficult to reach, again because of the negative stereotype.

Another problem is that we elect politicians to solve problems, and then promptly make it impossible for them to accomplish the task. A good example is the seemingly intractable problem of immigration. We have a pressing need for workers due to the historic expansion of our economy coupled with the imminent retirement of the baby boom generation and the reduction in the birth rate (thankfully we don't have as much of a problem as the Europeans, whose birthrate is even lower and who must draw on culturally incompatible populations to grow their economies). This is a simple supply and demand problem. We have not supplied the people we historically needed to sustain our economy by natural birth, so the only way the demand can be met is with immigration.

Unfortunately, the majority of the population, being somewhat protectionist, ethnocentric, or isolationist, wants elected officials to ignore the supply problem and restrict the number of immigrants, which is the status of current law. If a politician tells those who elect them that they will act in opposition to these sentiments, it is a good bet that they will not be re-elected. The result is that most elected officials have chosen to ignore the problem, hoping that it will just go away. However, the law of supply and demand abhors a vacuum as much as nature does and so instead of controlled legal immigration designed to maximize its benefits and minimize the problems associated with it, illegal immigration with all the attendant security risks and social costs has solved the supply problem for them. Instead of large numbers of legal immigrants with college degrees, (often earned in American universities) we get large numbers of unskilled workers who put tremendous burdens on our social safety system and the college educated would-be immigrants return to their home countries to help give the home country the benefit of their education, which makes the United States less competitive in the world economy. Of course, the majority is even more convinced that politicians are corrupt because of the massive numbers of illegal immigrants pouring across the borders even though it is the public's fault that we cannot solve the problem.

Another result we see is the recent demand on the part of some for term limits. Whenever I hear people calling for term limits I have to resist the impulse to rap them on the side of their head and ask if anyone is home. Let me see if I have this straight; we are going to prohibit people who are repeatedly reelected and who have experience, wisdom, and are honest from governing because we cannot figure out how to get rid of bad politicians? We have term limits! They are otherwise called elections! If a politician is corrupt, do not reelect him or her. If someone's ideology is different than the majority, do not reelect him or her. If someone is reelected in spite of your opposition, you can assume you are in the minority and some accommodation is in order. Term limits are an attempt to throw the baby out with the bathwater, again partially because of our negative stereotyping.

All that is needed to see the colossal stupidity of this trend is to look and see who has been prohibited from running for an office in which they have governed wisely for years. In Clark County, Nevada there is a former County Commissioner who is no longer on the Commission simply because of term limits. Sadly, he is no longer in office even though he was one of the best Commissioners ever elected in the County. But he was forced from office because the Nevada electorate could not figure out how to get rid of bad politicians through the election process, and instead imposed term limits on most elected officials. In the long term, this will significantly increase the power and influence of un-elected bureaucrats (I know, I was one of them).

Most politicians try as hard as they can to serve their constituency and make a real difference in the lives of those they can. In the absence of proposals that conflict with core principles, they are generally responsive to public pressure, making decisions that they feel the majority of their constituents desire. I remember a specific instance when I worked as an intern for a prominent senator from Nevada. Many years ago, before the Senate approved the Genocide Treaty, the treaty was again coming up for a ratification vote. The Senator did not have strong feelings about whether the treaty should or should not be ratified, so he listened to the input that he received from his constituents and accordingly voted against ratification.

Ironically enough, if a politician demonstrates flexibility in his or her decisions, this is also a reason for cynicism. Any elected official who changes a position on an issue in order to respond to changing circumstances or accommodate the will of his constituents is immediately branded as a flip-flopper and therefore unreliable. This tendency is also lamentable. We expect people to be elected to office, and then promptly close their minds to new information and experiences that should affect their decisions as leaders.

To be sure, some try to be all things to all people. Such efforts are doomed. Abraham Lincoln said it best when he said "You can fool all the people some of the time, and some of the people all the time, but you cannot fool all the people all the time." The word "please" can be substituted for "fool" and the statement is just as true. Any attempt to please some will inevitably alienate others. First and foremost, it is important that elected officials do what they believe is right and resist political pressure to do otherwise with polite but firm resolve. Those that hold their finger up to determine which way the political wind of the day is blowing, and then make decisions based on that temporary climate, are doomed to suffer the wrath of the same constituency later when the wind has turned the opposite direction. When interest groups learn that an official's reaction is based on the majority sentiment at any given moment they immediately learn to distrust him or her, and those that supported the candidacy will be alienated.

Those who elect people to represent them have a right to expect their leaders to follow through on campaign promises. Acting in accordance with the core values that resulted in a candidate's election defines leadership and integrity. Promising one thing and doing another is another justifiable reason for cynicism. However, we must let leaders govern as best they can with the information and knowledge they accumulate while reacting to changing conditions. We also must realize that it is impossible for the official to make decisions on a wide range of issues that everyone is in agreement with, including those who share the politician's core values.

Some may think that I am being hypocritical by not standing for office myself. It is for other reasons that I would never run. I am the person who would tell those who I wanted to vote for me that which they do not want to hear. For instance, if I ran for an office that could have an effect on illegal immigration, I would attack Hispanic groups that seek open borders, lax enforcement of existing immigration laws, or impediments to rapid assimilation of immigrants. I would attack politicians for the cynical manipulation of the debate for political gain. I would attack most of the population for the protectionist, ethnocentric, and isolationist tendencies that make it nearly impossible to solve the problem. In short, I would systematically alienate every possible constituency or ally needed to be elected. That is not a winning formula to which I or anyone else would contribute time and effort to.

I have worked directly with many politicians in a career as a government official, some of whom were imprisoned for corruption. My experience has taught me that there are indeed two types of politicians; one honest and altruistic, the other corrupt and dishonest. The corrupt and dishonest, in spite of the seeming odds in favor of their election, are few and far between, while the honest and altruistic are common. They are people, of course, with the normal failings of people. If we expect them to be perfect, we are being just a tad unrealistic. Most politicians are people who have sacrificed much for the sole purpose of serving the public, and they do not deserve to be reviled as crooks. In addition to the personal damage inflicted on real people, this stereotype damages our political traditions and is a threat to the long-term survival of our republic.

Chapter 4

"The Constitution is a Living Document"

Many insist that the Constitution is a living document. The theory is that it has survived over two centuries as the governing charter for this nation because it is flexible enough to allow for change within its framework. However, the net effect is the theory has been used as justification for the judiciary to interpret the document in conflict with legislative decisions that properly belong to the legislative and executive branches of government. As such, this theory has been a tremendous disservice to this nation and its people.

There are two assumptions underlying the propensity to use the judiciary to usurp legislative functions. The first is that change must be accommodated. That the world has changed considerably over the past two centuries is a given. The political, culture, social, and technical environment literally forces us to change our government and its procedures to be able to react to, or anticipate if possible, the challenges that we face and the ever evolving values that guide us. The second assumption is that the document should not be changed except under rare and extraordinary circumstances. The thought is that the Constitution has such gravity and solemn dignity associated with it that it should not be changed lightly. In today's political climate, I question the effect of the combination of those arguments.

First, it is worth noting that change was anticipated from the inception of the document. A process for amending the Constitution is clearly described. If those who drafted, compromised, and eventually recommended the document to the States thought that changing it would be a normal event, why should not we also think so?

Frankly, I also believe that it should not be changed on a whim, but the process required to amend the Constitution itself guarantees that cannot happen. An amendment can only be included if both houses of Congress approve the amendment by a two-thirds majority, after which three-quarters of the States must ratify it. Alternatively, the States can call a constitutional convention; amend (or develop a new constitution) which again must be ratified by three-quarters of the States. Neither of these two procedures is possible without the support of a significant majority of the population.

Absent major cultural and political changes, is there really a frequent need to change the Constitution? The established framework accommodates most of the legislative changes we need make to react to changing circumstances. The Congress and President can adopt and sign legislation that can address the needs of the nation. The framers wisely constructed a governmental system that divides power, protects fundamental rights, and allows the legislative branch to adopt laws and the executive branch to enforce them. Not many of the world's problems will find a better solution by the modification of this foundational work.

Examples of our continued ability to function within the framework the founders established in spite of technological and cultural changes are many. I will focus on one in which I have personal experience. I have a background in planning, and worked for a government with a population over 800,000. My responsibilities included interpreting the zoning code for this jurisdiction. As such, it was easy for me to see how our zoning code worked, what it was designed to accomplish, and how the Constitution permits and affects local government's ability to regulate land use.

The Constitution allows State and local governments to establish laws and regulations that protect the health, safety, and welfare of the state and community, also known as police power. With this authority, state and local governments can and do establish laws to protect the public from the effects of decisions of property owners that can deleteriously affect those that occupy adjacent property. For instance, smokestack industry, pig farms, and sexually oriented businesses can be prevented from locating where they will adversely affect incompatible uses such as residential development. These laws also create a stable economic environment in which people can invest billions of dollars in capital improvements without the fear of incompatible uses undermining the investment. In spite of the many changes in land use trends and technology over the years, this clause has been flexible enough to accommodate the changes.

To be sure, many court decisions have attempted to ensure that state and local governments do not infringe on the rights granted to individuals in the Constitution, including defining the line between when such regulation becomes an uncompensated regulatory taking of property. However, this particular example of self-government by communities is included in the Constitution, which functions well if federal, state, and local institutions follow its direction and process. The same is true of innumerable other governmental functions.

45

Political

If our Constitution provides the framework needed to accommodate technological and cultural change, amendments should be rare, as they are. However, in the recent past a legal climate has evolved that has created a need for amendments, not because of the lack of foresight by the architects of the document, but rather because of the informal amendments that have been forced upon the nation by the judiciary.

Because the Constitution cannot be easily amended, those who cannot win at the ballot box have concluded that they need an alternative method for amending the document. This process is called an informal amendment, and it involves using the judiciary to interpret what the Constitution means, sometimes without much regard for the original intent of the founders. Originally, the intent was to determine the original intent of the framers; however, this process has evolved to become a means of circumventing the intent of the framers. In short, judicial activists have used the power to interpret the Constitution to impose legislative actions on the rest of the nation without the consent of the people as represented in Congress. They have succeeded in imposing their political goals by judicial fiat.

The widespread use of this device is bringing us to a point where the plain words of the Constitution are meaningless. The effect of the judiciary substituting its will in place of the language of the Constitution is that there are no concrete objective standards that can be relied upon over time. Every word is malleable and subject to change on a moments notice. In effect, we have no Constitution upon which we can rely; any change can be made at any time. The Kelo[9] decision is a good example of this. In direct contravention to the clear language of the Constitution and over two hundred years of political tradition, the Supreme Court ruled a private use of property can be a governmental use. Not only was the decision easily one of the egregious examples of judicial activism in the history of the nation, it also has spawned a political backlash that is being used by the opponents of all land use regulation to undermine legitimate and constructive land use law. For example, Oregon is faced with significant problems resulting from this backlash.

If we cannot rely on the clear words of the Constitution nor the documented intent of the founders, we have nothing to rely upon when making long-term cultural, political, or economic decisions. The value of anything we have can be swept away at the whim of five un-elected justices

---

[9]http://en.wikipedia.org/w/index.php?title=Kelo_v._City_of_New_London&oldid=132814084

(assuming the argument reaches the Supreme Court). This leads to political instability; no one can count on stable laws. Indeed, the only thing that separates us from a third-world dictatorship is the fact that we have at least five dictators telling us what to do. This includes land use, gay rights, abortion, and other subjects that mandate a result that cannot be found in the language or documented original intent of the Constitution. In making these decisions, the court has circumvented the will of the people and the political process that invariably leads to compromise and accommodation. Instead, we have political decisions that cannot be reversed by any means other than a Constitutional amendment.

This leads us to the most ironic and perverse result of judicial activism. If the Supreme Court legislates from the bench with a result that is in conflict with the intent of the Constitution, the restoration of the original law can only be made by Constitutional amendment, along with the difficult process that comes with it. Suddenly those who seek to reinstate a traditional constitutional interpretation are in the position of advocating amending the Constitution to restore it, and the opposition paints those advocates as dangerous extreme ideologues who are trying to change the Constitution radically or whimsically. Because a minority can easily thwart the will of the majority, the result usually stands, and part of our culture is permanently changed. In the case of unborn children, millions of lives are lost. In effect we have a "tyranny of the minority" instead of majority rule, a situation much worse than the "tyranny of the majority" which we attempt to keep within proper bounds.

Shakespeare and Charles Dickens both make a valid point that poorly reasoned law is an ass[10]. In other words, laws can and often do subvert themselves and the good of the public. When this occurs, the law must be changed. The Constitution has whatever is necessary to establish, amend, change, or repeal laws that are necessary to govern the people of this nation. If the law is an ass, it is not because of the Constitution, but because of subsequent legislation that can be altered within the framework of the Constitution or interpretation that can only be altered by amending the Constitution.

The Constitution is indeed a living document. It established a system of government that has lasted for over two hundred years, and can last another two hundred if the system as designed is allowed to function. The only way

---

[10] CHARLES DICKENS, *Oliver Twist*, chapter 51, p. 489 (1970). First published serially 1837–1839.

Political

to bring the law of the land back into conformance with constitutional principles is to ensure that jurists do not succeed in usurping the power of the people as they are represented by Congress and the President. The only way within our system to accomplish that is to ensure that judicial appointees are not going to attempt to legislate from the bench. Indeed, the most important aspect of national elections today is the power to appoint and confirm judges and justices. Our ability to govern ourselves depends upon justices that will allow us the freedom to continue that right.

Chapter 5

"Give Peace a Chance"

John Lennon plaintively appealed for society to choose peace over war in his 1969 song lyrics. At the time, the Vietnam War was in full swing, and body bags were being filled at the rate of 181 dead soldiers, marines, sailors, and airmen a week. Here I will disclose that I served in the Marine Corps from 1968 until 1970, and remember the carnage well. The United States seemed to be trapped in a war that had no hope of ending. With this backdrop, Lennon wrote and the Beatles performed the song, the title of which has since served as a rallying cry for the peace movement.

What effect has the emphasis on peace had on our pursuit of peace? As a percentage of the world's population, there are very few who prefer the horror, destruction, and curse of war to the tranquility, prosperity, and blessing of peace. It certainly seems reasonable that we should do as the lyrics suggest and "give peace a chance". However, what the lyrics do not bother to point out is that if we are required to resort to war, peace has been given a chance and is, for one reason or another, not a viable option.

It is important to understand that while it is only a very small percentage of the world's population that prefers the horror of war over peace, these people do exist. More important is their ability to affect the lives of all the others in the world that value peace. It does not take a majority to start and prosecute an offensive war, to be clearly distinguished from defensive wars. Defending against those who would enslave, coerce, plunder, or destroy is not waging offensive war.

What are some of the purposes of offensive war, or rather what justification is used to rationalize its use? There are some who know that their maintenance of personal power is contingent on keeping their population convinced that they are engaged in a just cause against oppressors that would destroy them. For these people, an informed and educated population is the kiss of death. Some are cold and calculating, using war as an instrument to further national objectives, including economic objectives, against their enemies. Some have irrational fears based on racial and religious biases. Some seek to exalt, at the expense of other groups, their own ethnic or cultural group. Some see it as their calling to spread religious ideals, even if it takes killing or coercing non-believers to do so. There are many reasons used to justify war.

First, let me make it as clear as possible that there is no justification for war based on the reasons listed above. The leadership of any country that commences or prosecutes war with these objectives deserves to be defeated and ignominiously executed. However, the question being discussed is how we can give peace a chance knowing that there are those who seek our destruction, and indeed the destruction of the civilization that seeks to give peace a chance. My answer would be that we have given peace a chance and it did not work. Meanwhile, we cannot sit by and allow our society to be overcome by those working against our interests, which incidentally coincide with world interests, just because some of us want to keep giving peace an indefinite number of chances in the face of malevolent forces that cannot be reasoned with.

I believe that most informed individuals have come to similar conclusions, which explains the widespread support for the maintenance of armed forces and their use in protecting our interests. However, a vocal minority continues to insist that peace needs a chance in spite of recent attacks and the clearly stated intentions of those who have attacked us.

These people are incredibly naïve. They cling to an idealistic notion that no one wants violent conflict and that if only given the chance everyone will lay down their arms, embrace, and sing Kumbaya together. I love the song too, but in the real world there are many who will not join in the refrain no matter how idealistic our intentions or altruistic our motivations. The "give peace a chance" advocates ignore the fact that conflict between individuals, communities, and nations is inevitable, and that some individuals, communities, and nations will resort to violence to achieve their goals no matter how desperately these idealists want peace. Yet they advocate that we cease fighting to protect ourselves in the misguided assumption that if we stop fighting our enemies will also stop fighting. I am unaware of any example in history where catastrophic consequences of surrender were not the result of one group in a war deciding to cease fighting, except for Russia's cessation of fighting in World War I. However, that example is not normal; Russia avoided national subjugation because Germany still had to fight on the Western Front. On a much lower level, if a victim of violence decides to capitulate to a bully, the long-term effect is constant abuse.

In addition to being naïve, they are also locked into a 1970's Vietnam War mentality. They refuse to believe that military defense is possible no matter how grave the threat. Every conflict we become involved in is followed by weeping and wailing about another Vietnam. This is true no matter how improbable the likelihood of defeat. Military operations in Grenada, Panama, the Gulf War, Afghanistan, and Iraq all were preceded by dire predictions of the doom of another Vietnam. It seems we are obsessed with making Vietnam the perpetual pattern for military action. The only operation I can remember which broke that pattern was our military intervention in Bosnia (Hmmm…I wonder why that could be?).

The attitude that we cannot prevail in a military conflict creates a self-fulfilling condition. The wails of defeat of the few undermine the will of the general population and serves to ensure defeat. If the majority allows this to occur, our defeat will be self-imposed, not a result of actual defeat on the battlefield. In addition, our enemies hear the wails and take heart because they know that soon their victory will be assured if they can just stay alive long enough for the politicians to pull the funding plug for the troops as Congress did to end the Vietnam War.

We also seem to be determined to limit our military options to ensure defeat. We are not willing to use interrogation techniques that are not torture because we are afraid of offending minority or world opinion. I am willing to bet that if a military unit were to execute a Muslim terrorist today with a bullet coated in pork lard (as General Pershing did in the Philippines) the anti-war activists would go berserk. If we were to summarily execute terrorists, as we did following the occupation of Germany and Japan after World War II, we would also be castigated. Those that want to coddle the adversary and seek to placate them fail to realize that all's fair in war, that war is Hell and will be forever, and that we must do what it takes to win. The only restrictions should be the Geneva and other relevant conventions that we are signatories to.

I submit that the "give peace a chance" advocates of today are the appeasers of yesterday. History has repeatedly taught us that aggressive enemies will not cease their aggression simply because those that value peace want them to. Indeed, aggressors view the desire for peace as a weakness to be exploited. Poland, Norway, the Netherlands, and Belgium learned this lesson the hard way leading up to and at the outset of World War II. Their desire for peace made no difference to Hitler. They were invaded, conquered, and subjugated anyway. Indeed, large numbers of their citizens were subsequently deported and systematically exterminated as a part of Hitler's "final solution" to rid the world of what he perceived to be inferior races, undesirable groups, and "useless eaters".

Political

The western powers just before World War II sought to make whatever accommodation Hitler wanted, short of selling out their own national interests, in order to avoid war. This was done in spite of clear indications that Hitler was convinced that war was inevitable. Neville Chamberlain, the Prime Minister of Great Britain, negotiated a settlement at Munich that he proclaimed would result in "peace in our time". Unfortunately, for Czechoslovakia it meant annexation for much of their population. Chamberlain was willing to trade peace for the liberty of the Czechs. In the end, the Czechs lost their liberty and Chamberlain got war anyway. In less than one year, Hitler invaded Poland, and the allied nations finally learned the bitter lesson that appeasement is a fatally flawed foreign policy strategy.

For many years after World War II that lesson was not lost upon us. In spite of the threat of or commencement of war, we took a hard line against totalitarian forces arrayed against us, and ultimately won. The Korean War, the Cold War, the Vietnam War (a battle in the overall conflict that we went wobbly on and lost) together with numerous smaller conflicts gave the enemy to know that we were willing to make the sacrifices needed to ensure our continued liberty, in spite of Nikita Khrushchev's assertion that Communism would bury our culture. That we succeeded in our long-term goal even though we allowed ourselves to be defeated in Vietnam is a testament to the enduring legacy of the lesson that Hitler taught us in addition to the enlightened leadership under President Reagan that finally forced the demise of the Soviet Union during the 1980"s.

Since the collapse of the Soviet Union, the lesson seems to have become a distant memory to some recent leaders. We have allowed interests aligned against us to demonstrate that we do not have the resolve necessary to defend ourselves in a protracted conflict. The withdrawal from Somalia and the inaction surrounding the first bombing of the World Trade Center and our overseas embassies are examples of this. At a time when we could demonstrate resolve and act to punish those who were instigating these atrocious acts, we chose to be indecisive instead. This encouraged those arrayed against us, who in turn plotted additional violence against us.

North Korea is a particularly egregious example of failure of appeasement, especially because when United States acted the North Koreans did not have the ability to significantly affect our national security. In 1994, the North Korean government was teetering on the brink of collapse. Their rice crop had once again failed, ostensibly because of drought, but oddly enough, the South Koreans across the 38th parallel were able to produce much more than they needed to survive. The North Koreans were in such dire straits that all that was needed was for us to sit by, watch them collapse, then go in afterward and help China, South Korea, Japan, and Russia deal with the resulting humanitarian crisis. This was at a time when the North Korean nuclear weapons program had not progressed to a point where it was a threat to anyone. Indeed, it seemed for a brief time that the Clinton Administration was going to take that approach.

Suddenly Jimmy Carter, the former president, decided to be a hero and rescue the world from this impending crisis. He successfully negotiated (from a position of strength) an agreement that gave the North Koreans the food needed to continue feeding their army, the fuel needed to keep their army, ruling class, and secret police warm and mobile, and technology that could be used against us in the future. In exchange, the North Koreans were allowed to continue to enslave and starve the general population. They also promised to cease their nuclear weapons program, but were not required to demonstrate compliance in any meaningful way. What a deal. It is no wonder that the North Koreans want to deal with us bilaterally; they still have the vivid image in their mind of Jimmy Carter graciously giving them everything they wanted with no real expectation of reciprocity. I am sure they would like to negotiate another similar deal with the stupid, naïve Americans. I hope that they have not.

As a result, we now have a rogue nation controlled by an intellectual midget that has nuclear weapons it developed in direct contravention to the promises it made to the United States. The North Koreans have made it clear that they may use them either as bargaining chips in a future deal with the United States or as a source of foreign currency by selling them to the highest bidder. All this because we decided to appease the North Korean leadership when they were in the weakest possible position. Jimmy Carter would be expected to deal naively with the Koreans; he has consistently demonstrated a lack of judgment with respect to foreign affairs. The real blame lies with the Clinton Administration, which foolishly accepted the agreement to avoid short-term foreign instability. No doubt other nations, especially Iran, have concluded from this experience that the United States and United Nations are weak and will not stand up to a nation determined to acquire nuclear weapons even though these actions are in direct conflict with international treaties.

The North Korean agreement, together with other actions described since the end of the Cold War, can be construed to be altruistic attempts to give peace a chance. However, when the long-term effects of the actions are considered, it seems clear that these actions are much closer to attempts to achieve peace at any price and have subsequently brought us much closer to war than we would have been if we had chosen the alternative course. I have yet to see an example in history when appeasement has led to peace. On the contrary, it has always had the opposite effect; war is eventually inevitable against a determined aggressor. This works out to be a "pay me now, or pay me later" situation (remember the car care commercial?). We can endure short-term pain and instability at a relatively low price in exchange for long-term peace, or we can cave in to the demands or aggressive actions of an aggressor only to have to pay a much higher price later.

Even more ridiculous is the statement "war never settled anything". I beg to differ. War generally settles almost everything. There is nothing quite so final as defeat or victory in war. The victors have triumphed, along with their ideology. The losers are consigned to oblivion, along with their ideology. Historically, the conquered group suffered unspeakable horror in the course of and after the war, and subsequent rebellion and dissent from the subjugated was dealt with using harsh, brutal, and final methods.

This has always been the pattern, except for recent wars that prematurely ended without a winner or loser. Typically in these cases, diplomatic pressure to end the war for the sake of ending the war forces a ceasefire but does nothing to remove or resolve the underlying source of the conflict. The assumption now is that war is always bad; therefore, we must stop all wars no matter what the long-term cost of delaying the resolution of the underlying conflict that defies resolution by diplomatic means. The underlying conflict is never resolved, and the parties continue the war by other means until the next inevitable conflagration erupts, only to be prematurely ended again. The standoff between Israel and the Muslim countries surrounding it is an excellent example of this. In spite of three generations of diplomatic efforts and the forced cessation of five shooting wars, peace is further from that region than it has been since before the establishment of the State of Israel.

We are living in a world where fanatical ideologists seek the destruction of our culture, religion, and way of life. Holy war is being waged against us, whether we want to live in peace or not. Those waging that war are willing to die to kill us because we are infidels and because they believe our way of life is decadent (unfortunately true to some extent, see Chapter 10). Indeed, they believe that martyrdom in their cause leads to happiness in the afterlife. This is an extension of the extended conflict that started in the 8th century in which Christian and other populations in the Middle East,

Southern Europe, and North Africa were systematically conquered and forced to convert, die, or live as second-class citizens.

In this war, our only choice is whether to fight or capitulate. If we capitulate, we should expect to see a culture that values freedom and liberty replaced with one that values strict adherence to religious dogma, including the honor killing of rape victims and the torture and execution of women whose only crime is their need to work to sustain their families. Granted, this is a worst case scenario, but because it seems that many mainstream Muslims either sympathize with the extremists or they fear death if they oppose them, it is not irrational to conclude that if the extremists win we could have a society that is a world-wide mirror image of Afghanistan under the Taliban.

Even then, we will not live in peace. If fanatical Muslims are successful in imposing their religion on the world, the next series of wars will be between different Islamic sects, races, or ethnic groups because they are different, or wars to gain economic advantage. There will always be differences in ideas and people, which will be used as an excuse to wage war on the part of those that seek it. This is easily demonstrated by the atrocities and conflicts between competing Muslim ideologies today even as they ostensibly seek unity against the West.

Many no longer believe in the principles that made this country great. If someone quoting Patrick Henry says, "Give me liberty, or give me death", they regard the person as a fanatical ideologue who is just as dangerous as the extremists we are currently fighting. They place a higher value on life than they place on principle. This means that nothing is more important than staying alive. Those that believe this may eventually learn the hard way that life without liberty is not really living, and that under an intolerant ideologically driven regime life is cheap and easily forfeited.

In addition, many think that because they sympathize with those who oppose us they will somehow be exempt from the terrorist carnage. They have yet to understand that the freedom to protest governmental action is a nearly exclusive characteristic of western democracies, and that their sympathy is largely interpreted as weakness. At best, these people are "useful idiots" to those who seek our destruction, and when they are no longer useful they will be just another segment of a decadent society that needs to be purged.

Those who effectively undermine our ability to defend ourselves include several groups. Many pacifists seek peace at any price; for this group there is no cause or value more important than the avoidance of violent conflict.

55

Another group is those who are convinced that the United States is evil, and believe our defeat is justified (isn't that treason?) Then there are those who cannot focus on a long-term problem and fail to realize that liberty is a condition that must be constantly maintained, most often with the sacrifice of members of our society that value their and our liberty more than their own lives. These people react with horror when the bombs explode and the body bags start coming home, and seek to end the horror no matter what the long-term cost. An umbrella of strength that they disdain and work to subvert protects all of these groups.

A group that has recently brought contempt upon themselves are mainstream media representatives who claim they cannot take sides in the current conflict, in spite of the fact that terrorist actions are deliberately designed to destroy what they value most, including diversity, freedom, and dissent. This is in stark contrast to the stance that the media has taken in every war before the Vietnam War. When has the American media ever declared themselves neutral in a war that seeks to destroy the foundation of their existence? Even if they now consider themselves a global media responsible for global welfare, they should still be interested in the preservation of the culture that allows them to exist and flourish.

Much of the impetus behind the cries to give peace a chance is the lack of fortitude needed to persevere in a conflict that will take years, if not decades, to win. We think that our wars should be like watching a movie or ordering fast food; all that is necessary is to pay the bargain price, go to the drive-up window in a car (bomb from afar), and wait for the result. Or we watch as Sylvester Stallone single-handedly rescues the nation in two hours, then goes home to dinner and a romantic evening. This is incredibly unrealistic, and we have been watching way too many movies for our own good. In the real world, just because Hollywood can save the world in a two hour movie does not mean that wars can be fought and won in a short period of time or without suffering and hardship.

I believe we have given peace a chance, and it has not worked. It is now time to give strength, resolve, courage, and determination a chance. We should give standing up to our enemies a chance. Showing them that life, liberty, and the pursuit of happiness are still principles worth living and dying for is worth a try. It certainly will be a dramatic change for a significant minority of our population that is convinced that we are weak and without moral authority to act in our own interest. I also believe that history has taught us repeatedly that this is the only road to peace.

Chapter 6

"The Sky (Environment) is Falling"

The Chicken Littles of the world have predicted doom and gloom continuously for centuries. However, in recent years the voices have become ever more shrill in their insistence that not only is the sky falling, but that human activities are making it fall. Consider that over my short lifetime, I have been told that human and environmental disasters are looming because of:

- Global cooling and an impending Ice Age;
- Global warming and catastrophic polar melting;
- Depletion of oxygen due to estuary pollution;
- Depletion of oxygen due to deforestation;
- Depletion of the ozone layer because of chemical pollution;
- Widespread destruction of species due to the actions of humans;
- Population growth that will result in resource wars and mass starvation;
- Unsustainable economic models;
- Technology

If there is anything we can be certain of, it is that the Chicken Littles of the world will continue to run around hysterically shouting that the environmental sky is falling. This in spite of the fact that most of these dire predictions were either wrong or that technology (one of the sources of fear for the doomsayers) has solved or at least postponed the problems. Some examples are as follows.

Climate Change

While in college in the mid 1970's, I was taught that the earth was entering an extended period of cooling that would lead to another Ice Age. Many were convinced of this, including professors (and I graduated from Brigham Young University; not exactly a bastion of liberal thought) who propounded it in classroom lectures and who were supported by text authors. The degree to which they were convinced that global cooling was real was just as intense as the depth of conviction that holds global warming is occurring now. Concerned as everyone was, because the cooler temperatures were supposedly a result of cyclical forces of nature it seemed that there was nothing that humans could use to reduce the possibility of widespread starvation and suffering.

However, that teaching was soon replaced with the supposition that we were not entering into another Ice Age, but rather that global temperatures were increasing. This will ostensibly lead to the melting of our polar icecaps, the inundation of coastlines, climactic disruption, and, of course, widespread starvation and suffering. Remarkably enough, some of the climatic repercussions of global warming seem to be nearly identical to the repercussions of another Ice Age if Hollywood propaganda is to be believed. Also remarkable, this theory holds human activity as the culprit for global warming; if we but stop burning fossil fuels and return to a Walden-like agrarian lifestyle we can circumvent the suffering.

As a side note, I do not know for certain whether global warming is real, or if it is real whether it is a result of human activity. Based on what I have read, it may or may not be. However, even if it is not real nor the result of human actions, we should not use that as justification to avoid minimizing the impact we have on our environment, and reducing the economic drain and subsidization of enemies associated with imported fossil fuels. In this case, the Chicken Littles may be hysterical in their reaction to the prospect of global warming; however, the net effect of their histrionics may be useful in weaning ourselves from fossil fuels, the purchase of which undermines the economy and security of the United States.

However, whether global warming is real and a result of human activity or not is beside the point of this chapter, which is that much of what we accept as scientific fact at one point in time is replaced with other conflicting facts at a future date. Unfortunately, it seems that all too often the change in facts conveniently coincide with radical environmental interests. While I like to think that science is based on honest scientific inquiry and analysis, I tend to get skeptical when science suddenly produces facts that support popular ideology, especially when the previously accepted facts supported the polar opposite of the latter.

Oxygen Production

On to the next subject. While in college I was taught that a preponderance of the world's oxygen was produced in estuaries by enormous numbers of algae fed by the nutrients washing from land into the ocean. I had serious doubts about that fact, and questioned whether the massive numbers of trees and other vegetation on land wouldn't produce the bulk of oxygen. I was assured otherwise with the condescending demeanor the professor thought I deserved. Remarkably enough, at the time estuaries were threatened by pollution generated by human activity, which threatened the production of algae and species that depended on the algae for food, whether first hand or further up the food web. Of course, humans depend not only on the species further up the web for food, but also for the oxygen the algae produced.

A funny thing happened after the Clean Water Act was adopted, properly enforced, and had a positive effect on polluted estuaries. I am now told that the vast majority of oxygen is not produced in estuaries, but by forests; especially rainforests. I guess I was right to question the estuary fact while I was in school. Also remarkable is the fact that there is significant logging within the rainforests, and that environmental organizations are intent on limiting the exploitation of these resources. Here is another factual shift that conveniently supports an environmental cause in conflict with the facts that were used to support previous environmental policy.

Population Crisis

Yet again, while in school I was taught that there was an impending crisis because of the projected exponential increase in population and our inability to produce the food needed to sustain the population. Energy and other resources were also alleged to be limiting factors on how large a population could be accommodated on our "fragile" planet. Zero population growth was the rallying cry of the day, and those who produced more children than the replacement rate were demonized and ostracized. This in turn led to political and social pressure to limit family size and relax restrictions on abortion and euthanasia. Euthanasia was not condoned then; however, the states of Oregon and Washington now allow it. Abortion in the United States has resulted in the premature death of 45 million human beings that could have been productive citizens. China, in addition to forced abortions, practices infanticide to ensure that couples do not have more than one child. The push for zero population growth has lead to one of the largest worldwide losses of potential human life that has ever occurred in recorded history. Even worse, we have adopted Adolph Hitler's practice of killing the handicapped; the only difference is that we do it before the handicapped baby is born.

Political

However, a funny thing happened on the way to our population crisis. For some reason, food production was able to keep up with population growth, and populations that were threatened with mass starvation in the 1950's and 1960's were not only saved, but world population tripled and we still have enough food for all[11]. Indeed, if obesity rates in much of the world are any indication, we may have too much food available for all (for those who are humorless, that last comment is a joke).

It turned out that technology created a "green revolution" that enabled massive increases in food production, which forestalled the predicted Malthusian crisis. The problems we face with starvation today are associated with war, economics, distribution, and storage, not with our ability to produce the food needed to feed the world adequately. Indeed, we still pay farmers in this county to limit food production in order to prop up food prices and use a significant percentage of food for fuel. In the recent past, more than half of all food produced was lost to insects, rodents, decomposition, and waste.

That said, we must not become complacent about our ability to provide food for future populations. Indeed, by 2030 it is expected that world demand for food will increase by 50%. That is a lot of food. For that reason we must take steps to increase food supply, including increasing production and decreasing the loss of what is presently produced. We should eliminate the use of food for fuel, allow irradiation of food to prevent spoilage, and mount an aggressive genetic engineering program to minimize the use of energy and pesticides and to increase production in difficult climates and soil types. For more on this see the technology section of this chapter.

The exponential increase in population was also supposed to lead to massive environmental problems, especially problems related to clean air and water. Remarkably enough, technology and strict regulation has also led to a decline in pollution within industrialized nations as compared to the initial phase of the Industrial Revolution, or even thirty years ago for that matter. It has been a long time since the Cuyahoga River caught fire. The doomsday scenarios that we are constantly bombarded with have been demonstrated to be inapplicable when technology is allowed to solve problems.

Because we have been indoctrinating our young to limit the number of children they bear, we now have the opposite population problem; that is many western nations are not replacing themselves, and are suffering

---

[11] http://en.wikipedia.org/wiki/Special:Cite?page=Green+Revolution

cultural and economic decline as a result (see Chapter 13 for more on this). Those nations and cultures that did not buy into the arguments of the Chicken Littles are producing lots of people. Those cultures are ascending, which should be a concern to those who are in decline because of declining birthrates. Even worse, many of those reared in western cultures have concluded that their culture is inferior because it is not perfect and therefore they are not willing to promote it in the face of increased competition for the allegiance of our youth and other cultures. But I digress.

Ozone Depletion

Another crisis that seems to have come and gone is the thinning of the ozone layer and its potential effect on the earth's climate. Chemical pollution was blamed, especially chlorofluorocarbons. The solution was to ban the use of the chemicals, although the doomsayers routinely lamented that the effects of the chemicals were irreversible, and that once the chemicals were in the atmosphere they would remain indefinitely. Because the interaction of the chemicals in the atmosphere with ozone not only destroyed ozone but left the chlorofluorocarbons intact to continue to destroy ozone into the indefinite future, we were told that it was only a matter of time before our protective ozone layer was gone.

The political campaign was successful, and chlorofluorocarbons are largely a chemical of the past. We are now told that ozone layer degeneration is slowing and may recover. In fairness to the Chicken Littles of the world, this is one time where the action taken seems to have had a beneficial effect. Indeed, even the economic disaster predicted by those who did not want to see chlorofluorocarbons banned did not materialize; the accusation that the ban would result in discomfort because chlorofluorocarbon replacements would not cool efficiently was overblown. Still, the doomsayers prediction that the destruction of the ozone layer was inevitable seems to have been hyperbole.

Species Protection

Last, it was and still is predicted that human activity, specifically habitat destruction and over harvesting of species for food, would lead to the extinction of many species. While this is clearly a concern, it is not the environmental disaster that has been predicted. Many species are being protected and are in recovery. Others are doing just fine, regardless of human activity, indeed, some species of wildlife survive well even in

61

suburban settings. Coyotes in Las Vegas eat very well with the abundance of cats and dogs here that are unable to defend themselves against these wily animals.

Is it possible to save all species? Of course not. Some species will become extinct no matter what we do. Some species must become extinct if our scientific belief in the theory of evolution is to be taken seriously. Some species will be lost simply because of inevitable environmental changes that are not the result of human actions. In nature, the extinction of species is inevitable, in fact ordinary. The only question is whether a particular species will disappear entirely or be replaced by a similar species that has adapted to changed circumstances or conditions. After all, if only the fit survive in a Darwinian system, it stands to reason that as environmental changes occur some species will not adapt while others will. Most species do not become extinct because of human activity.

Other species will be lost because of human manipulation of the environment; however, this result is not inevitable. Governments have taken action to preserve species, often with favorable results. With this effort, our society must balance the needs of the human population with the cost of preservation. Some argue that if there is a choice between human progress and the extinction of a species we should forego progress. Almost always we do not need to make that choice; if technology and reasonable regulation cannot prevent extinction it is likely the species was not selected by the natural environment to survive.

Environmental species protection is an area where an agenda to stop development is evident. There are those who are using species protection as a means to reduce or eliminate economic growth. They seek to protect species that are not threatened as an excuse to stop growth and human use of property, and even worse, to effect a regulatory taking of property. The justification is that the figurative sky will fall because some obscure and inconsequential insect genetically identical or similar to other robust insect populations will be unable to survive the construction of a home needed to provide shelter for humans. Those that take these extreme positions do incalculable damage to their environmental cause.

We can and must take reasonable steps to preserve species and habitat. But not to the exclusion of all else, including housing for those who need shelter and jobs to feed their families. A happy medium can be reached to the benefit of all. The tendency of radical environmentalists to overreach in their attempts to save species that are not really threatened considerably undermines the cause of responsible environmental policy.

There are some on the radical fringe that take species protection to a ludicrous extreme. For instance, do all species have a right to exist? To question whether a distinctly human right is applicable to plants and animals of itself reveals an unreal anthropomorphic view of nature (these people have been watching way too many cartoons that depict mice, deer, and other animals with human characteristics). When did we conclude that species have rights, as if they were human beings with our awareness of nature? The political stance of PETA[12] notwithstanding, we have never granted rights to other species. Laws regulating the humane treatment of animals do not confer rights; they merely prohibit unnecessary cruelty, and are as much to protect humans as they are to protect animals.

Conferring rights to other species would present significant problems for the human population. If we grant rights to animals and prohibit their use as food, we eliminate a substantial portion of the food available to us. If we grant animals these rights, do we also do the same for plants? Fruitarians would only have us eating food that can be harvested without killing the plant. And if we protect plant life, what is to stop us from conferring rights to potential plant life, specifically seeds. That would remove all grains as a food source. It's not hard to imagine a substantial reduction in the food supply if we go down this road.

By the way, much of this food is not, as is represented by PETA and others, grown at the expense of better food. While much grain is used for animal husbandry, it is also true that these animals eat much that humans cannot eat. Food waste fed to pigs and grass consumed by cattle are notable examples. Because humans cannot digest cellulose, growing cattle is a means of using cellulose for human food (and other carnivores).

In addition, if we decide to grant animals rights, where do we draw the line between which animals have rights, or do all organisms have rights?. Does that mean we would not be able to use chemicals and drugs to kill microorganisms that pose a threat to human life? Bleach may become a prohibited chemical, and antibiotics could be prohibited due to their effect on species that have the right to exist and grow within human bodies. For that matter, would we be forced to stop drinking acidic orange juice, stop walking to make sure we don't inadvertently step on an ant, and stop breathing to ensure we don't inhale and kill microscopic life in the atmosphere? While these seem to be ludicrous policies that would result in

---

[12] People for the Ethical Treatment of Animals

63

the extinction of our species, it is still appropriate to explore the potential ramifications of the arguments that are being foisted upon us.

We are a component of a natural environment in which animals eat plants and other animals to survive. Carnivores eat animals, herbivores eat plants, and omnivores eat both plants and animals. Humans are omnivores, and assuming the theory of evolution to be valid, we have evolved and survived as a species by eating both plants and animals, with genetic mutations over time that maximized survival with the diet we had available to us. Very few will argue that we should force lions, tigers, and bears (Oh my!) to accept vegetarian or fruitarian diets because they have evolved as they have with the diet to which they have genetically adapted. By the same token, it is illogical to argue that we should ignore millions of years of evolution in our current food choices notwithstanding the vociferous campaign waged by PETA to get us to stop eating meat.

What about species that pose a threat to human survival? If all species have a right to exist, can we destroy smallpox or tuberculosis as a species? That we did not eradicate tuberculosis when we could has now resulted in antibiotic resistant strains that cannot be cured with the drugs we have at this time. Smallpox would devastate the world's population similar to the epidemic that decimated the Native American population along the eastern seaboard of North America in the early 1600's if the few remaining samples were allowed to be reintroduced into the human environment. A good argument can be made that any species that presents a threat to human survival should be destroyed if possible. While I recognize that there are rational arguments against doing this, if human survival is dependent upon the destruction of a species, I would choose the destruction of the species in a heartbeat. I'm sure that misanthropes will disagree.

In addition, environmental groups have in the recent past influenced public policy makers to stop the attempted control of species regarded as pests. The argument was that we should let the natural environment take its course. An example of this is the bark beetle, which burrows into the trunks of evergreen trees, deprives the tree of sustenance, and eventually kills it. There are vast tracts of formerly lush green forests across the west that are now composed of dead and dying trees. This because those who allegedly cared most about the preservation of the natural environment cared more about the prevention of human intervention to protect that environment. Ironically, for many years they also prevailed upon policy makers to prevent the harvesting of the trees, which not only ensured that the bark beetles had unimpeded access to the entire forest ecosystem, but also led to the senseless waste of precious resources, and created conditions ripe for extremely large and destructive wildfires. You know the rest of the story with the news reports and videos of wildfires burning in the Western United States. Only in the past few years has this idiotic policy been reversed.

The net result of this policy is typical of the result of acting to protect the environment without considering the total effect of a policy. Because of the lack of action to stem the onslaught of the bark beetle infestation, many forests that were formerly a visual, economic, and environmental resource are now visually blighted and a hazard. The forests that burned not only resulted in a significant loss of valuable species and habitat, but also the loss of resources that could have been utilized for lumber and paper products at the same time that these resources are in high demand, and which will need to be filled by cutting trees elsewhere that otherwise would have been saved. The result is we have the worst of all possibilities; that is we have none of the resources associated with the original forest, we are cutting forests elsewhere to obtain needed products that could have been provided by the blighted forests, plus the burned forests put additional heat and carbon into the atmosphere, something the environmentalists decry in their ostensible quest to reduce global warming. Habitat restoration will take years.

Some species deserve protection, but much of the time there is little we can do. For example, the desert tortoise, a protected species, lives in southwestern deserts. This animal has been decimated by 1), a virus that killed large numbers of the animals, and 2), natural predators that eat them. There has been much ado about restricting the development of private land in the southwestern states; however, compared to the vast tracts of undeveloped pristine federally owned land the developed and developable private acreage is miniscule, and the development of that small percentage of land should have no material effect on the long-term survival of the tortoise. If we really want to preserve the species, we need to somehow prevent the spread of the virus and reduce the predatory raven population.

Even more perplexing is the fact that the protected tortoises eat protected flora. Herein lies a conundrum for environmental extremists; if we do not allow the viruses and ravens to propagate by destroying tortoises, are we practicing species discrimination? Do we kill carnivores that eat protected herbivores, or kill protected herbivores that eat protected flora?

In the end, most of our efforts at manipulating the natural environment that ignore the complexity of nature will have little long-term effect, if they have any effect at all. Instead of using data that may be flawed to dictate public policy, we should be carefully considering the totality of the implications of proposed policy on the natural environment, upon which we depend for our survival, including our economic survival.

Sustainability

Much of the current efforts of the Chicken Littles are focused on policies that result in sustainable populations and environments. The effort is well intentioned; however, the underlying assumptions about global sustainability do not account for the resources that humans have to ensure the availability of everything needed to sustain large populations.

First, let me observe that I am in the business of promoting sustainable environments. I am a planner, and recently retired from a position that had significant responsibilities in a large political jurisdiction in the Southwestern United States. I am also a member of the American Institute of Certified Planners, and so I have some level of professional expertise and a considerable interest in promoting sound and sustainable planning practices. These practices seek to maximize the efficient use of land, air, water, human, ecological, and economic resources to promote efficient and livable environments that are in the best interest of present and future populations. I firmly believe that these are goals that most people share, whether considering a local or global environment.

That said, some of those who promote sustainability are surreptitiously advancing a radical agenda that seeks to undermine individual rights while not significantly contributing to sustainable environments. Conversely, others advocate in favor of sustainability, but actually promote unsustainable practices. Still others advocate in favor of sustainability but do so while laboring under the false impression that the resource base available for human and ecological benefit is much more limited that it actually is, which results in a substantial devaluation of potential.

On a global scale, what constitutes sustainability? The best analysis that I have read to date is a paper produced by World Watch titled "What is Sustainability, Anyway?"[13]. In it the authors present a cogent and thoughtful analysis of the planet's ability to sustain large human populations taking into consideration various lifestyle and quality of life factors. However, even this analysis fails to comprehend the ability of the planet to sustain not just very large human populations, but also maintain with

---

[13] What is Sustainability, Anyway?, Thomas Prugh and Erik Assadourian, Oct 2003 World Watch Magazine

minimal impact the complex and essential environment and ecological system that nurtures and fulfills human existence.

A principal flaw in arguments in favor of sustainability is the assumption that the Earth has a finite amount of resources and that this limited resource base presents limitations on the amount of life, including human life, that the planet can sustain. The next part of the discussion invariably leads to a discussion of these limited resources, their scarcity, and the unsustainable rate at which the resources are being consumed, fossil fuels being the most notable example. Indeed, given the economic system that has developed with fossil fuels providing the energy needed to sustain the economy, that conclusion is not surprising. However, once again, these arguments do not present a holistic picture.

My principal argument is that we really do not have a finite amount of resources, but rather we have nearly infinite resources. This seems counterintuitive, even to me. I recognize that the Earth is essentially a closed system, with little matter being added to its mass compared to its existing mass. The few meteors and ice chunks that are injected into our ecosystem from space are insignificant when compared to the current mass of the Earth, and certainly are not a major factor in improving our resource base. For all practical purposes, the Earth is composed of a finite number of elements. Here I need to make a clear distinction between a limited number of elements and a limited resource base. A finite number of elements does not necessarily mean that the resources we have available to us are finite when energy is added to the equation.

Life on earth was made possible because of the combination of energy and element in just the right amounts. Indeed, one argument of secularists is that the evolution of life is possible without a creator and without contradicting the Second Law of Thermodynamics because of the energy rained down upon the Earth by the Sun. Whether one believes that this is a creative process instigated by God or random chance does not change the indisputable fact that life would not be possible without the energy from the Sun. The energy received has resulted over time in countless life forms having lived and died on this planet. Many of the remnants of those life forms constitute the fossil fuels that we currently extract to sustain our economy.

The energy that is still being rained down on the Earth is the reason we have such a vast resource base. The interaction of element and energy can be and is being used to create everything we need to not just survive, but to

67

thrive. These include the life created by propagation and photosynthesis without any human influence whatsoever. It also includes matter and life that is manipulated by technology to create materials and modified life forms that enable us to more efficiently produce the food that we and other animals need, products that protect us from and heal us of disease, materials for shelter, and the tools needed to perform work, just to name a few.

Even though our economy is currently dependent upon fossil fuels, we are not obligated to continue this dependence. Energy is everywhere, and as the price and scarcity of fossil fuels increases the probability of alternative energy sources becoming economically advantageous increases. Extracting energy from the myriad sources around us, including solar, magnetic, and atomic, is not a matter of solving intractable technological problems; rather it is a matter of cost and political will. If the past is any indication of future success, almost any technological problem can be solved if enough money is thrown at it. That being the case, no matter what limited amount of fossil fuels we have available for extraction we can assume that the energy needed to fuel our economy and create resources we need will always be available. The only question is how much it will cost.

Sustainability is not a matter of limiting population to match a perceived limited resource base. Elements are neither created nor destroyed; they do not suddenly disappear merely because humans have discarded resources and used them to fill massive landfills. The resources will always be there for use whenever society recognizes the materials as resources rather than toxic waste. The same is true of carbon, along with oxygen and hydrogen it is one of three elements that form the building blocks of life. It is a resource not to be treated as toxic waste and buried to mitigate the effects of global warming, but as an element that can be utilized over and over again to create food, clothing, medicine, building materials, extremely strong and lightweight fiber that is far superior to steel, and a myriad of other products that support life, including wildlife and threatened species. All that is needed to continuously support this process is the energy that is everywhere around us.

It is important to remember that we are not producing carbon when we burn fossil fuels. We are merely utilizing the energy stored in the chains of carbon, oxygen, and hydrogen molecules, which then breaks up the molecules into simpler molecules. If it is true that the carbon dioxide that is produced as a byproduct of combustion is changing our climate, perhaps we should consider how we could efficiently use the resource over and over again. Remarkably enough, nature has already solved this problem for us.

Instead of burying carbon dioxide, would it not make more sense to use it for plant production? The plants can be harvested and used, after which the cycle can be repeated, mimicking the natural environment. If not plants, carbon is one of the most useful elements we have available to us, and technological advancements may result in its use in high strength cables and solar cells just to name a few.

Humans have been wildly successful beyond any other species because of our ability to 1) transmit and accumulate knowledge using symbolic speech, 2) utilize fire as a tool, 3) construct tools, and 4) adapt. Using accumulated knowledge and manufactured tools, we have adjusted to problems in the past that threatened our existence. We face similar problems now. Indeed, some human populations have chosen poorly when it comes to managing their resource base in a sustainable manner. Easter Island is a good example. We can follow their example and squander valuable resources without planning for the future populations that depend upon them. Alternatively, we can recognize the value of all the recourses at our disposal and plan to utilize them for the benefit of our society and ecology.

Technology

Other Chicken Littles insist that we are threatened by technology, especially technology that promises to significantly expand our ability to feed larger human populations. However, the combination of technology and energy is the only reason this planet can sustain more than around four hundred million people at a time, and that population would be living hand to mouth in a subsistence economy without technological intervention.

Why is it that there is such a vociferous campaign to stymie technological advances in food production and preservation? Could it be that radicals are so frustrated with their inability to predict the demise of our species that they are trying to stop advances in food production and preservation technology to make their predictions of disaster self-fulfilling? I wonder.

There is much technology available that will allow us to increase food supplies in order to meet future demand. There are many bio-engineered foods that have been developed that could transform nutrition, allowing fresh fruits and vegetables to be grown year around in all but the harshest climates and providing food resistant to disease and pests. Other genetic engineering projects have produced strains of crops that can grow on marginal soils, thereby significantly increasing the ability of developing countries to feed their populations. Radiation technology can substantially reduce food spoilage while at the same time reducing the risk of food poisoning. Yet, there is a nearly hysterical campaign to prevent the use of these technologies. Indeed, those who insist that their use gives us "frankenfoods" that will somehow irreparably harm us have successfully prevented the use of irradiation and frost resistant strawberries, to name just a few.

By the way, this negative reaction to genetically engineered foods is profoundly illogical. Very few of the foods we consume have not been genetically engineered. Any person who refuses to eat genetically engineered food is in serious trouble. To be sure, this engineering has occurred over significant periods of time, but the engineering has occurred nonetheless. Maize is a good example. When first discovered and domesticated many millennia ago, the plant was small and yielded a comparatively miniscule amount of grain. Over time, selection, crossbreeding, and the creation of new strains resulted in the tremendous increase in crop yields and the myriad of varieties we use as food today, some varieties better suited for human consumption and some for animals. The same process has occurred for all domesticated crops and animals grown for food. The only difference between the genetically engineered food we buy with an "organic" label and the food produced as a result of genetic manipulation in the laboratory is that the laboratory makes the changes occur much, much faster.

I personally resent the effort of those whose meddling affects my ability to make choices. Not only does the blocking of effective technology threaten our ability to feed our future population, but it is also personally depriving me of strawberries that I can grow in the winter and irradiated food that I don't need to refrigerate. Because I must continue to refrigerate food that has not been irradiated, I am forced to continue using energy that impacts national security and climate change in order to eat. I can understand why some may choose not to buy these products. They have no right to take away my ability to do so just because they are hysterically and irrationally opposed to the technology.

Conclusion

I understand that there are indeed problems that face our species, planet, and other species on a global scale. I am not necessarily saying that none of the aforementioned "crises" are grounded in fact; indeed, the chlorofluorocarbon issue was a problem that needed to be addressed.

What is clear is that environmental arguments on the opposite side of an issue cannot be accurate. Also clear is the propensity of the Chicken Littles to hysterically decry human attempts to solve problems that will demonstratively improve the human and natural environment because the Chicken Littles fear technology or seek the disaster they predict. I am willing to listen to objective evidence and reason, but the scientific community has cried wolf way too many times for me to just jump up, stand at attention, salute, and run off to implement their latest environmental fix. I am not from Missouri, but I still want the scientific community to show me that the effect they describe is real, and is a result of human activity that can be mitigated by behavioral change.

Last, hysterically complaining that the sky is falling and calling for a knee-jerk reaction that does not consider a holistic solution to a problem is shortsighted and foolish. We can and must do better.

Chapter 7

"America is a (or the) force for Evil in the World"

You must be kidding! This has to be one of the most ludicrous assertions I have ever heard. Yet, with apologies to Dave Barry, I am not making this up; there are really people out there that believe this. In and of itself, it is a statement as to how extreme viewpoints have polluted public discourse and reason that I actually feel a need to write a chapter defending the moral status of the United States.

The first thing we should evaluate is whether in fact the assertion is true. It is a simple test. Overall, does the history, current domestic policy, and current foreign policy of the United States of America have a destructive impact on the people of this nation and the world? As you can tell from the opening paragraph, it is obvious that I believe they do not. I believe that a rational examination of the facts would similarly persuade any open-minded individual who accepts real facts as a basis for their opinion instead of the propaganda being spewed by left-wing loons.

History should be the first criterion for determining what impact the country has had. I believe that the history of this nation has been one extended experiment in and struggle to allow unprecedented freedom to its population, the immigrants who came (and still come) seeking a better life, and eventually the whole world.

The visionary statement that served as the foundation for the establishment of this nation, the values of which are reflected in the government and rights established by the Constitution of the United States, is the Declaration of Independence. The Declaration asserts that all men have inalienable rights bestowed upon them by God, affirms the equality of man, and explains that government's proper role is to secure those basic rights for its people. It also insists that people have the right to replace a government that does not accomplish those purposes for its citizens. These words did not just give a final cause to the conflict that evolved into the Revolutionary War; they were in fact revolutionary concepts that were anathema to the rulers of the day. Even so, these principles were held to be self-evident by those who put their lives on the line when they signed the document. The founders of this nation were not evil, nor were the results of their inspiration and the sacrifice needed to effect its implementation.

In recent decades, there has been a concerted effort to denigrate and marginalize the founders. They have been accused of all manner of indiscretions and selfish motivations, and we are expected to be shocked, shocked that those human beings would actually act like, well human beings. Of course, they were people with failings and problems. In fact, that makes their achievement even more meaningful and significant. In spite of their failings, they drafted documents that have served as a model for humanity the world over, and resulted in the establishment of a nation that has almost single-handedly transformed the political, cultural, and economic environment of the globe. That the framers were unable to secure equality for all does not diminish their accomplishment, they did the best they could with the political environment they were in.

Another criticism is that the founders were hypocritical, racist, and sexist. Well duh. Many citizens today would stand convicted on the same charges in spite of two hundred years of cultural conditioning. We are expected to be shocked that eighteenth century men would actually exhibit behavior that reflects the cultural values common in, well the eighteenth century. Even then, not all were hypocrites, especially with respect to race. The compromise on slavery that was adopted in the Constitution was the best that could be expected given the political realities of the day. The legacy that the founders of this nation bequeathed its citizens is not evil.

The Constitution was an attempt to implement the vision of government expressed in the Declaration of Independence. It was designed to divide power among the various branches of government in order to guard against the abuse of power by any one branch of government; all the better to help ensure that government remained responsive to those governed. There is flexibility built into it; it can be amended through a deliberately difficult process. It has worked well, has survived over two centuries intact, and I believe it can last indefinitely if allowed to by the people governed by it. Importantly, the Bill of rights was also adopted, which set stage for unprecedented freedom for individuals and the economic prosperity that was to follow. The Constitution of the United States is not a force for evil in the world.

Following the Revolutionary War and the ratification of the Constitution, the people of many nations aspired to the liberties evident in the newly created United States of America. Revolution swept across Europe, some successful, others not initially, but eventually the political landscape was transformed. As time wore on it became apparent that not only was this experiment in democracy beneficial from the standpoint of liberty, but it also set the stage for unprecedented prosperity, innovation, creativity, growth, and the improvement in any nation's quality of life. In time, a majority of the countries of the world adopted institutions designed to accomplish what the United States had achieved. It is clear that the model presented to and emulated by the world is not a force for evil.

Unfortunately, the reality of human politics, culture, fear, and greed meant that often we did not live up to the ideals expressed in the Declaration of Independence nor its proposed implementation in the Constitution. Already mentioned is the compromise on slavery. In addition, we have had a constant struggle to ensure the civil rights of minorities, including African-Americans after freedom from slavery was granted by the Emancipation Proclamation and Thirteenth Amendment. Historical biases against giving rights to women meant that half the population was treated as second-class citizens at best. Those with different religious beliefs were feared, and in at least one instance the weight of government was brought to bear against a group in a deliberate attempt to eliminate the organization. Mormon citizens were forcibly expelled from Missouri under an extermination order issued by the Governor of the state largely because the slaveholding interests in the state feared them and their political views. Later they were forcibly expelled from Illinois, and an army was sent to the relocated community in the Salt Lake Valley to quell a non-existent uprising. The nation's treatment of Native Americans was particularly abominable during the nineteenth century, especially under Andrew Jackson's morally bankrupt presidency. It was much worse than the treatment accorded African-Americans, in effect a policy of genocide against that population. California even paid bounties for the scalps of Native Americans unlucky enough to be born in that state.

These and other historic problems have resulted in the perception in the minds of radical ideologues that the history of the United States is a study in immorality, extermination, oppression and the abuse of power. This is their opinion in spite of the majority's prolonged and consistent opposition to the base human tendencies that resulted in the injustices they decry. They use today's moral positions to condemn the practices of long ago and at the same time ignore the fact that the oppressors lost.

They also disregard the fact that human history the world over is replete with societies that practiced the same policies that are condemned, in addition to even worse customs, which have occurred repeatedly. The only thing that changes is the time and place. As an example, Native American tribes, specifically the Ute tribe, would conduct raids on other tribes in what is now the Southwestern United States. They would capture and sell into slavery those they could and kill those whom they couldn't sell. This practice in particular decimated the Southern Paiutes. In one account, a group of Mormon settlers was approached with two captive children. When the Mormons indicated to the Ute band that they would not participate in the slave trade, one of the children was immediately killed by bashing its head against a boulder. The Mormons quickly reconsidered and bought the surviving child. This example illustrates that all people have the propensity to do what we now consider evil because of cultural conditioning, including those that many want to romanticize as noble savages.

The fact is that eventually the nation did or is trying to live up to the ideal set forth in the Declaration. We fought the Civil War to eradicate the practice of slavery (those that still claim it was a state's rights issue are wrong, the issue was whether the southern states could continue to practice slavery which they considered a right and were willing to destroy the nation to continue the practice). The suffrage movement gave women the right to vote. Later, the Civil Rights Act and Supreme Court decisions were used as a hammer to force the cessation of rampant discriminatory practices, especially in the South. Religious freedom is extant as all religions are welcomed to practice as they please so long as they adhere to the law. As time marches on this nation has come closer to the ideals expressed in the Declaration. In all these events, it is clear that the progress we have made is not evil.

The United States has been a beacon to those who have sought either liberty or economic opportunity since its inception. Over the past two centuries tens of millions of people voted with their feet in agreement with the proposition that this country was not evil. This stands in stark contrast to very real evil repressive governments from which populations sought to escape. By the way, this trend is not something that occurred only in the distant past. Today, millions of people attempt to legally immigrate while millions of others are so desperate that they immigrate illegally. I submit that if the United States was or is evil, we would not have people beating down our doors to get in.

Aside from the direct beneficial impact that the government has had on its population and the migrants who have flocked here over the years, the United States has also played a major role in the liberation of hundreds of millions of people in countries across the globe. Most often, this has been accomplished only with a significant sacrifice of life, and less importantly, treasure. Admittedly, our involvement in the wars that resulted in the overthrow of repressive regimes was motivated by self-interest; nevertheless, that involvement still had the effect of liberating those who suffered the horror of totalitarianism, and in some cases genocide. These included World War I, World War II, the Korean War, the Vietnam War (our only failure), the Gulf War, and most recently the campaigns in Afghanistan and Iraq. Sprinkled here and there are small actions such as Grenada, though while affecting a small number of people still resulted in a liberated population. In each of these actions, the United States did not establish political control over the liberated countries in order to establish an empire. These are not the actions of an evil nation or government.

In addition to our historical tradition of supporting human rights, current domestic policy also refutes the notion that we are an evil nation. The best example of this is the rights granted by the Constitution. With some exceptions, the rights guaranteed by the Bill of Rights and subsequent amendments are as meaningful today as they were when they were adopted, in particular the First Amendment. In fact, with respect to the First Amendment, it is probable that we have more rights under it now than those who lived in the eighteenth century. If there is one thing we can count on in this country it is the ability to say almost anything we want to, no matter how idiotic, insipid, irrational, or irresponsible, without fear of government retribution (market sanctions are a different matter). For instance, Supreme Court decisions have considerably affected the way government enforces law, providing protections that ensure the rights of the accused are not abused. I am always comforted with the knowledge that our most cherished freedoms are alive and well when I hear someone complain bitterly about how we have lost our freedom. People who have lost their freedom do not complain about it and live freely to complain again.

Beyond basic freedoms, we also have social systems designed to ensure that nobody wants for basic human needs, including food, shelter, emergency health care, and legal services. Nobody is starving to death, and not many even go to bed hungry. If some are hungry, there is no excuse for it given the extensive social safety net that private and governmental organizations have established. Almost everyone has shelter, and government guarantees basic health care. In spite of the oft-repeated claim that vast numbers of our citizens are suffering because of neglect, the truth is that the vast majority of the population lives well by the world's standards. Many people in third world countries would (and in some cases do) die attempting to come to this country and share to some degree in the prosperity that is widely enjoyed by the poorest among us.

Yet, we still hear a steady drumbeat of dissatisfaction with the way the country treats the disadvantaged. While it is true that we are not perfect in that regard, it is also true that no other country with similar challenges is. It is also true that the disadvantaged among us do have opportunities that they can utilize to survive and eventually prosper if they seize the opportunity.

Many of the most vociferous domestic critics of the United States are those who have an economic or political motivation for convincing the electorate that there is rampant discrimination, repression, injustice, and suffering. They place the blame squarely on the lack of action or spending by the federal government. Leaving aside the issue of whether the federal government should be involved in efforts that are best left to individuals, families, religious and community organizations, or state and local governments, the fact is that the federal government is acting to ensure that all members of our society have the necessities of life. In reality, much of what is passes as fighting discrimination and other injustices are really race and class baiting for political purposes or economic extortion.

The foreign policy goals of the United States are designed to advance the interests of this country. That is of course as it should be. No government will survive very long if it does not. Remarkably enough, what is in the interest of this country is identical in almost all respects to the interests of the world community as a whole, in spite of the parochial and self-serving complaints to the contrary on the part of other countries with which we compete. We have learned that what is good for the United States is good for the world, and even more important is the companion lesson that what is good for the world is good for the United States. We enjoy the political equivalent of a symbiotic relationship with countries across the globe with which we trade and jointly prosper, and that is not evil.

The United States is a stabilizing influence in the world. Stability creates a political, cultural, and economic climate that is beneficial for all. Having said that, it is an illusion if we think that tyrannical regimes offer long-term stability, a lesson it seems we are finally learning. For many decades, our foreign policy took the shortsighted view that a stable dictatorship was preferable to instability.

That has changed in the recent past, with efforts to create democracies in countries that do not have a democratic tradition. These efforts serve us as well today as they did after World War II when Germany and Japan were transformed into stable democracies in spite of a drumbeat of pessimistic opinion that democracy could not survive in those authoritarian cultures. Short-term instability is worth it if it results in a political system that serves the people of a liberated country, especially if liberated because of our action. Even if we ultimately fail to establish a successful democracy, it is still preferable to the hypocrisy and future problems of supporting a tyrant whose regime is ultimately doomed anyway. Our support for the Shah of Iran is one of the better examples of this shortsighted policy. Still, even though there are past examples that illustrate shortsighted foreign policy, overall the foreign policy goals and accomplishments of this country have served to spread democracy and freedom through most of the world, and those are not the actions of an evil government.

This nation has been an active participant in expanding economic opportunity and trade throughout the world. It has helped to establish educational systems and contributed to health care initiatives that improve the lives of and significantly increased the lifespan of populations within third world countries, and has aided many nations suffering from the effects of natural disasters and political upheaval. These actions cannot be construed to be evil on the part of any thinking person.

The nation has recently been active in opposing the corruption and paralysis in the United Nations. Some nations have economic and political incentives to maintain the status quo even though it means the world comes ever closer to the time when nuclear weapons fall into the hands of terrorists. The United States has been actively working to minimize the risk through diplomatic means, contrary to the perception of detractors. We are led to believe that from the beginning of the Bush administration the country has been transformed by the administration to an evil nation. This is asserted in spite of close collaboration with other nations to accomplish clearly stated and actively sought objectives in furtherance of peace and freedom throughout the world.

If the assertion that the United States is evil is demonstrably inaccurate, why is this perception so widespread throughout the world, including within the United States? I believe there are three groups who are propagating this idea, all of which seek to undermine the power of the country, not because it is evil, but because it stands against evil and thwarts the objectives of the groups. This is the big lie all over again, and it is being told as often as possible to convince as many non-thinking persons as possible.

The first group is comprised of foreign nations, groups, and individuals who seek to destroy the United States. Nations such as Iran, Venezuela, and North Korea, groups such as Al Qaeda, and individuals inspired by political and religious causes seek the physical destruction of the country in order to implement their vision of utopia in the world. This vision generally involves the destruction of Israel and the United States to begin with, and ultimately the total subjugation of the West. Yet they call us evil, rail against the open society that we enjoy to the benefit of all, and threaten to bring us down by whatever means possible, including nuclear weapons if they can be obtained.

For radical Islamic jihadists, the only option we have is to convert to Islam. This group would have us believe that we are evil because we support freedom of religion and they are good because they want to force one religion on all. Is it just me, or does this seem backwards? While this is a very dangerous group, which we must fight by any means at our disposal, they are very direct in their approach and we have no reason to be confused about their mission if we simply listen to what they are telling us.

The next group consists of foreign nations and people who envy us, either for cultural or economic reasons. This group does not necessarily seek our destruction; however, they would not object if our influence in the world dramatically decreased. The argument that the United States is an evil influence is designed to marginalize our goals and us. Very often, this group will work with us when it is in their interest, but otherwise they view us as competitors. Competition is expected, and countries and individuals are obligated to act in their interests; however, the hyperbolic accusations ultimately undermines not only the United States and its competitive position, but often undermines the effectiveness of those who seeking advantage by this strategy even more.

The last group is the most insidious. These are those citizens of the United States who have either become so propagandized about our present and historical role in the world that they seek the destruction of the nation, or who dislike the Bush administration so much that they attempt to tear down the entire country to destroy the President. I believe that this group is very small and insignificant in terms of numbers; however, their influence is wildly disproportionate to those numbers.

They are particularly destructive for a number of reasons. First, they give aid and comfort to foreign interests that would either destroy or marginalize us. Second, many of them have substantially benefited by the economic opportunity that they despise, so they have resources to spend in their pursuit of the denigration of the country. Third, they have a sympathetic cadre of journalists in the mainstream media that repeats their propaganda almost verbatim while ignoring even the most obvious arguments that counter the reasoning of the detractors. Fourth, they largely control entertainment mediums, and use these to indoctrinate as many as they can. Last, they have hijacked the Democratic Party and turned it into a group that on the national level is complicit in their attempts to undermine our national interests and survival.

It is worth noting that most of these people probably believe they are actually acting in the best interest of our country. That they have not learned some very simple lessons from history is alarming at best; however, it is clear that they have a worldview that is different from the traditional view that I have expounded here. However, the road to the theological place of eternal punishment is paved with good intentions. Just because they fervently believe that their actions serve either the country or mankind in general does not mean that the result of their efforts will have that effect. Good intentions count for nothing; the only thing that matters is the actual effect that the denigration of this nation will have on it and its long-term interests. Of course, the long-term interests of all who live here (and the rest of the world for that matter) are inextricably linked to the long-term interests of this nation. In effect, these people are undermining their own interests along with everyone else's.

The use of social and entertainment institutions and mediums to indoctrinate (or attempt to indoctrinate) young and malleable minds is common. Schools are prohibited from teaching traditional moral precepts under the guise of ensuring an impossible separation of church and state that was never anticipated by the founders. What this means is that the unorganized religious traditions called secularism and atheism have unfettered ability to advance their point of view, but opposing opinions cannot even be discussed because that would ostensibly violate the constitutional prohibition on the establishment of religion. Without coherent competition in the marketplace of ideas, the secularists are convinced they will eventually replace a population that believes in traditional values with one that has been trained to think the way they want them to think. Organizations that have been revered in the past as providing worthwhile role models, such as the Boy Scouts of America, are castigated and reviled because they continue to adhere to traditional values. Even churches are under assault for believing that some behavior is wrong, including homosexual behavior; there have been judicial and legislative attempts to enforce the morality of the day in spite of long held religious doctrine. Much of this tradition is held up as justification for contempt for America and the belief that it is evil.

For those who think religious morality will never be dictated to churches by the state, think again. If the Supreme Court can restrict religious organizations from practices that are deemed to be abhorrent, as they properly have, they have effectively dictated morality. It is a short leap from declaring that homosexual behavior is a fundamental right to telling churches that they must recognize that behavior as moral. This makes selecting judges all that much more important.

Hollywood, a common reference for the entertainment industry as a whole, is a principal component of the effort to undermine the country and its moral status. It is easy to see this in the choice of antagonists and protagonists for movies and television series. When was the last time you watched a movie that portrayed the Central Intelligence Agency as a force for good? I am not talking about a single individual uncovering deceit or corruption in the Agency, but the Agency itself. Even though the men and women of the CIA are working hard to ensure the safety and survival of the United States and its citizens, the entertainment industry cannot bring itself to paint any kind of a flattering picture of this organization. If the CIA is not involved in an evil plot, the next favorite villains in descending order are politicians, (particularly the president) various military organizations, political organizations, and Christian organizations. Invariably the protagonist is fighting diabolical or fanatical forces that seek gain or dominion, and these forces are almost always the institutions that currently protect us or those that form the moral core of the population.

Unfortunately, their propaganda campaign is working if my experience is any barometer of the shift in public opinion. As a teenager in the early 60's, I don't remember seeing a movie or television program that portrayed American institutions as evil. If there was such a movie or program, it did not make much of an impression or sell many tickets. At the same time, I don't remember ever hearing some loon assert that America and its institutions are evil. In fact the opposite was the case; the overwhelming majority believed that America was good and Hollywood supported that belief. Since 1968, when the counterculture attempted to take over the Democratic Party by violent means, Hollywood has consistently portrayed American institutions in at best a bad light. It is therefore no surprise that we have indoctrinated so many to the belief that America is evil.

The standard response when confronted with these facts is "this is fiction", "nobody is influenced by movies or television" (or music for that matter, but that is a different topic). That assertion is absurd on its face, which can be easily seen by the effect the medium has and the economic demonstrations of their effect. A simple test of its effect is to ask a few pertinent questions, including the following:

81

- Do we go to movies to be disengaged and detached from what is happening? That would be no. We are driven by the plot to sympathize with the protagonist and detest the antagonist. The productions we see are designed to entertain, but they are also frequently designed to shape our attitude about issues and institutions. Anyone who has listened to Academy Award winners pontificate as they accept praise for their latest propaganda piece is aware of this.

- What was the general purpose of the movies made during World War II, and do the movies that have been made since the Vietnam War have the same effect? That would also be no. Look at the shift in attitudes between World War II and the post Vietnam era with respect to war and peace. The movies made during World War II were designed to boost morale and encourage us in a very bleak time in history. Most of the movies made since Vietnam are designed to show us how immoral our national goals are per the perception of Hollywood, and how those goals pervert the people who are involved. The result is that many of us (especially younger citizens who did not grow up in the earlier cultural climate) are now convinced that we are evil, and that those that would oppress us are good. It also has the effect to discouraging us from committing lives and treasure toward protecting our interest because confidence in our ability and appropriateness of acting in our interest is undermined by this perception.

- What was the attitude of the world toward us before Hollywood's shift in attitude, and what influenced world opinion before and after? During and after World War II, the United States was held in high regard, except by the Axis and Communist blocks. Remarkably enough, Hollywood's campaign to demonize American institutions tracks very closely with the rise in virulent anti-American sentiment across the world, including in the United States. We now have substantial numbers of people across the globe who go to see American made movies or watch American television programs and are told (by us!) that we and our governmental institutions are evil, corrupt, and oppressive. Then we cannot figure out why the international attitude toward us is poisoned so badly.

- Do those who produce entertainment believe it has the effect of influencing behavior? That would be a resounding yes. Once again, listening to Academy Award winners is illuminating. In addition, it is clear that producers have convinced advertisers that movies and television affect behavior. The producers of movies practice product placement, and collect a lot of money on the premise that people will be influenced to by a product because is featured in a move. Advertisers continue to spend the money to place products so it is logical to conclude that at least both the producers and advertisers are convinced that behavior and attitude is affected by their entertainment products. Even more obvious is the advertising associated with television. Indeed, the ability of networks and advertisers to manipulate consumer behavior has resulted in a medium that is financially sustained by the advertising dollars that are brought in as a result of the public response to the advertising. Last, entertainment executives and advertisers both know that the most effective form of advertising, whether it is a product or entertainment medium, is word of mouth. The only way this is possible is for the product or medium to be so appealing that people are willing to modify their behavior to the point of advocating for the product or medium. How can anyone argue that this has no affect on behavior?

I'm sure that there will be many who will immediately attack this position, hysterically accusing me of wanting to censor the entertainment industry and force them to say only nice things about the government. Nothing could be further from the truth. All I can desire and hope is that rational people will see the effect of what they have been doing and voluntarily project a more rational and accurate picture of American institutions. In addition, ordinary citizens can have an effect on entertainment mediums by refusing to economically support subversive programming and content.

The effort to define this country as evil is evil in itself. This is another example of a big lie being repeated to the populace so often that many have come to believe it. We accept these lies as truth at our peril. If we succeed in undermining the faith we have in governmental institutions and those who protect us, we will soon find few willing to make the sacrifice willing to protect the rest of us.

Chapter 8

"Capital Punishment is Not a Deterrent"

I routinely yell at the television whenever I hear someone make this ridiculous argument. Let me see, if we take someone who has committed a heinous crime and execute him, will that person ever be able to commit another atrocity against another person? That would be a resounding no! (notwithstanding the insipid horror movies we see that indicate otherwise). It is impossible for capital punishment not to have a deterrent effect on crime.

It is probable that capital punishment could have a significant deterrent effect on others who may consider committing atrocious crimes if we would actually make the punishment for such activity certain and relatively swift. When the length of the appeals process results in convicted murderers getting old and decrepit before their sentence is carried out, we send a message that crime does indeed pay. Or at least that punishment is less of a hazard than those who may kill them for substantially less than what we would.

Direct evidence of the deterrent effect of capital punishment is the effect that the threat of execution by organized crime organizations or gang members has on the public and members of their organizations. How many criminals have not been prosecuted because either the criminal or his associates in crime have intimidated witnesses? These witnesses are rightly convinced that their testimony in court will result in a death sentence for them or their families. And the organization will not wait until twenty or thirty years have passed. Their retribution is swift and sure. In this environment, the deterrent effect of that threat is obvious to the most casual observer.

Having said this, I do believe that we should use every means at our disposal to determine the guilt or innocence of those accused. Capital punishment is final, and someone being executed for a crime that they did not commit is particularly egregious. In particular, the best technology available should be used to determine guilt or innocence where possible. I have occasionally read of zealous prosecutors resisting efforts to use DNA[14]

---

[14] Deoxyribonucleic acid

testing to substantiate the convictions of murderers convicted before such testing was possible. I simply cannot understand why anyone would resist corroborating a conviction with this evidence. Any effort to suppress such evidence gives the appearance that the prosecution has something to hide.

Even so, no human activity is going to be foolproof, including criminal investigation. If we make mistakes that ultimately lead to an innocent person being executed for a crime it is a tragedy, but still does not justify not ensuring the general population is protected from predators who will kill, or cause to be killed, others whether in or out of prison.

Those who use this argument are really arguing that punishing criminal activity will not work because punishment does not deter the activity. We are to believe that the numbers of crimes that warrant capital punishment are not reduced by the threat of execution and therefore we should not execute people. Using that logic, we should repeal all laws because they are all routinely broken, and therefore are not a deterrent.

Another argument is that the criminal does not deserve to be executed because it is not his or her fault. This is the "Devil made me do it" argument (see Chapter 32). We are expected to forgive the miscreant, no matter how egregious the offense and no matter how unlikely the prospect of rehabilitation because society or genetics is responsible. This argument is fatally flawed in that it ignores the principal purpose of punishment.

In the end, punishment is not really about punishing the miscreant. It is about protecting the innocent in our society from those who would prey on them. There will always be people who will act in conflict with societal values in spite of the threat of punishment. But if there is a credible threat that capital punishment, or for that matter any punishment, was a swift and sure penalty for a behavior, there will be others that will be deterred by the threat. And if one guilty of a horrific crime is executed, the population will be forever protected against future crimes by that individual.

Chapter 9

"The Second Amendment Does Not Give
Individuals the Right to Bear Arms"

No honest person can study the early history of the United States and conclude that the founders intended the Second Amendment to grant the right to bear arms only to formally organized state militias (National Guard units). A cursory review of the literature of the time, especially the Federalist papers, makes clear the intent to allow all able-bodied men the right to bear arms of military consequence. An examination of the role of the militia in the defeat of the British in the Revolutionary War does the same. Those that argue otherwise are simply uninformed or dishonest. I will not recreate the research that other capable historians have developed; their work makes the argument very well.

Since I initially wrote this chapter, the Supreme Court has issued a decision in the District of Columbia vs. Heller case that firearms ownership is indeed an individual right, supporting historical tradition and original intent. The ruling wisely said that some regulation was appropriate. That is the good news. The bad news is that there were four justices that dissented, meaning only one justice was the determining factor in whether future citizens would be able to defend themselves within political jurisdictions hostile to gun ownership. Once again the importance of judicial nominations is evident.

I have no problem with debating whether the Second Amendment is justified two centuries after the clear need for it that existed in the late 18th century led to the amendment being included in the Bill of Rights. If the argument is that times have changed and the amendment should be repealed, that is a legitimate debate. I would vociferously disagree; I believe it is just as important today as it was in 1787. However, to lie and say that the founders did not intend this amendment to be an individual right is simply an attempt to repeal the amendment without the benefit of debate or a vote, other than the vote of judges willing to usurp the authority of the people as vested in their duly elected representatives.

Another legitimate debate is what constitutes an arm that individuals are entitled to bear. During the Revolutionary War that would have been the musket. It does not follow that the framers intended the right be extended to include cannon. By extension, considering technological advances, it seems that today the weapons commonly used to arm infantry would be protected by the amendment; however, arguing that an individual right to possess nuclear weapons is guaranteed by the amendment is irrational. This brings us to the fact that a line must be drawn between the weapons necessary for individual defense and the weapons that only our military services should possess. The line is clear and defendable in my mind, but I concede that this is the subject of reasonable debate.

Another point of further debate is what constitutes appropriate regulation. Indeed, the Heller decision leaves that question unanswered, and there will yet be much litigation before this is sorted out. Some restrictions seem to be appropriate, for instance historically convicted felons have not been allowed to own guns. In addition, reasonable registration restrictions to make it more difficult for felons to obtain guns seem reasonable. Unfortunately, the gun control movement has indicated that they will use this as a point of future attacks on the amendment itself. They believe that they can make registration restrictions so unreasonable that most people will give up their attempts to obtain defensive weapons.

The Second Amendment is one of the least defended amendments by the intellectual elite, but it is also one most important to the maintenance of our freedom. "Political power comes from the barrel of a gun", an expression uttered by Mao Zedong in the 1960's, was blunt and offensive; however, the expression is an accurate evaluation of the effect of weapons. Those who have weapons can protect themselves against those who also have weapons. Generally speaking, those with the best and most weapons will prevail in a conflict. Those who do not have weapons are at the mercy of those who do, and a long history of murder, domination, war, and genocide across the globe and throughout history documents the folly in depending on the mercy of those who have such power.

While Mao's statement was made long after the Revolutionary War and the drafting of the Bill of Rights, his statement was just as true then as it was in the 1960's. This truth was not lost on those who had utilized large numbers of citizen soldiers to win a war against the strongest political power on the earth at the time, the British Empire. The battle at Saratoga was particularly demonstrative of the value of the farmers and villagers who responded to the threat from General Burgoyne and flocked by the thousands to the aid of Generals Gates and Arnold. They were the decisive difference in the defeat of the British Army. While it is true that throughout the war the majority of these armed citizens were ill trained and ill-equipped to fight, it is also true that without them the Revolutionary War would have been lost.

Before, during, and after the Revolutionary War, the people of the original colonies and country began a tradition of sharing the duties of a common defense. This originated by necessity; if groups settling the land did not band together and fight against the various threats they faced they would not have survived. The tradition of a citizen soldier willing to leave hearth and home to defend that home was more than a myth. The inhabitants of this land demonstrated time after time that they were willing to respond to threats to their security and overcome them together. That tradition has served us well. It is supported by the Second Amendment, which fosters a sense of responsibility to country and a willingness to use the arms to which we are entitled to own in support of it.

Since the Revolutionary War, history has demonstrated the wisdom of the First Congress for including the Second Amendment in the Bill of Rights. A long history of genocide in particular vividly illustrates the foolishness of having a general population without the means to defend themselves with arms. Millions of Armenians were slaughtered by the Turks in the early 20th century, most of whom were simply marched into the desert without food or water until they died. The rise to power of Adolph Hitler and the Holocaust was facilitated by the strict gun laws in effect in most European countries. Genocide in Cambodia, Uganda, China, and Rwanda has demonstrated the wisdom in having a population that is educated in the proper use of weapons and who have the weapons needed to preserve life and liberty.

A notable exception to the people of European countries being unable to defend themselves is Switzerland, which has considered able-bodied men their militia since the origin of their federation in the late 13th century. An important requirement of the citizens of that nation is that all members of the militia are required to be armed with military grade weapons. This has been a major factor behind the fact that Switzerland has not been invaded for over eight centuries. That includes World War II when Hitler swept over all of Continental Europe except Switzerland and the Iberian Peninsula. Spain was spared because its government was sympathetic to the Nazis. Switzerland's government, while neutral, was not. It is true that there were other political and geographical reasons that helped the Swiss maintain their neutrality in the face of a megalomaniac who wanted to conquer the world. However, it is also true that the fact that almost the entire Swiss male population was trained, armed, and willing to fight was a significant deterrent to Hitler's desire to conquer Switzerland.

Many argue that if there were not so many guns that we would not have the genocide and atrocities that are common throughout the world. I strongly disagree. While it is true that guns provide an efficient means of killing, it is also true that people, being people, will kill with or without guns. Rwanda is perhaps the most vivid illustration of this at the level of genocide, although the thousands of people murdered by means other than guns is also demonstrative. The vast majority of the 500,000 to 1,100,000 of the Tutsi's killed in the genocide were hacked to death with machetes. The Hutu population did not need guns to perpetuate one of the largest genocides in history. Guns make genocide easier, but the root of the problem is not guns, but hatred, bigotry, and jealousy that results in one group deciding to kill the members of another. If the Tutsi's had been armed, the story would have been dramatically different.

This brings me to an important point. Guns do not kill. Left to itself, a gun will sit in a secure area and do nothing. It takes a human being to actively use the gun to kill someone. Guns are tools, just like any other. They have a purpose. They can be misused, just as any other tool can be. The attempts to litigate them out of existence is an exercise in futility; we may as well try to litigate knives and axes out of existence (oh, wait a minute, trial lawyers are trying to litigate all manufactured products out of existence – but that is the subject for a different day). If those opposed to gun ownership are successful in forcing law abiding citizens to give up their right to self-defense, it will be open season on the law abiding citizens that will no longer be able to protect themselves, both from criminals and from politicians who recognize that coups have never been possible in this country because of the Second Amendment.

There is a two pronged attack on gun ownership in the United States today. Because gun control advocates know they have no chance of success at the ballot box, they have chosen to attack the Second Amendment through the judiciary. First, they have attempted to persuade the courts to rule that gun ownership can be restricted to formal militia units, specifically the National Guard. This has now been met with failure as a result of the Heller decision. However, because what level of regulation will be held to be reasonable has yet to be determined, it yet remains to be seen as to how successful they will be in intimidating those who want to protect themselves. Second, they have attempted to sue gun manufacturers out of existence through the use of liability claims. That has also been defeated with the passage of federal legislation exempting manufacturers from liability resulting from the improper use of their products. This was exceptionally wise, because a successful claim would have set a precedent enabling any manufacturer of any product to be subject to litigation because some knucklehead misused their product. This is truly good news for average citizens who only desire the ability to defend themselves.

Many people have an irrational fear of guns. That is largely because they have not been exposed to them or been shown how proper handling makes them as safe as any other tool. It is natural to fear the unknown. The media demonization of them has been successful to a large degree because of the fear of these simple and useful tools. If taught about the proper handling and safety of these weapons, I believe that almost all people would conclude as I do that guns are not as scary as Hollywood would have us believe. I was presented with a high power hunting rifle at the ripe old age of twelve, was taught the proper use and handling of the weapon, and it has safely been in my home continuously along with other weapons accumulated since then. My children have also been taught gun safety (critical if there are children in the home), and each of them has a healthy respect for the usefulness of these weapons.

Another example of the value of the Second Amendment to Americans is the effect that an armed group of African-Americans had on when faced with the threat of violence during the civil rights conflicts in the 1960's. The "Deacons for Defense" vividly demonstrated that political power does indeed come from the barrel of a gun when they successfully intimidated the racists who threatened the black population in Louisiana. Other chapters were organized in other southern states, which contributed to the political pressure brought on the Federal government to properly enforce the Civil Rights Act.

There is a popular notion that seems to be prevalent, even among gun rights advocates, which should be debunked. The Second Amendment is not and never has been about hunting rights. The founders did not intend for the militia to have weapons so that they could go deer hunting, or to protect their communities and country from animal populations that threatened their liberty, although defense against predators was a useful byproduct of the right. The Second Amendment was about ensuring that all capable individuals could own weapons with which they could defend home, family, community, and country against all enemies, both foreign and domestic.

Hunting was an incidental benefit to the primary purpose of the amendment. It still is.

Many years ago, I participated in a informal discussion with friends about the theoretical probability of the government of the United States being overthrown with a military coup. I was in the Marine Corps at the time, and the Vietnam War was raging. A group of Marines, including myself, considered why it was that military coups were common in many other countries of the world, but not in the United States. We recognized that our democratic tradition was strong, and that the military had long ago accepted its subservient role to civilian authority. But we concluded that was only a minor part of the equation. Everyone in the group uniformly agreed that there were two additional reasons why a military coup had not been attempted and, more importantly, would never be successful in the United States.

The first reason was that the military was composed of citizen soldiers who were fighting for their country only because of what the country stood for. These citizen soldiers would never allow themselves to be used to overthrow that government. The second was that even if there were some loony enough to try, there were so many people armed and ready to defend our constitutionally established government that the effort would be doomed.

Since that day, I have never heard or read anything that would persuade me that the group's conclusion was wrong. In fact, I am more convinced of it today than I ever have been. We owe our lives and liberty to those who either bear arms or are prepared to bear arms in service to the ideals that made this nation great, both in the branches of the military services, national guard units, and in the unorganized militia comprised of all citizens who are willing and able to answer the call to service. Those that seek to disarm individuals seek, unwittingly or not, to facilitate the future use of force to oppress the population. Ironically, those who seek to undermine the traditional values of our culture with respect to the obligation to participate in the common defense and gun ownership also unwittingly undermine the foundation for the values that protect their ability to freely hold and express their views.

Chapter 10

"Pornography is Constitutionally Protected Speech or Expression"

Against my better judgment, I'm going to venture into the quagmire of pornography, speech and expression, and the effect that Supreme Court decisions have had on the ability of federal, state and local governments to regulate offensive speech and expression. These have been controversial decisions, and I recognize that many intellectually honest and principled people will oppose my reasoning. I will even concede that what has happened is not idiotic; it is easy to understand how honest people came to the conclusions they reached.

I recently retired as a planner from Clark County, Nevada, the political jurisdiction that has planning and zoning authority over the Las Vegas Strip. Among other things, my responsibilities included interpreting the zoning ordinance. Much of my reasoning and some of my examples will be drawn from this professional background. I apologize for the planning jargon here, but I believe it is the best means of communicating this subject matter in a relatively inoffensive manner.

First, I recognize it is very difficult to know where to draw a line between what is pornographic and what is not. What is obscene to some is perfectly acceptable to others. In some cases, nudity is accepted by the mainstream. Very few object to a famous Goya painting hanging in an art museum. Likewise, most are amused and not offended when they see the old Coppertone billboard that displays a child whose swimsuit is being pulled down by the dog. In addition, many people, including myself, consider the male and female form to be a marvelous wonder of creation that is not obscene in and of itself. These facts make if difficult to differentiate between material that is art and material whose emphasis is on arousing sexual fantasies or debasing sexual practices. Establishing regulations that have the effect of prohibiting such speech and expression would even offend me.

By the way, attempting to regulate content that arouses sexual fantasies is also a quagmire. Men are easily aroused by visual stimulus, which can also include fully clothed women (or men) in modest dress. For that matter, women in a burka or a brown burlap bag can be the subject of sexual fantasy (we are a sorry lot, aren't we?). It would be a tad difficult to regulate fully clothed women out of all media and public view, although that has not stopped some Islamic regimes from trying.

The First Amendment guarantees free speech. The suppression of speech is fundamentally at cross-purposes with the maintenance of a free society. The free exchange of ideas is most responsible for the cultural, intellectual, and economic climate we enjoy in this nation, including the attendant education, invention, innovation, growth, freedom, knowledge, protection from corruption, and prosperity associated with a people that can freely express ideas while others can challenge and expose them to critical analysis. Free speech is the foundation of our society.

What is the purpose of the free speech clause? I believe that the intent of the founders was to protect core speech, including political, religious, motivational, scientific, and other expressions that foster debate about human relations and activities in addition to the world around us. Core speech is in the best tradition of the democratic process; it is easy to visualize missionaries, philosophers and others standing on a soapbox in Hyde Park or any other public square expounding on their ideas with listeners free to accept or reject their message.

That said, the Amendment does not confer an absolute right. A person does not have an absolute right to say whatever he or she wants to say by whatever means they want to use whenever they want to say it. As is true for any right, free speech has limitations. Even non-commercial speech can be limited; yelling fire in an enclosed area, or threatening the life of the President are two notable examples. I mention these facts to illustrate that the question is not whether we will exercise some control over expression and speech but at what point.

Commercial speech does not enjoy the same protection afforded core, or non-commercial, speech. The Amendment itself does not differentiate between types of speech; however, over the years decisions and laws have allowed commercial speech to be restricted more than core speech. For instance, commercial speech can be prohibited if it is demonstrably false, misleading, or dangerous. If someone wants to sell snake oil and represent that it will cure all manner of ailments, government has a right to demand evidence of its benefit and restrict the sale of the product if it is found to be harmful. Commercial speech advertising products can even be limited as to its placement, for instance, commercial signs in residential areas can be prohibited, and permitted signage may be restricted to advertise only the goods and services available on a commercial property.

Political

In addition, if a person attempts to enrich himself using public property, the public has a right to restrict that speech. In particular, a commercial entrepreneur does not have the right to use public property for personal gain absent the consent of the public entity that owns the property. If government allows such a use by one person, it must allow it for anyone subject to whatever restrictions it may place on the activity to guarantee public safety. Public property is public for a specific reason, and commercial uses are often at odds with that purpose. Streets and sidewalks are the best example. Government obtains these public properties for the sole purpose of ensuring legal access to property and allowing the free flow of vehicular and pedestrian traffic from one place to another. If a vendor sets up a booth to sell hot dogs or t-shirts on public property, or if mobile billboards create traffic congestion, traffic and pedestrian movement will be adversely affected and the public purpose of the land will be subverted.

If we conclude that speech can be properly limited, the only question is where to draw the line in terms of what is limited. Between the extremes of total suppression and no control at all lies reasonable middle ground. We must determine where that appropriately lies. I believe that because of the importance of speech in maintaining our culture and liberty that we should only prohibit speech that can be demonstrated as dangerous to society or have a perniciously destructive cultural effect. This chapter will attempt to demonstrate that the line that has arbitrarily been drawn by the Supreme Court with respect to pornography was drawn in an excessively permissive way that has had the aforementioned pernicious effect.

Pornography and erotic dancing has been determined to be forms of speech and expression protected by the First Amendment as determined by the Supreme Court. These rulings represent a significant departure from the past. Before the mid-1960's, these were largely state and local issues left to be resolved through state and local regulation. Federal restrictions also applied where interstate commerce was affected. However, beginning in the mid-60's, there have been a string of Supreme and appellate court decisions, the net effect of which is to require federal, state, and local governments to allow the sale and distribution of pornography and the establishment of strip clubs. Governments can regulate to ensure that non-consenting adults and minor children are not exposed to such material and activities and that the threat of crime in neighborhoods in close proximity to these uses is mitigated. However, if the net effect of regulation is to establish a barrier to pornographic outlets, hereafter referred to as adult uses, the regulations will be and are regularly overturned.

The most obvious problem that I see with the cumulative effect of these decisions is that the courts have for some reason erased the distinction between commercial speech and core speech. Pornography is commercial speech. This content is not given away; magazines, DVD's, videotapes, and internet access to pornographic web sites are sold. The purpose of the content is not core speech, but simply a product to obtain commercial gain. If the speech is commercial speech, it stands to reason that the same rules that apply to snake oil will also apply to pornography. All that needs to be accomplished to restrict content is to determine that the content constitutes a health, safety, or welfare problem for society. I am not the first person to go down this road; indeed many of the arguments before the court emphasized this point. The problem is in developing evidence that there are health, safety, or welfare problems associated with the content.

By the way, some argue that adult uses are no different from newspapers, news magazines, and almost every other media that clearly is core speech because these medias function in a commercial world and accept advertisements to raise revenue for their operations. I disagree, there is still a distinction between these medias and pornography. Pornography can and frequently does exist commercially independent of advertisements. Those who do advertise merely publicize other pornographic sources, which are incidental to the commercial success of the enterprise.

Given court rulings, at this point there are three categories of pornographic speech. The first is fully protected speech, that is speech that has been deemed to be not offensive by reason of what the content displays. This speech is characterized by a lack of display or reference to specified anatomical areas, and is further defined as content that does not have as its principle purpose an emphasis on sexual content. In this construct, not all inoffensive speech is inoffensive as I will illustrate below.

The next category of pornographic speech is also protected but to a lesser extent. This is speech that is required to be permitted; however, it can be regulated to prevent its exposure to non-consenting adults and minor children. The placement of commercial establishments can also be regulated to ensure neighborhoods are not blighted and subject to crime associated with the blight.

The last category is prohibited speech, which includes child pornography. This is important, because it shows that the courts recognize the threat to public health, safety, and welfare that child pornography presents. That this speech is prohibited demonstrates that the issue with all pornographic content is where to draw the line between protected and prohibited speech.

While this is not an easy task, it still should be the decision of legislators to make. It is not. In analyzing the effects of court decisions, the first problem is where to draw the line between non-offensive protected speech and offense protected speech that can be regulated. In order to meet court-imposed standards, governments have attempted to define adult uses to include offensive speech only, thereby establishing no restrictions on non-offensive speech. Here, what is offensive or not is ostensibly determined by the governing body; however, there is a de-facto standard that has been established by court precedent. There will be many in a community who object and will pressure elected officials to establish more restrictive standards; however, such efforts are doomed because they are invariably overturned. Elected officials are caught between a rock and a hard place because they are forced to alienate their constituents in order to establish any regulation that will survive judicial review.

Local governments are also caught between court-imposed requirements to allow adult uses, but then are promptly made the focus of criminal corruption investigations by the executive branch. As far as the federal government is concerned, local governments are damned if they prohibit adult uses, but are also damned if they allow them.

Local governments find themselves caught between frustrated citizens and court imposed restrictions on their ability to restrict pornography. Indeed, Clark County attempted to make it difficult (but not impossible) to establish adult use establishments, only to have the ordinance thrown out by a court as too restrictive because it had the result of no adult uses being established for the fifteen or so years the ordinance was in effect. This was quite a reach for the court, especially because there were no adult use applications submitted that gave the governing body the ability to approve an application and thereby demonstrate that the regulations were not excessively restrictive.

The definitions of adult uses are very graphic and detailed. I will not describe them here except to say that they attempt to remove all ambiguity from the decision-making process used to establish what level of protection the speech or expression is afforded. In response to court precedent and the danger in overreaching and losing the entire regulatory scheme in court, they generally err on the side of allowing unrestricted speech or expression that can be crude and offensive to many, but do not rise to the level of legally offensive speech, which while protected can be regulated.

This can be a significant problem for the general population, especially when outdoor advertising is considered. If a government approves the placement of a billboard, after the sign is constructed the government cannot control content unless it is false, misleading, dangerous, or obscene. As the definition of what is obscene is restricted to the definition of what constitutes an adult use, much tacky, tasteless, and offensive speech cannot be enjoined.

Many adults, especially parents with children in the car, are offended by such displays when they observe them; however, government can do nothing to restrict them. By the way, size and placement make ignoring these signs exceptionally difficult if not impossible. I recall reviewing numerous complaints about billboard content over several years, and all except one was determined to be legally appropriate. Those who complained were left with only market sanctions and protest to address their concerns. Under these and similar circumstances, non-consenting adults and minor children cannot be protected from content that is offensive but not pornographic.

Handbill distribution is similarly a problem. Attempts to restrict the thrusting of objectionable materials into the hands of male tourists have been ruled unconstitutional. If an advertisement allowing an escort service or erotic dancing outcall service is distributed on the Las Vegas Strip and the advertiser carefully designs the handbill to ensure that it does not constitute an adult use, government cannot prohibit the distribution of the handbills. That is true even though the circulars are extremely offensive to the tourists walking up and down the Strip, many with spouses in tow. Most throw them away in disgust, creating a significant litter problem. In this situation, the public is forced to allow the commercial use of their property where no other commercial use is permitted, the blighting of the visual landscape as a result of litter, and the degradation of pedestrian movement because the actions of the handbill distributors impede pedestrian traffic in conflict with the public purpose of the property.

Even if the sidewalk is on private property with only a public access easement over it, the property owners cannot prohibit the handbill distribution. Thus, property owners are forced to allow the use of their own property for advertising their competition (in terms of where entertainment dollars are to be spent) and offending their customers, thereby undermining their businesses. In addition, they are required to clean up the resulting mess at significant cost.

Political

Repeated attempts to prohibit these handbills have been overturned by the court of final jurisdiction. With these handbills, even market sanctions and protests are ineffective because the escort or outcall erotic dancing service is unaffiliated with the resort hotels, don't care if they offend the resort hotel customers, and could not care less about someone protesting the content of their handbill. Most of those who have these offensive handbills thrust into their hands are offended, and it is likely (if editorial comment is any indicator) that many will chose not to return to Nevada as a result of the experience. In this case, the courts have mandated that Nevadans allow the subversion of Nevada's major industry.

By the way, it is worth noting that prostitution is illegal in Clark County. While the underground practice is evident, prostitution is prosecuted. Escort and outcall erotic dance services are thinly veiled prostitution services; however, their businesses are also protected under free association rights. The owners of the businesses disassociate themselves from the independent contractors who are prosecuted for illegal acts when they are caught, so even if those whom they send in response to a call are arrested, the operators are immune. Thus, the service and their advertising continue to be legal in spite of repeated prostitution violations.

Even though governments attempt to define what is obscene unambiguously, and attempt to uniformly enforce regulations, challenges abound. Definitions are frequently challenged as ambiguous regardless of how graphic they are. Regulations are routinely challenged as unnecessarily restrictive, no matter how many legal adult use establishments are permitted to be established. If a business is denied, the propensity is to sue the jurisdiction to impose a court judgment in conflict with the regulation established by the governing body. Sometimes the regulations survive; however, all too often the judge decides in favor of the plaintiff. Sometimes the government, fearing a much worse loss in court than the effects of a concession to the plaintiff, will settle the matter out of court. It is better to concede one use than to risk having the entire adult use regulatory scheme overturned. In other words, courts have taken over the legislation and regulation of adult uses.

Perhaps even worse are court imposed public subsidies of pornographic access. Libraries have been enjoined from establishing filters on computers, so anyone can go to the nearest library and view content that has been determined should only be available to consenting adults. Of course, libraries are general public places, so non-consenting adults and children are regular patrons that are routinely exposed to this content. The only option for a non-consenting adult or child is to stay away from the library. This has the doubly negative effect of teaching adults and children that libraries are places to be avoided (unless you want to view pornography) and forcing the general public to subsidize the distribution of pornography. Those that access the content are shameless; I recall a recent article in which a mother respectfully requested that a viewer consider the effect he was having on her children only to be profanely berated and dismissed.

As a cumulative result of court imposed decisions, no regulation is reliable. In the case of the billboard determined to be inappropriate that was previously mentioned, the billboard company voluntarily removed the offensive content and replaced it with appropriate content. They could have just as easily sued. Even if they did not win the legal lottery, with a routinely granted injunction they could still easily keep the sign up for as long as the advertising contract stipulated. A court decision on such a matter takes many years to finally resolve, and of course, once the sign was removed because the term of the advertising contract expired, the case would be dismissed as moot. Even if the community wins, it loses.

In the future, it is easy to imagine hardcore sexual acts displayed on billboards. Indeed, several years ago the publisher of a major men's magazine announced his candidacy for the presidency, then promised to put up hardcore pornographic displays on billboards across the nation. He eventually voluntarily withdrew his threat; however, he or someone else could attempt to do the same thing in the future. If they did, what would the courts decide? Is such speech protected political speech?

Even content not associated with a political campaign could be established at least temporarily. Remember that government generally does not regulate content, so billboard operators display messages without the review of government. The first inkling that there may be a content problem on a sign is when the complaints start to come in. If the content is pornographic, by that time many would have been forced to view the patently offensive content. Then it takes time to investigate the complaint, notify the property owner, and give adequate time for voluntary abatement of the offensive content. If the operator decides to fight the citation, the courts get to take whatever time they need to decide the case, possibly issuing injunctive relief for the sign. We live in a political climate where the practical ability to enforce regulations designed to protect non-consenting adult and minor children from exposure to this content is questionable.

As if adult use regulation was not difficult enough, we also have court decisions that have forced jurisdictions to allow sex (swingers) clubs. For those unaware of these uses, they are establishments that allow patrons to pay an admission fee, then engage in all manner of sexual activities on the premises. Most often, the individuals within the establishment will agree to sexual activities based upon agreed upon remuneration. If this sounds like prostitution, you can be forgiven for being confused.

Even so, because the businesses routinely disguise their admission fees as voluntary contributions, some courts have been sympathetic to sex club operator's claims that they are merely allowing free association between patrons. These clubs tend to locate wherever they think they can get away with the use, and often locate in residential neighborhoods where adults and minor residents are supposed to be able to quietly enjoy their homes and property. In the case of Clark County, a court ruled that a specific sex club is permitted, and the use exists to this day. The net result is that a court allowed a de-facto brothel in spite of state and local laws prohibiting prostitution within Clark County.

The fact that courts impose decisions that conflict with adopted ordinances results in what many consider to be a double standard. Even though Clark County has attempted to consistently and even handedly enforce its ordinances, it is left with court granted exceptions and settlements to avoid risk to the overall ordinance. The only alternative for the County is to continue to enforce the regulations, or throw in the towel and allow the uses without regulation with the attendant social, health, and criminal impacts associated with the uses. This leads many in the community, especially the press, to castigate the County because it "allows" some sex clubs to exist but refuses to allow others. Because good reporting and research is much harder than repeating unfounded allegations or idle speculation, they hypothesize about the possible reasons while ignoring what is obvious to any informed individual. They whine about a double standard and theorize that corrupt politicians have deals with some operators at the expense of others. In this situation, the courts have mandated that Clark County subvert public confidence in its government.

In this regulatory climate, the question is what court-imposed regulation comes next? Is public sexual expression protected speech? If sexually suggestive dancers are protected, why aren't overt sexual acts in public? Will the courts decide that indeed there is a double standard as is alleged, even if the double standard is one of their own making, and will they force jurisdictions to allow de-facto brothels? As the legislative functions related to pornography have been usurped by the judiciary, longstanding restrictions on sexual activities are subject to being vacated.

It is easy to go from allowing sex clubs at which remuneration is routinely paid for sexual services, to overtly allowing prostitution. Prohibitions on sodomy have already been overturned without regard to the health implications of the practice, and regulated prostitution is, from a public health standpoint, less risky. After that, the next domino to fall may be the restriction on consensual sexual contact between adults and children. If NAMBLA has their way, that will occur sooner rather than later. If consensual minor sex is permitted, what stands in the way of voiding child pornography restrictions, which is the only form of prohibited pornographic speech we currently have? Would legal incest be further down the road?

As you can see, it is a relatively short trip from where we are now to a culture that is forced to allow practices that have traditionally been repugnant to the majority. Over time, the sexualization of women and children can only have long-term negative consequences for all of society, including mental and physical well-being. If the majority through their elected representatives were allowed to regulate these behaviors, it is exceptionally unlikely that the behaviors would be permitted. As it is, all it takes is an un-elected judge to allow the establishment of the use, and therefore the behavior. In some cases, because of the lack of legal resources or lack of successful prospects for an appeal, the decision is not even taken to the appellate or Supreme Court. This is a direct result of court imposed judgments that have overruled the will of the majority, especially decisions related to adult uses.

Technology has facilitated the widespread availability of pornography. I don't need to elaborate on the ease with which anyone can view this kind of content, either on cable stations, the internet, or in print media. Pornography is a multi-billion dollar industry.

What other effects result from the widespread availability of pornography? There seems to be conflicting results from studies; however, some effects are abundantly clear. First, a limited study found a correlation between prolonged exposure to pornography and the self-admitted propensity of the participants to consider actual participation in the acts that they viewed, which included rape and other forced sexual acts. This result seems reasonable, especially when considering the natural progression of events leading to such behavior. People are what they think, and fantasizing about criminal and violent coercive sex is the first step that anyone will take

Political

toward actually performing the act. If an individual repeatedly fantasizes about forcible sexual behavior with the fantasy facilitated by pornographic content, it may well result in the person eventually acting out the fantasy on an unwilling and innocent victim.

Others argue that prolonged exposure to pornography results in broken marriages, dissatisfaction with the sexual performance of partners, debasement of women, sexual addiction, and promiscuous sex. There are others, particularly those enriching themselves through the sale of this content, who argue that these effects have not been proven. However, given that epidemiological experiments to measure these effects are nearly impossible to design, even if there was a direct causal link between the content and destructive behaviors it is likely that these links could never be proven. In other words the smut peddlers want those who question the effects of pornography to prove the unprovable. That said, the lack of proof does not mean the effects do not exist. We cannot prove a link, but then I can't prove that the sun will rise tomorrow. We should be able to use inductive reasoning as a tool for determining the effect of content, and there is a mountain of anecdotal evidence that supports these allegations. Worth noting is that each of these effects each have associated social and public health implications.

It is appropriate to inject a word about personal responsibility. Just as a claim that "the Devil made me do it" (see Chapter 32) is not a basis for avoiding personal responsibility for repugnant and illegal behavior, so is the argument that "pornography made me do it". No matter what the underlying motivation is, people have an obligation to conform to the law, and excuses for indefensible behavior do not justify it. That said, if the use of a product repeatedly results in negative consequences, most rational people will avoid the use of the product, and most ethical business people will avoid trafficking in the material.

The material seems to have a substantial effect on child behavior. As young children obtain easy access to proscribed (for them) material over the internet, they are learning and performing destructive behaviors. Young girls and boys are demeaned and regarded as sexual objects. Unfortunately, some children lacking in self-esteem swallow the propaganda and allow themselves to become sexual objects, sometimes to peers, but all too often to adult predators. I recall recent news broadcasts detailing sexual intercourse occurring in elementary schools. Most of the emphasis in the report centered on the teacher's reactions, left largely unaddressed was the student's behavior. Then there are the children who are forced into sexual relationships.

These and other effects are described in the report of the Meese Commission, which include the following:

- "Children and adolescents who participate in the production of pornography experience adverse, enduring effects,"
- "Prolonged use of pornography increases beliefs that less common sexual practices are more common,"
- "Pornography that portrays sexual aggression as pleasurable for the victim increases the acceptance of the use of coercion in sexual relations,"
- "Acceptance of coercive sexuality appears to be related to sexual aggression,"
- "In laboratory studies measuring short-term effects, exposure to violent pornography increases punitive behavior toward women[15]

Another effect could be that pornography undermines our national security. While I would never argue that we should capitulate to competing ideologies a principle that should be defended, indefensible practices are another thing. Much of the underlying argument for violent Jihadists is that our culture is decadent. Pornography and its associated effects are one of the principal examples of this decadence, in effect making pornography a national security issue. While we must defend our national interests in any case, we would be better served if we had moral high ground with respect to culture. Defending cultural decadence is a difficult sell to Muslims (or almost every other cultural group for that matter) living in the United States that we are attempting to socialize and integrate into our culture.

Underlying the question of what effect the material has is the question of demand. Is pornography a major industry because the courts have merely allowed the demand for this content to be met, or did the court rulings allowing the content create the demand? While I will concede that there has always been a demand for pornography, I do not believe the demand would be anywhere near what it is now without the judicial intervention that served to make it available to every adult (actually to every adult and child when the ease of access over the internet is considered). Indeed, studies have shown that repeated exposure only creates more of a demand for ever more

---

[15] Koop, C. Everett. "Report of the Surgeon General's Workshop on Pornography and Public Health." American Psychologist. 42 (October 1987) : 944-945.

salacious content. I believe that if the courts had allowed the legislative will of the majority to be implemented, the demand, and therefore effect, of this content would be dramatically reduced.

That said, we cannot turn back the clock; we are where we are now. We are awash in a tidal wave of smut that has substantially affected our culture. In the absence of replacing liberal jurists with those unwilling to legislate from the bench (not a likely scenario given our current political climate), what are our realistic options now? For communities, states, and the nation, not much. From a regulatory standpoint, the status quo is going to continue into the indefinite future, unless it gets worse. It almost certainly will not get better.

For individuals there are things we can do, most of which involve the power of the purse. Above all, people who want less pornography in their communities should make sure they do not subsidize the material. If nobody bought the material or visited strip clubs to view exotic dancers, they would be out of business in a very short time. Also important to note is that just because adults have the right to view this material does not make it beneficial. People routinely destroy themselves with the rights that they are granted; this is another right that has negative consequences for the participating individual.

Next, we can inform the sponsors of objectionable material that we will boycott their product(s) if they continue to sponsor the offensive content. I recall one particularly offensive billboard, which I ruled to be appropriate, became the subject of protest by a vocal community group. The group was eventually able to persuade the sponsoring entity (a radio station) that their sponsorship of the sign was not in their economic interest and removed the sign. Market sanctions work.

We can pressure media to alter their coverage and their emphasis on the subject. While media types are generally defiant and claim that they are above the influence of those upon whom they depend for their existence, the fact is that media organizations are subject to market forces, as is any other business.

Better still are the free speech and assembly protections that we all enjoy. Protesting these establishments may work under the right set of circumstances. I recall an adult use established in the small town of Mesquite, Nevada (under false pretenses by the way, their business license was for a regular bookstore) which was granted injunctive relief from being shut down. In spite of that, community residents and supporters from a three state area banded together and organized a systematic and round the clock protest of the business, which included attempting to shame patrons. At first, the operator dug in his heels and refused to close the store in spite of massive economic losses directly attributable to the protest. Nevertheless, the community did not give up, they kept up the protest for over a year. In the end, the operator went out of business and the establishment closed. Protest can work. (By the way, this story would have made a great movie, but Hollywood would never make a movie showing smut peddlers being defeated).

We can stigmatize the behavior. Not all behavior is equal, and the non-judgmental "I'm okay, you're okay" philosophy should not go beyond petty and trivial differences that do not affect others. If we continue to tell people that their behavior is acceptable, or is the result of genetics or socialization, we will continue to reap the consequences of the unstigmatized behavior.

While difficult, we can teach our children the destructive effects of this material, and give our children the confidence and grounding they need to avoid the material when it is presented to them (note I did not say if the material is presented to them). Most important is to instill the confidence they will need to avoid becoming caught in the web of those who would prey upon them as sexual objects in order to gratify or enrich themselves.

In a perfect world these uses and material would disappear because of the lack of economic incentive to continue producing the material and maintaining the uses. Yes, I know that this is not going to happen. However, we can each try to have a positive effect on our culture by refusing to reward the smut peddlers and stigmatizing the behaviors of others. While we cannot dissuade the determined individual, we can affect those that will listen and respond to reason.

Eventually, that perfect world would also be a place where judges allow legislatures to implement that which is in the interest of the health, safety, and welfare of the community, state, and nation in accordance with majority will. Even if the uses survive the legislative process, the eventual result would be in accordance with the result expected through a healthy debate about the issues and compromises to protect the rights of individuals.

In conclusion, we should not be communicating to the young women (or men) of this country that they are no more than the sum of their anatomical parts. Women have been the nurturers of upcoming generations for millennia, and as such have been the principal civilizing influence in human relations. If we demean women as sexual objects and the procreative act as only a means of sexual gratification, once women learn and accept that role we may have a generation of children who believe the same. Instead of a civilizing and nurturing role, we may have a generation of children brought up to be subservient sexual objects to be exploited. While NAMBLA would be pleased, I don't believe that most of us would like to create that kind of a hell on earth for our children.

The courts should allow legislatures to regulate commercial speech that has pernicious effects on society, including the effects that I have described in this chapter. Specifically, if content is so offensive that it can be regulated to prevent exposure to non-consenting adults and minor children, government should be permitted to prohibit it entirely, just as it can prohibit child pornography. At a minimum, government should be able to prohibit content that contains real or simulated illegal acts, such as rape. The line currently drawn at child pornography is unjustified if other illegal acts can be legally depicted. If the argument is that child pornography can be prohibited because of its pernicious effects on the health, safety, and welfare of children, the same argument can be made for the health, safety, and welfare of women.

Chapter 11

"Do Nothing Congress"

One of the first things heard whenever someone describes the effectiveness of Congress is that they do not do anything to solve the problems facing the nation. This is a popular perception; however, is it true? By the way, the conclusion I reach in this chapter can be reasonably disputed; this is one instance where the term is not as idiotic as the title of this book suggests. Honest and thinking adults may conclude that the term is an accurate description of the Congress.

The expression has been used derisively for many decades. I vividly remember the disgust expressed by my Grandmother when she accused the Congress of this when I was not yet a teenager. It seems that the much of the population has perceived the Congress to be useless for quite some time. My respect for my Grandmother notwithstanding, I do not believe the expression is entirely accurate, nor does the perception serve us well. I will focus my attention on what the Congress has done lately to evaluate the performance of Congress.

Actually, the first question we should ask is whether or not they should be doing something. Many insist that the Congress has done enough damage to the country and that gridlock is preferable to making matters worse. On one level I agree with that sentiment; no bill is preferable to a bad bill that will have a destructive effect on our freedom, economy, or culture. The actions of Congress over the years has added legislation over the top of legislation until we now have such a mass of confused and often conflicting laws and implementing regulation that it is impossible for any one person to know what federal law requires let alone how to comply with it. I often worry that I am unknowingly breaking a federal law or regulation just by breathing and exhaling carbon dioxide (after all, it is the greenhouse gas most responsible for global warming). This condition is harmful to our nation on many levels.

In addition, the old saying that whenever Congress is in session you should hang on to you wallets is as true now as it ever was (perhaps even more so) Earmark happy senators and representatives out to buy their re-elections are not bashful about spending other peoples money to do it.

Political

Sadly, this was as true of Republicans when they controlled the 109th Congress as it is of the Democrats in the 110th Congress.

However, a good bill that can have a beneficial effect on the economy or culture is much better than no bill. If nothing else, the Congress should be acting to simplify federal law where appropriate so as to free the nation from counterproductive regulations. Efforts have been made in the past to do this with limited success because entrenched interests have a political or financial stake in perpetuating the status quo. The Grace Commission is a good example of that. Only a relative few of its recommendations were implemented in the 1980's.

In addition, it is critical for the Congress to adopt legislation to meet the challenges that this nation is faced with. Technological change creates opportunities to revolutionize the way that government can work for its people. At the same time, it creates significant challenges with respect to our ability to compete in the global economy, and more importantly, it forces us to alter security systems to be able to defeat those who would attack us. Change is inevitable no matter what subject or facet of life is considered, and that includes political change. The Congress must act to respond to the challenges that we face together and take advantage of opportunities to improve government when they arise; if they do not then they will truly deserve the scorn associated with this accusation.

So, how have the 109th and 110th Congresses performed? Excluding minor housekeeping bills, and appropriations bills, which are for the most part are annual funding bills, here is a bullet list of major congressional bills adopted to date, courtesy of Wikipedia, with my brief description of the bill's effect:

- 2005 February 17 - Class Action Fairness Act of 2005, This act, which forced major class action lawsuits to be filed in federal court instead of the various state courts, was a modest attempt to reign in out of control lawsuits that punished manufacturers and consumers alike. The only winners in these suits were the lawyers who brought the class actions. While the act can only be considered the first step in tort reform, at least the first step was taken. Tort reform remains a major problem for the United States, both in terms of making our manufacturers uncompetitive in the global market and consumers liable for the cost of litigation and punitive awards. These awards must be passed along to the consumer if the company is to remain a viable entity contributing to the economic health of the nation by providing goods and services in accordance with the demand for them.

- <u>2005</u> <u>April 20</u> - <u>Bankruptcy Abuse Prevention and Consumer Protection Act</u>. This act was a major reform of bankruptcy law that should have the effect of making those who incur debt more responsible for its payment. It should result in a decrease in consumer costs passed along to innocent consumers who are responsible in their payment of debt.

- <u>2005</u> <u>April 27</u> - <u>Family Entertainment and Copyright Act</u>. This act is designed to prevent the unauthorized photography and release of copyrighted material. It should help protect the rights and economic interests of artist and producers.

- <u>2005</u> <u>July 28</u> - <u>Dominican Republic-Central America-United States Free Trade Agreement Implementation Act</u> (**CAFTA**). This act implemented the creation of the Central American Free Trade Agreement, an international treaty designed to reduce trade impediments on the part of all countries involved in the treaty. The treaty and its implementation should have the effect of decreasing consumer costs in the United States, improving our ability to export goods to the countries involved, and improve the economic opportunities in these countries. As with other agreements which facilitate trade between willing partners, this is a win-win agreement for all.

- <u>2005</u> <u>July 29</u> - <u>Energy Policy Act of 2005</u>. This act provides significant tax advantages to energy producers that are designed to make the United States less dependant on foreign energy sources. Compromises on several key provisions make the bill less effective than it could have been; nevertheless, it should have the effect of encouraging the domestic production of energy and the growth of alternative energy technologies. This is critically important for the national security interests of the United States to avoid being held hostage to the interests of antagonistic energy producing countries and the funding of those regimes and their political partners.

- <u>2005</u> <u>August 10</u> - <u>Transportation Equity Act of 2005</u>. This act provides for long-term funding of transportation infrastructure within the United States. It is critical to the maintenance of our ability to move people and goods to meet market demands. Funded with energy taxes, it puts those monies into the public improvements for which they were intended.

- <u>2005</u> <u>October 26</u> - <u>Protection of Lawful Commerce in Arms Act</u>. This act is another tort reform measure, designed to prevent frivolous lawsuits designed to ensure that citizens would be either prevented from purchasing firearms for their protection or would be forced to pay exorbitant prices for them. This was a wise response to an attempt to emasculate the Second Amendment by judicial and punitive economic means (see Chapter 9).

- <u>2005</u> <u>December 30</u> - Department of Defense Appropriations Act, (including <u>McCain Detainee Amendment</u>). This act funded the Department of Defense for fiscal year 2006, but also included an amendment that addressed and required the humane treatment of prisoners held for acts against the United States in the current war on terror. This was a response to the attacks on the administration by domestic and foreign critics who insisted the United States was torturing these prisoners.

- <u>2006</u> <u>May 17, 2006</u> - <u>Tax Increase Prevention and Reconciliation Act of 2005</u>. This act prevented the sunset of various tax provisions designed to provide tax relief and encourage economic growth and stability.

- <u>2006</u> <u>May 29</u> - <u>Respect for America's Fallen Heroes Act</u>. This act was designed to ensure a reasonable distance be maintained by war protesters who sought to disrupt the funeral of military service members who were killed in action.

- <u>2006</u> <u>July 27</u>- <u>Adam Walsh Child Protection and Safety Act</u>. This act creates a national database for registered sex offenders designed to inform parents and communities about convicted felons living within their neighborhoods.

- <u>2006</u> <u>October 13</u> - <u>Safe Port Act</u>, including title VIII, <u>Unlawful Internet Gambling Enforcement Act of 2006</u>. The Safe Port Act establishes procedures designed to guard against the importation of weapons that can be used against us domestically, especially weapons of mass destruction. The internet gambling bill which was attached as a rider has good intentions; however, it is likely to have little or no effect on internet gambling; technological loopholes are likely to be found to undermine the intent.

- <u>2006</u> <u>October 17</u> - <u>Military Commissions Act of 2006</u>. This act establishes a procedure for the trials of terrorists held by the United States. Adopted to comply with a Supreme Court ruling, if largely legitimizes the procedures previously used by the Bush Administration.

- <u>2006</u> <u>October 26</u> - <u>Secure Fence Act of 2006</u>. This act authorized the construction of a security fence between the United States and Mexico. It did not comprehensively address immigration reform; however, its emphasis on border security is a necessary first step in controlling our borders.

- 2007-05-25 - Fair Minimum Wage Act of 2007. This bill increased the minimum wage.

- 2007-06-14 - Preserving United States Attorney Independence Act of 2007 This bill was designed to insulate U.S. attorneys from undue political influence in the performance of their duties.

- 2007-07-26 - Foreign Investment and National Security Act of 2007. This bill strengthens pre-existing requirements for foreign investors.

- 2007-08-03 - Implementing Recommendations of the 9/11 Commission Act of 2007. This bill enacted the recommendations of the 9/11 Commission that could not be implemented by executive order.

- 2007-08-05 - Protect America Act of 2007. This bill allowed warrantless surveillance of foreign intelligence targets reasonably believed to be outside of the United States. It was passed with a sunset clause, but was extended by subsequent legislation.

- 2007-09-14 - Honest Leadership and Open Government Act. This bill strengthened disclosure requirements for members of Congress.

- 2007-12-19 - Energy Independence and Security Act of 2007. This bill mandated increased energy efficiency measures.

- 2007-02-13 - Economic Stimulus Act of 2008. This bill approved economic stimulus checks to be sent to those who filed tax returns.

- 2008-05-21 - Genetic Information Nondiscrimination Act. This bill prohibits discrimination based on information obtained through genetic testing.

- 2008-05-22 - Food and Energy Security Act of 2007. This is the reauthorization of the five year farm bill. It provides for agricultural subsidies and research.

- 2008-06-30 - Post-9/11 Veterans Educational Assistance Act of 2008. This bill increased veterans educational benefits (GI Bill).

- 2008-07-29 - Tom Lantos Block Burmese JADE (Junta's Anti-Democratic Efforts) Act of 2008. This bill bars the import of Burmese gemstones.

- 2008-07-30 - Housing and Economic Recovery Act of 2008. This bill provides subsidies and incentives to homeowners facing foreclosure.

Political

Clearly, the Congress and the President working together over the past three and one half years have done something. Many will argue that the actions of Congress have not addressed the pressing issues of our time. That is true; however, that makes the Congress a "Didn't-do-enough Congress", not a "Do-nothing Congress". In my opinion, while the Congress could have done much more, because of the procedural constraints in the Senate, which allow the minority party to dictate legislation to the majority party, what was adopted was probably the best we could hope for. Others may argue that much of this legislation creates more problems than it solves. That is unrelated to the topic of this chapter. For good or bad, Congress acted, which means they did something as opposed to nothing.

What has the Congress not accomplished and why? The following are issues of critical importance that need to be addressed:

- Energy. We need to create a short-term bridge between the energy sources we have now and those that can be developed in the future. This means we must spend much more money on not just the development of alternative sources, but actual construction and investment in current technology. However, while we are doing this we need to develop current energy supplies in order to reduce and eliminate if possible our dependence on foreign energy. We must stop funding those hostile to our culture and values; this must be a national priority. Eventually we will be held hostage by unstable or radical regimes that use energy as a political weapon if we do not. Unfortunately, it seems that will occur sooner rather than later given the geopolitics of the time. Sadly, there is environmental opposition not just to the development of traditional fossil fuel sources, but to the development of alternative energy projects also. They seem to object to the development of anything that enables the growth needed to accommodate future populations.

- Social Security and Medicare reform. Demographically, the system is unsustainable. The only options are to increase the tax burden on future workers who will be unlikely to see any benefit from it, extend the retirement age to keep senior citizens working and contributing to the systems, reform the way the money is used to create additional revenue, or some combination of the three. If a private company established a pension system similar to the Social

112

Security System, the principals would be arrested for creating an illegal pyramid scheme, where those who get in early do well but those who get in late lose their investment. Unfortunately, the Democratic Party, as they have for decades, has killed any hope for meaningful reform with their time tested fear mongering.

- Tax simplification. The tax system in this nation is so complex and unwieldy that collection, accounting, filing, and enforcement has become a major drain on the economy. We must simplify the system to provide incentives for savings and disincentives for conspicuous consumption. A national sales tax would be the easiest to implement; current technology would make it easy and the system could exempt staple foods and medicine to ensure it would not be unduly regressive. Here also, entrenched interests have made it difficult to effect reform, including the accounting and legal professions which stand to lose much under a simplified system.

- Tort reform. As I indicated previously, much needs to be done to protect our citizens and industry from the litigating classes who seek to reassign responsibility for the simplest actions. A multi-million dollar award to someone careless enough to spill hot coffee on him or her is an excellent example. The litigious climate we find ourselves in imposes enormous costs on every citizen in this country, most especially for health care. Punitive damages should be capped at not more than three times actual damages. Non-binding arbitration should be required, and those who refuse the arbitrator's decision and proceed to trial should be forced to pay all court costs and the attorney's fees for both sides if they lose. Remarkably enough, the Trial Lawyer's Association is adamantly opposed to reform, and their contributions to the Democratic Party have been effective in stymieing reform except under limited circumstances.

- Educational reform. It seems that the purpose of education now is to either socialize children to be sensitive to all the latest social fads, or to ensure that they have a healthy self-esteem by not challenging their minds or demanding accountability for what they learn. This is a recipe for disaster. Other nations are not so foolish, and we may find that our technological advantage may disappear unless we take teaching seriously. Charter schools, incentive pay for teachers, accountability for results, and a challenging curriculum can all help. We must value teaching and teachers more; I have always found it amazing that we value our teachers so little that we pay them less than garbage collectors. Unfortunately, the National Education Association, and their supporters in the Democratic Party, is largely responsible for the lack of meaningful reform.

- Health care. Our health care system is one of the best in the world. However, much can be improved. Insurance is largely out of the reach of many because of legislative mandates as to what is required to be covered. Most cannot get coverage for basic needs without being required to pay for coverage that they will never use. These decisions largely belong in the hands of consumers, not legislators. In addition, insurance companies must be allowed to compete nationally; this is another instance of government mandates that maximize health care costs. Further, the tax code is designed to penalize those who can't get insurance in the workplace. Last, frivolous lawsuits are a major factor in runaway health care costs. In return, people should be responsible for ensuring that they have adequate coverage for their needs, much as drivers are required to have coverage when they drive. Massachusetts has established a system that could have been a model for others if the legislature had instituted the reforms I list above. Nationally, most legislators advocating health care reform tend to support Canadian style systems, which have been shown (in Canada!) to be unresponsive to health care needs and technological advancement.

- Drug laws. Our approach to drug addiction and abuse is a woeful failure. We seem to think that we can legislate away the law of supply and demand. It is time to recognize that it has not worked. We need to remove the monetary incentive for drug cartels and pushers to entice people to become drug-dependant, and the necessity for drug addicts to feed their addiction through criminal acts. I seems to me that the best chance we have of accomplishing this is to provide drugs at low cost to addicts through medical prescriptions, and to mount a massive educational campaign to show the effects of drug use while continuing to prosecute drug traffickers vigorously. Nancy Reagan was ridiculed for her "Just say no" slogan, but it worked while it was used. Both the Democrats and Republicans are jointly responsible for the failure to reduce drug dependency.

- Immigration. The security of our borders is critical to ensuring that 1) we control those who we allow to enter the country and 2) enemies do not have the means of importing weapons to destroy us, particularly weapons of mass destruction. To this end, the Secure Fence Act was adopted. However, this can only be the first step in immigration reform. As with drug dependency above, if we think that we can wave our legislative wand and eliminate the demand for labor in the United States that is unfilled by the current population and which will get progressively worse as the baby boom cohort moves into retirement, we are bound to be disappointed. We must allow adequate immigration to meet our needs, and in addition provide the haven to oppressed people that we have historically provided. Here again, both parties are responsible for the current immigration fiasco; the Democrats want voters, the Republicans want workers, and neither group is particularly fussy about whether the voters and workers are legally entitled to do either. Unfortunately, most citizens want neither. The result is we ignore the problem, allow virtually unfettered illegal immigration, and hope it does not come back to bite us. This is not the way to make us safe.

- Cultural preservation. There is much derision and ridicule heaped on religious organizations (always referred to as right-wing zealots, bigots, or radicals) who seek to preserve traditional values and institutions. Cultural elitists want to transform our society and law to accommodate historically radical views. What these people fail to understand is that the traditional values and institutions they seek to replace are what brought us to a point where we have the freedoms we do. We replace them at risk to all the underlying values of our society. Government should be seeking to increase confidence in these values, not undermining them. Democrats have largely become the party of special interests at the expense of mainstream values.

As can be seen, the Congress has not been effective in many respects with addressing the legislative priorities the country faces. Unfortunately, the political environment is so polarized that significant problems have been ignored. It is so bad that when George W. Bush took office promising to work with the minority party that the minority party went out of its way to oppose and ridicule him at every opportunity, then promptly accused the president of breaking his campaign promises. However, it is still inappropriate to say that Congress has done nothing.

Why is it that most people are unaware or unappreciative of the actions that Congress and the President have taken to make our society safer, encourage responsible behavior, and promote economic growth and prosperity? A large part of the problem can be laid at the feet of the mainstream media, which has a tendency to focus on bad news in order to sell newspapers or attract a viewing audience. The media also focuses an inordinate amount of coverage on trivial items, especially the escapades of celebrities, which are truly meaningless in terms of their importance to our lives. Ultimately, it is the responsibility of all citizens to become informed and to make decisions based on factual information rather than popular perception.

The Congress deserves more credit than most people are willing to give them, largely because of perception and misunderstanding. Over the long term, perpetuation of the perception that the Congress does nothing will have the effect of further undermining the effectiveness of our government and its ability to meet the challenges that face our society.

The perception that Congress does nothing feeds the ambivalence toward government felt by the general population. It contributes to the perception that politicians are crooks, and undermines confidence in the government. If the trend continues, it is possible that enough people will perceive Congress to be so ineffective that the institution should be replaced with a more effective legislative organization. All it would take to accomplish that would be a constitutional convention. I do not believe that would be in the best interest of this country.

Chapter 12

"There is Not a Dimes Worth of
Difference Between the Two Parties"

In the United States, two political parties dominate the political landscape. The Democratic Party has been in existence formally since the days of Andrew Jackson, but has its antecedents in the Democratic-Republican Party formed by Thomas Jefferson. As with any political party, it has evolved over the years, changing positions to cater to core constituencies. The Republican Party, formed in 1854 in opposition to the expansion of slavery, also has morphed in principle since its organization. Transitioning its mission to accommodate the concerns and desires of its constituency is essential to the continuation of any group; a party must stay relevant or it will go the way of the Whigs. Many argue that both of the predominant parties have transitioned their missions to a point that there is no material difference between them. I disagree.

First, it is worth considering the obstacles that a party has to overcome in order to form an effective governing coalition. There are approximately 300 million people living in the United States, and this population is diverse in every conceivable way. Included within this population is almost every cultural, religious, ethnic, and racial group on the face of the earth. Each of those within each group generally share similar values with the rest of those in the group; indeed these values often form the basis for the existence of the group except for groups that are based on genetic differences such as race. However, almost all, if not all, individuals will differ in their individual specific beliefs, traditions, and values, or they will differ in the intensity of their conviction. In turn, most groups share some values with other groups.

In addition to the effect of cultural indoctrination, there is also the effect of environment. Crime, education, economics, nature, and random chance gives every single person a unique perspective on life and how the problems of life should be solved. Because of all the factors that contribute to individual philosophy, I believe that each person is as culturally unique as he or she is genetically unique. If I am correct in that belief, the net result is we have a nation of 230 million adults over eighteen years of age with somewhere in the neighborhood of 230 million different specialized philosophies. The standard joke that if you put ten people in a room and ask for an opinion you will get ten opinions is true.

A political party must persuade enough people to accept its political positions and vote accordingly to enable it to control the direction of legislation. The party must persuade a majority to its cause, or a least a plurality in the case of a fragmented multi-party system. In addition, it must persuade that majority to hold together as it is taking positions on a multitude of issues that range across the spectrum of political debate. It is truly a wonder that any party is able to do this given the complexity and diversity of the population.

What is a party trying to accomplish? It is formed based on an ideology a group proposes to advocate. The ultimate purpose of the party is to educate and persuade enough people to accept its ideological principles and vote for people who will implement the ideology in policy. To accomplish this it must persuade many people. In order to attract support in numbers sufficient to govern, parties try to be as inclusive as possible. The party must attract support from people holding a wide variety of opinions so, in addition to their core philosophy, they attempt to convince citizens of the benefits of their positions while at the same time adjusting their political goals to accommodate the wishes of key constituencies. However, if the party tries too hard and attempts to be all things to all people, it will undermine their credibility with everyone. Holding true to core principles is essential to the survival of a party.

It is clear that in order to be an effective force in politics, a party must make numerous accommodations to groups that share its basic values but differ in the details of exactly what is to be done, how it is to be done, and to what degree. This involves compromise, which is a dirty word in politics. This is where each of the two major parties begin to loose people, who become disenchanted with the party's departure from what is essentially a core philosophy of the constituent. Those disillusioned either realign their allegiance to a minority party or separate themselves from politics entirely. Either choice is a mistake.

Those that are so disillusioned with politics that they divorce themselves from political participation have a destructive effect on the political process. Instead of advocating for what they believe in and supporting those who are the closest to their philosophy, they support no one. They cry and moan about how they cannot affect government or politicians, so they let a small minority of the population make decisions for them. Edmund Burke's famous truism is applicable; "All that is necessary for evil to triumph is for good men to do nothing". Those who allow themselves to give up also allow themselves to be taken wherever those who are active in politics take them, and if the result is contrary to their interests they have no one to blame but themselves.

Those who join a minority party are permanently relegated to insignificance. They cannot possible hope to win politically. The most they can do is to fragment the vote of those they are in general agreement with (but from whom they have separated) frequently ensuring the defeat of those to whom their philosophies are most closely aligned and the election of those who they are opposed to. They make the perfect (in their view) the enemy of the good. Examples of this abound. The Green Party siphoned enough votes from Al Gore in the 2000 presidential election to make a difference in the outcome. Harry Reid beat John Ensign in his 1998 Nevada senatorial race by a few hundred votes, while thousands of conservative voters in the American Independent Party threw away their vote on a candidate that had no chance of being elected. A more significant example of this effect is the results of Ross Perot's failed independent presidential bids, which fragmented the generally conservative vote and ensured the election of Bill Clinton to the presidency twice with a minority vote. Those who vote with minority parties generally undermine the ability of those they would prefer to govern in favor of those with whom they are diametrically opposed.

In some societies, the fragmentation of political power has led to perpetual gridlock. The starkest recent historic example of this is Italy, which has a multi-party system that for many years could not maintain a governing coalition for more that a few months at a time. Although it has been more stable in the recent past, from the end of World War II to the present, the average government lasted only about two years. Other multi-party systems are similarly paralyzed, unable to address the problems they face because a majority cannot agree on solutions. Remarkably enough, we actually have people here in the United States advocating for a multi-party system, which will inevitably make political progress here even more difficult than it presently is.

In a sense, the United States already has a gridlocked government in that often we split our votes, giving one party power over the executive branch and the opposite party control over the legislative branch. Foolishly enough, there are those who actually think this is good in that it leads to a check on the power of the other branch of government. In the next sentence, they will decry the inability of the branches of government to resolve political differences and work together to solve the many problems facing our society. In this respect, the parliamentary systems of Europe are superior to our government organization; in those systems the party who wins the election has an unequivocal right to govern so long as they can maintain their working majority in parliament.

Even when we have the executive and legislative branches controlled by the same party, the tradition of the Senate still perpetuates gridlock. Senate rules, dating from 1806, allow the minority party to filibuster legislation, clearly thwarting the mandate of the majority party. Even worse, one single senator can put a hold on nominations or legislation. Astoundingly, this single senator can remain anonymous. This means that one single senator can ensure legislative gridlock and thwart the will of both houses of congress and the executive branch without anyone knowing who is preventing the business of the people from being accomplished. When the minority party obstructs legislation with a filibuster, they promptly accuse the majority of legislative paralysis because of the majority's inability to get the minority party to allow them the opportunity to pass legislation. Is it just me, or is something profoundly wrong with this picture?

The party who has the majority in Congress should be permitted to govern. Rather continuing perpetual gridlock, the Senate should eliminate or severely restrict filibuster or hold rules and allow the majority to have up and down votes on all legislation and confirmations. Both parties fear this because the majority party today may be the minority party tomorrow. Big deal. That is no reason to perpetuate an anachronism that ensures bad government and thwarts the will of the majority of voters. If the majority party passes legislation that is then signed into law by the President which does not have a constructive political end, they will be out of power in two to four years and the new majority can rewrite the legislation. We must allow government to work for the people.

So what are the ideological goals of the two dominant parties? What follows is a side by side comparison of the respective positions on issues as taken from a summary of the 2000 and 2004 Democratic and Republican party platforms arranged in alphabetical order; I have removed references to past action preferring to focus on future goals and have included my commentary on the effects of the listed policies. It should be evident that even though there are a few issues with which there is little difference, with most issues the difference is dramatic.

Democrat	Republican
Abortion	
• Pursue embryonic stem cell research.	• Promote adoption & abstinence, not abortion clinic referrals.
• Support right to choose even if mother cannot pay.	• Human Life Amendment to the Constitution.
• Choice is a fundamental, constitutional right	• Ban abortion with Constitutional amendment.
	• Alternatives like adoption instead of punitive action.

The Democrats support the right to obtain abortions under all circumstances, including partial birth abortion, though this is not included in the platform. The Republicans oppose abortion and support constitutional amendments to ensure the protections of unborn children. There could not be a clearer difference between the two parties.

Democrat	Republican
Budget and Economy	
• Cut the deficit in half over the next four years.	• None

The Democrats want to cut the deficit in half; however, this is an instance where the platform position does not match legislative action. The impulse to spend the Federal government into oblivion is at least as much of a problem with the Democrats as it is with the Republicans. In addition, they have been denigrating the economy for years, which until recently was doing well. This was a lot like trying to turn a silk purse into a sow's ear. Unfortunately, the Republicans have removed the goal of a balanced budget amendment, leaving us to conclude that balancing the budget is no longer a priority for the Party. Republican spending habits which approximate the spending of past Democratically controlled congresses unfortunately support this conclusion, which most likely is the principal cause of their loss of the majority in both houses in 2006.

Democrat	Republican
Civil Rights	
• Strengthen some parts of Patriot Act and change other parts.	• The Patriot Act is used to track terrorist activity.
• Support affirmative action to redress	• Homosexuality is incompatible with

Political

discrimination.

- Racial and religious profiling is wrong.
- Keep marriage at state level; no federal gay marriage ban.

military service.

- Support the advancement of women in the military.
- States should not recognize gay marriage from other states. (Sep 2004)
- Affirmative Access, without preferences or set-asides.
- Constitutional Amendment banning same-sex marriage.
- Strong support for traditional definition of marriage.
- Let Boy Scouts exercise free speech (ok to ban gays).
- Women exempt from combat; "candid analysis" of military gays.

The differences on these issues are significant, including gay marriage, homosexual rights, and affirmative action. The Democrats support affirmative action to redress discrimination, which generally amounts to quotas to try to achieve equal results; the Republicans support affirmative access, which seeks equal opportunity for all. The Democrats seek to avoid the federalization of the gay marriage issue, normally a Republican position but in this case an obfuscation of the issue. It is already federalized by the action of the Massachusetts Supreme Judicial Court, California Supreme Court, and the effect of the Full Faith and Credit Clause. The Republicans seek to prevent the legalization of gay marriage by any means. Democrats view homosexual rights as equal to other protected classes, while Republicans view these rights as more limited in that private institutions and the armed forces should not be obligated to accept this lifestyle choice.

Democrat   **Republican**
Corporations

- Tax credits and investment support for small business.
- Transparency in corporate accounting.
- End corporate welfare as we know.

- None

No stated position from the Republicans; the Democrats profess support for small business and seek to eliminate corporate welfare and accounting practices that lead to fraud.

Democrat   **Republican**
Crime
- Crack down on gangs and drugs   - Support the death penalty.
                                    - Best way to deter crime is to enforce existing laws.

Generally, each party's public position is an attempt to be harder on crime than the other is. This is an area where there is little substantive stated difference.

Democrat   **Republican**
Drugs
- Bring to justice those bringing drugs to America.   - Jail time and school drug testing deters drug use.

Same comment as crime above.

Democrat   **Republican**
Education
- Support lifelong learning and distance learning.   - Promote school choice and home-schooling.
- Bush broke promise of NCLB by not funding it.   - Support voluntary student-initiated prayer in school.
- Standardized tests to advance learning, not bureaucracy.
- Charter schools OK, vouchers not.

The policy differences are significant here. Democrats make a silly accusation as if it constitutes a good statement of public policy. They also oppose vouchers, one of the most effective means of ensuring accountability in education. Republicans support educational choices leading to a decentralized learning system.

Democrat   **Republican**
Energy and Oil
- Energy independence to avoid dealing with repressive regimes.   - No Kyoto, no mandatory carbon emissions controls.
- Develop renewable energy and efficient vehicles.

Political

- We cannot drill our way to energy
  independence.

The principle difference is in the respective party's approaches to current energy sources. The Republicans believe that we need to develop current oil reserves to decrease dependence on foreign sources and avoid the transfer of wealth to nations that often use the income generated against us. In addition, the Republicans repudiate the Kyoto protocol, although to be fair Democrats joined Republicans in a unanimous vote repudiating the treaty before it was finalized, and President Clinton did not submit it for ratification knowing it would be defeated with a clear bipartisan majority. The Democrats want alternative energy now, and are willing to impose economic pain on the public to achieve it.

Democrat	Republican
Environment	
• Reject choice of healthy economy vs. healthy environment.	• Private property ownership key to environmental agenda.
• Honor hunting & fishing heritage via more conservation lands.	• Cap-and-trade market-based air pollution reductions.

In rejecting the choice of a healthy economy over a healthy environment, the Democrats clearly chose the environment. The Republicans emphasize the importance of property rights. The differences are obvious.

Democrat	Republican
Families	
• Family is the center of American life.	• Families are the cornerstone of our culture.

Democrats view the family as the center of American life, but are silent as to what form the family takes. Republicans hold that families are the cornerstone of our culture, and in practice they place a high value on traditional marriage and the foundational role the traditional family plays in the perpetuation of our society.

Democrat	Republican
Foreign Policy	
• Bush bullies when he should instead	• Nations that support terrorism are just

124

persuade.

- US leadership in Africa for economic & humanitarian goals.
- Commit to "One China" policy but support Taiwan.
- Asia: Enhance relations with Japan, S. Korea, India, Pakistan.
- Community of the Americas for US-Latin American relations.
- End Castro regime, but allow travel.
- Russia: work on nukes, human rights, and democracy

as guilty.

- Pursue a comprehensive strategy against WMD proliferation.
- Applaud the success in mobilizing international cooperation.
- The Broader Middle East Initiative spreads democracy.
- Provide new strategies to help poor nations.
- Objectives of assistance and the strategies must change.

Remarkably, the Democrats have a plank accusing President Bush of bullying other nations. This is silly beyond belief. Even if it were true, which it is not, why would they take such a negative approach? In addition, the Democrats seem to not link foreign policy with the war on terror that we are engaged in throughout the world. Republicans are focused on enlisting help in the war on terror, spreading democracy, and changing the paradigm of aiding those who may be stable but ultimately are a destructive influence on the spread of peace, prosperity, and freedom. Here, again, the differences are clear

Democrat   **Republican**
Free Trade
- Knock down barriers to free, fair and balanced trade.
- Review all trade agreements; investigate China rights abuses.

- None

The Democrats profess to want free trade, but their actions indicate that they are actually protectionist. Republicans are silent on the issue, but generally support free trade. Neither party addresses the trade imbalance and unfair trade practices that put this country's economy at a disadvantage.

Democrat   **Republican**
Government Reform
- Line-item veto to root out pork-barrel spending.
- Ensure accessible, independently

- Stop activist judges from banning Pledge & Ten Commandments.

auditable, accurate voting.

The Republicans for years sought for both the line item veto and for election reforms that preclude the manipulation of the vote. Historically the party advocating fiscal responsibility over the Democrats, who never met a social spending program they didn't like, they thought the line item veto could lead to fiscal restraint on the prolific spending habits of the Democratically controlled congress. Unfortunately, the bill that was adopted was ruled unconstitutional, although efforts continue in favor of a more modest line item veto proposal. With election reform, Republicans have had elections taken from them without a peep of protest from the Democrats, most notably the election of John Kennedy over Richard Nixon (contrary to the popular lie, the 2000 election was not stolen as demonstrated by even the left leaning media, but that has not stopped the perpetuation of the lie). That leaves judicial activism as the principle difference on this subject. The Democrats depend on judicial activist judges to make law that cannot be won in congress or the ballot box while the Republicans oppose it. There could not be a more significant difference between the two parties

Democrat	**Republican**
Gun Control	
• Reauthorize assault weapons ban, close gun show loophole.	• Open more public land to hunting.
	• No frivolous gun lawsuits, no gun licensing.

While the Democrats have not taken the position advocated by the most radical among them, they do seek to impose restrictions on the sale and use of many types for firearms that can be legitimately used for defense of life, property, and the nation. The Republicans are in favor of not adding additional restrictions on or impediments to the ownership of firearms.

Democrat	**Republican**
Health Care	
• Bush's Medicare drug program helps companies more than seniors.	• Government-run universal health care leads to inefficiencies.
• Expand coverage and cut healthcare costs.	• Ethical research yes; embryo cells no; cloning no.
	• ABC for AIDS: Abstinence, Be

faithful, Change behavior.
- No assisted suicide.

Here the Democrats want everyone to believe that the new Medicare drug benefit does not benefit seniors but rather benefits drug companies. Unfortunately for them, the program is widely accepted as beneficial to those who depend upon it. They also want to expand coverage and cut healthcare costs at the same time, which seem to be conflicting goals. Republicans prefer to allow the market and personal responsibility solve healthcare problems.

Democrat

Homeland Security
- We respect and honor our veterans.
- 3 challenges: War on Terror; WMDs, stable world democracy.
- Reform intelligence community internationally and locally.
- Safeguard nuclear material and stop creating new material.
- Add 40,000 new soldiers and keep military all volunteer.
- Focus on cargo containers and border security.

Republican
- Keep our homeland safe by taking action on multiple fronts.
- Establish minimum safety requirements at chemical plants.
- Greatly increase the federal bio-terrorism budget.
- Recapitalize and enlarge the Coast Guard's fleet.
- Break down the wall between intelligence and law enforcement.
- Establish a National Counter terrorism Center.
- Provide Armed Forces better pay, treatment, and training.
- Cover all basic housing costs for average service members.
- Increased funding for VA health care.
- Equip our nation to fight 21st Century adversaries.
- Provide $10 billion to defend from ballistic missiles.

Here the stated differences are relatively insignificant. The general goal is the same; that is the protection of life, the first unalienable right listed in the Declaration of Independence which the government has the responsibility of protecting. Beyond the platform positions, the rhetoric is heated about how best to accomplish that goal. Democrats want to spend as

Political

much money domestically as possible, and would prefer that we wait for the enemy to come to us where we search everything everywhere that could possibly be a threat. They also castigate the Republican administration for what they call the incompetent prosecution of the war on terror. The Republicans prefer to spend the money in defending us where the terrorist threats originate. The policy differences are dramatic. It is worth noting that however difficult and problematic the prosecution of the war on terror, it is clear that we have not been attacked since 9/11, and that supports the axiom that the best defense is a good offense.

Democrat	Republican
Immigration	
• Path for undocumented aliens to earn citizenship.	• Only legal immigrants, through tightly controlled borders.
	• Amnesty encourages illegal immigration.
	• Use biometric data to better track foreign travelers.

The Democrats emphasize providing a means for illegal immigrants to gain citizenship while the Republicans are focused on reducing illegal immigration and permanently discouraging the behavior. In practice, the Republicans are conflicted because of the economic importance of immigration and the unwillingness of the public to recognize that we need immigration to sustain our economy. Nevertheless, there are clear differences in the two party's positions.

Democrat	Republican
Jobs	
• A strong America begins with good jobs that support families.	• None
• Change tax system to not encourage shipping jobs overseas.	

Democrats emphasize the importance of jobs to citizens and advocate changing the tax structure to discourage the export of jobs. Republicans are silent, but have historically held that the market generally should determine jobs and wages.

128

Democrat	Republican

Principles and Values

Democrat	Republican
• New vision for America: strong at home, respected abroad.	• We saw the spirit of courage and optimism on 9/11.

This is fluff on part of both parties.

Democrat	Republican

Social Security

Democrat	Republican
• Bar practice of keeping retirement funds in company stock.	• None
• Oppose privatization and oppose raising retirement age.	

This demographically doomed program desperately needs to be reformed; however, the Democrats decided decades ago that the short term political value of scaring seniors with Republican bogeymen exceeds the value of true reform. Any mention of meaningful reform is met with charges that the Republicans are bent on starving seniors. This political trick has kept the senior lobby in the Democratic Party's pocket for decades, giving them short-term political benefits that far outweighed the long-term benefits of fixing the system. Nothing much has changed; the Democrats still think this is 1976 and that the population is as gullible as ever while the Republicans (with a few notable exceptions) are still too cowed by the effect of past Democratic demagoguery to address the systemic problems of Social Security. Past attempts to fix the system ignored the underlying problems (the fact that it is essentially a Ponzi scheme and that Congress spends the surplus for current needs) and simply raised the payroll tax.

Democrat	Republican

Tax Reform

Democrat	Republican
• Cut taxes for middle class, not the wealthy.	• None

The Democratic position officially is that they want to cut taxes for the middle class while ensuring that the wealthy pay their fair share. In practice, the Democrats classify almost all tax relief proposals as benefiting the rich (wealth redistribution is not a tax cut for the beneficiaries). The Republicans are silent, but have a long history of tax relief and reform proposals, some adopted and some successfully killed by the opposition.

129

Political

Democrat	Republican
Technology	
• Put science ahead of ideology in research and policymaking.	• Support do-not-call and do-not-email lists.
• Vigorous federal highway and transit initiatives.	

Democrats want to make science the determining factor in technological policy. This is remarkable; they advocate setting aside ideology, which is the ideas that guide our society, in making this policy, regardless of whether it is right or wrong. They are so married to this concept that research that is less promising (such as stem cell) is favored over more promising technology because the less promising technology conflicts with traditional ideology.

Democrat	Republican
War and Peace	
• "Name and shame" terrorist sponsors, tough on Saudi Arabia.	• Terrorists seek weapons of mass destruction to kill us.
• Focus on Afghanistan to avoid renewing terrorist haven.	• Shrink the space in which the terrorists can operate.
• Focus on preventing terrorism by education in Muslim world.	• Total and complete destruction of terrorism is needed.
• Need a plan to "win the peace" in Iraq.	• Afghanistan is liberated and the American people are safer.
• Internationalize Iraqi military and political presence.	• Saddam had capability to reconstitute his weapons programs.
• Committed to Israel but support Palestinian state.	
• Commitment to Israel is unshakable.	

These positions mask the policy differences of the two parties. The Democrats perceive that in international cooperation, education, and diplomacy are the solutions to issues of war and peace. The Republicans perceive that we are facing a determined enemy who is only willing to negotiate in order to buy time to prepare for their next tactical or strategic objective, and that the goal of Islamic jihadists is ultimately the forced imposition of their culture on the rest of the world. The differences are stark, and remarkable given the lessons so recently learned in World War II.

Democrat	Republican
Welfare and Poverty	
• Raise EITC & minimum wage to $7 & expand middle class.	• Faith-based welfare grants equal with secular groups.
	• Move more welfare recipients off the welfare rolls.

Here again the differences are clear; the Democrats believe the answer to poverty is top down government imposed solutions while the Republicans believe that personal responsibility and religiously motivated organizations offer the best solutions to these problems.

The two dominant parties are not the same. To be sure, not all elected officials or candidates of a party will agree with all of their respective party's platform positions. However, it is safe to say that most of them will agree with the majority of these positions. There are clear ideological differences between them, even though not all party representatives are united behind platform planks. The most effective way of influencing government to pursue a person's ideological goals is to become politically active in the dominant party that best represents the goals of the individual.

Chapter 13

"Limit Tax Exemptions for Children
to Penalize Large Families"

This seems logical to many at first blush, but a careful examination of the impact of this policy shows that it would have negative consequences for families, communities, and for the nation. First, I should disclose that I am the father of five children (now grown) who took advantage of these tax deductions for many years as my children were maturing. It is reasonable to say that because of personal experience I may be biased. However, just because I may be biased, it does not mean that I cannot be accurate in my evaluation of the impacts that this shortsighted policy would have.

In March of 2006, I was driving across the lonely countryside north of Yerington, Nevada on my way back to Reno where I was to catch a flight home. I generally listen to talk radio when in such circumstances, and as I am conservative I prefer conservative programs. I found such a program, the Lars Larson Show, where he was discussing a large family in Missouri. As described, although the children were well cared for, and indeed seemed to be extraordinarily gifted, the host of the show objected to the large number of children in general, and to the fact that each of the children earned the parents a tax exemption in specific. His objection was based on the premise that taxpayers should not be subsidizing the choices of those who want to have many children. I believe the logic of the host, and by extension many others both conservative and liberal, is flawed and myopic in its approach. (In fairness to Mr. Larson, he is normally on the side of traditional values. In this case, his argument has the opposite effect.)

First, the exemption is not really a subsidy. The tax code, however flawed it is in other respects, is ostensibly designed to provide minimum exemptions to ensure that the government does not take so much of a family's income that the family will be unable to make ends meet. If that were not the case, government would wind up subsidizing the family through food stamps, welfare, Medicaid, or similar programs. The exemption is simply a mechanism provided to allow the family to keep more of the money that they have earned. Note that this is the same argument that conservatives make in the defense of other tax exemptions or tax cuts.

Even conceding that it is a subsidy, it is not significant in terms of the amount. The tax exemption was $3,300 in 2006, which amounts to a total of $825 in tax dollars not withheld or returned to the family assuming the family is in the 25% tax bracket. That amounts to about 275 gallons of milk over the year, not a significant amount by almost anyone's standard. It certainly is not enough to actually support a child for a year. If the family is in the 15% bracket it is significantly less, amounting to $495, or about 165 gallons of milk (you can tell I have been conditioned to evaluate monetary value based on my ability to provide milk for my children).

While not insignificant arguments, the reasons above are not the most significant justification for the exemption. What is most important is the value of the children, including to the family, community, nation, and world. I do not understand how anyone can fail to see that it is in our interest to encourage the birth and responsible nurturing of children, but I will explain for those who do not understand.

One of the arguments Mr. Larson used against the exemption is that people will have babies anyway; why should they be subsidized? If this is true, why are birthrates are dropping like a rock? Mr. Larson implies that having babies is counter to the national interest and that providing financial relief to families is shortsighted. It also assumes that people will continue to have children regardless of tax policy. Nothing could be further from the truth. Mr. Larson demonstrates a woeful lack of knowledge about demographic trends, both in the United States and in other industrialized nations, including most of Europe. The simple truth is that people are not having as many babies as was formerly born, and that we should not be penalizing those who choose to bear children.

For many reasons, people in developed countries are not having nearly as many babies as they used to. These reasons include the widespread availability of contraceptives and abortion, social pressure to limit families, the desire of women to enter the workplace in response to social encouragement, the decline in marriage rates, economic incentives to entering the workplace instead of nurturing children, the actual economic cost of raising children, and cost of living increases that have resulted in inadequate wages for most single earner families. When you look at all the social and economic incentives in place that discourage child rearing, it is truly a wonder that any children are born in this nation. However, though there are still many children that are born, there are not enough to sustain our long-term interests.

133

Political

It is worth noting that in spite of the fact that there are currently over 6.5 billion people on the earth, technically speaking we are merely three or four generations away from extinction if all the women in the world decide to not have children. The survival of our species literally depends on the children we bring into this world. If we do not reproduce, we will not survive.

On a national level, the survival of our culture is dependant on our ability to reproduce enough of a population (or allow the immigration of culturally compatible groups) to defend us against the populations of competing ideologies that would destroy us if they could. Our military is an all-volunteer force, and must compete against private interests to recruit soldiers in numbers sufficient to sustain our ability to defend the nation. Given the demographics of our population, with baby boomers retiring and workers in ever more short supply (to the extent that we can employ what is estimated to be many millions of illegal immigrants), the Armed Forces may soon find it more difficult to recruit the numbers of men and women needed to secure our defense. For that reason alone we should stop stigmatizing large families and attempting to economically punish them.

As indicated above, the combination of an expanding economy and the reduction in the number of workers needed to sustain the economy is additional incentive to encourage the maintenance of our birth rate. We have hurt our ability to ensure continued prosperity because of shortsighted population policies, including the destruction of millions of unborn children through abortion, the emphasis on women entering the marketplace for the sake of equality which thereby reduced the birthrate, and the social stigma attached to large families justified by resource availability concerns. We are now in the position of, having for all practical purposes utilized all available domestic sources of labor, and we depend on imported labor to meet demand in spite of social pressure to limit immigration.

Since I first wrote this chapter the economy has taken a significant turn for the worse. Unemployment is increasing and our economic system is under considerable stress. Even so, this downturn will not dramatically affect the future need for human resources. Eventually the economy will come back as it always does, and we will still be faced with the same long-term problems we have had in the past.

As bad as it is here in the United States, at least we are not in as bad a position as most European countries. Their birthrates are so low that they are experiencing negative population growth, in other words they are loosing people in absolute numbers. To encourage their citizens to have more children, many of those countries grant direct subsidies for children amounting to many thousands of dollars. For instance, Germany allows up to a year of leave with 67% of a salary being covered, up to $1,800 a month. This is a phenomenal amount of money, far less than the $825 of their own money that we allow a family to retain annually. Other nations grant large payments with the birth of a child. Asian industrialized nations are also experiencing the same problem, especially Japan.

In addition to labor shortages, the declining populations in the industrialized nations have created a crisis with pension and social security systems. The retired workers of today are largely dependant on the contributions to retirement systems of current workers. If there are not enough workers contributing to the systems to sustain them, they are bound to fail sooner or later. In the case of the United States, the retirement of the baby boom generation will create a drain in the Social Security Trust Fund that will bankrupt it. Sad to say, in spite of the obvious train wreck that is approaching, the Democratic Party has created a political environment that has made meaningful reform impossible. As bad as the problem is in the United States, it is worse in other industrial nations. This is one more reason why we should not be discouraging people from bearing children.

European countries are also at a significant disadvantage because, in order to sustain their economies, they have encouraged the immigration of culturally incompatible immigrants. Muslims dominate immigrant groups in Europe, and their cultural influence has grown to the point where they are dictating to old Europe how they, their religion, and their prophet will be treated. If something does not go their way, they riot, burn cars and buses in France, threaten the lives of newspaper editors in Denmark, and murder filmmakers in the Netherlands who dare to be critical of their culture or icons. In the United States, we are fortunate in that the illegal immigration that we have is largely from culturally compatible nations, especially Mexico.

As time goes on, it is probable that the economies of Mexico and other Central American countries will improve. When that occurs, it is also likely that immigration from those culturally compatible areas will decrease. In the not so distant future, we may be lamenting the lack of immigrants willing to come to this country to work and help our economy grow. This is yet another reason for us to stop penalizing the birthing of children.

While we are on the subject of the value of children, it is worth noting that discrimination is not only legally and culturally unacceptable, it is also economically stupid. Anyone who would marginalize and deny opportunity to others based on genetic differences demonstrates a complete lack of understanding of the importance of maximizing available human resources. We should be encouraging all segments of our population to achieve their goals and become productive citizens, regardless of race, gender, or whatever. That includes the valuation of motherhood and fatherhood.

One of the saddest chapters in our history is the abortion debacle foisted upon the nation by an imperious Supreme Court. This has led to the destruction of millions of what could have been productive, responsible human beings while at the same time circumventing legislative compromise upon which reasonable people could have agreed. The lame excuse that these babies are better off dead is fallacious, there are so many people longing to adopt children that this is not a reasonable defense. We could have adopted policies that both ensured that unwanted children need not be brought up in a hostile environment while at the same time encouraging a culture that values life and preserves the precious resource that our human population represents. Instead, we have created a cultural setting that has so denigrated the value of children that we kill late term fetuses, advocate infanticide to get rid of the handicapped, and, in the case of the African-American population, seems to have the effect of genocide. The effects of this decision are finally catching up with us, and included among them are the lack of human resources needed to sustain our long term defense and economy.

Many insist that birthrates must be slashed in order to preserve the species. I recently read an article indicating that at current and projected consumption rates the world's population will require the resources of several planets in order to sustain that consumptive rate. This is one of many pieces designed to frighten us into believing that the sky is falling and the only means of preventing it is to reduce our population. What this article and other similar studies ignore is that resources are not really consumed. Virtually all of the elements used to create products, including food, industrial products, consumer goods, and shelter are still here on this planet. The metal in a junk vehicle does not magically get sucked into a black hole where it can never be used again. The same is true of every other element used in the production of goods. Actually, as time goes on we actually are gaining additional elements (and molecules for that matter) from space debris that winds up on a collision path with the earth.

The problem can be solved for the foreseeable future with better resource management. We have adequate resources to sustain a significantly expanded population, but economic incentives to utilize resources that are currently treated as waste and a nuisance do not exist (yet). Energy certainly is not a problem; we have an abundant supply of energy striking the planet every day that provides the means of producing food and power in many forms. The transformation of land use from agriculture to other uses, which reduces the land available for food production, is certainly a concern that needs to be addressed; however, it is clear that the Malthusian model was not a valid measure of past performance; the ability to produce food, for various reasons, has increased along with the population.

Indeed, technology, combined with the constant influx of energy, in addition to providing the means to feed an expanding population, holds out the promise to provide the raw materials we need for the production of goods, including substitutes for metals. The real danger to the survival of our species is our inability to get along with one another, not the ability to feed, clothe, shelter, and sustain an expanding population.

To summarize, we need to recognize that those who bring children into the world, and teach, nurture, feed, clothe, and shelter at great personal and economic sacrifice should not be penalized. The tax code should be tailored to allow them to keep an amount for each child proportional to the amount retained by any other person. More importantly, we need to change the destructive mindset that has lead to the cultural devaluation of people in general and children specifically.

Chapter 14

"We Have Lost Our Freedom"

It is amazing how often I hear people complain about how little freedom they have and what is left is being taken away. It seems like I hear the complaint in one form or another almost every day. Mind you, these complaints come from a very diverse group of people, including those who are well educated. They come from people who live their lives from day to day with minimal involvement with any government entity. They come (even more frequently) from those who are involved with government on a regular basis. Every time I hear the complaint I try to empathize, but in my heart I know that the person making the complaint has no clue as to what the lack of freedom means.

It is as if I am watching people who at a feast are engorging themselves while they complain about being hungry. We live in a country that has always placed a high value on individual freedom, and continues to do so to this day. Many of the rights we enjoy are enumerated in the Constitution, especially the Bill of Rights. Other freedoms were inherited through English common law, while more have been identified in an evolving cultural and technological climate. In comparison to most other countries across the globe, we are the beacon of liberty that other peoples have emulated whenever they have been given the opportunity.

Historically speaking, the freedoms we enjoy are unprecedented. History is replete with a constant pattern of war, slavery, oppression, extermination, subjugation, and death through the millennia. Human life was long considered to be cheap (unfortunately it still is in some places on the globe), and those who had power had had no qualms about killing those who represented a economic or ideological threat. This was standard practice through history; however, is not the environment in which we live here in the United States.

Before I begin this discussion, let me emphasize the necessity of vigilance to ensure that we in fact do not loose our freedom. It is important that we carefully guard against the gradual encroachment on our ability to pursue happiness as we see fit, and determinedly resisting real threats to our freedoms is imperative. This is one of the reasons that the constant refrain that we have lost our freedom is destructive; it tends to discourage people from learning and acting to ensure the preservation of rights.

With any discussion about rights, it is important to understand what rights we have. There has never been nor can there be an absolute right for an individual to do whatever he or she wants whenever he or she wants to do it. That is anarchy. Governments are instituted with the consent of the governed to secure the rights of the population (to paraphrase the Declaration of Independence), and that protection is to be from all enemies, both foreign and domestic. Laws are adopted to protect us from those who do not have the proper perspective on the extent of their freedom, or who are unable to control their behavior even with the knowledge of those limitations. Those that act in conflict with the law stand to lose liberty, their ability to pursue happiness, and (in extreme cases) life. Our freedom to act as we please is properly limited by the mores of society (that would be the morality discussed in Chapter 1).

Fortunately, the architects of our Constitution attempted to limit the ability of our government to restrict our activities any more than is necessary to protect our lives, liberty, and ability to pursue happiness. If it were not so, soon those who seek power could easily undermine the basic freedoms we enjoy, eventually leading to a state in which freedom is very limited. This is totalitarianism, on the opposite side of the political spectrum from anarchy. (Isn't it intriguing that polar opposite ends of the political spectrum result in misery for the population?) The only way to avoid the misery associated with either anarchy or a totalitarian regime is to strike the proper balance between individual freedom and proper restraint of individual and group behavior.

By the way, the proper balance for one society may not be the same for another. For example, in Japan, there is a tremendous emphasis on societal interests, and individual freedoms take a back seat to the good of the nation. That does not mean that individuals are subordinate to the state, but it does mean that the culture emphasizes what is good for the group and the group acts accordingly. Most Japanese are mystified (or at least were mystified thirty-six years ago when I lived in Japan) by our emphasis on individual rights, an emphasis that comes at the expense of societal priorities.

That said, I believe we have a good balance, including a tendency to err on the side of individual freedom. People can do pretty much what they want to so long as their activity does not physically or economically harm others. Most activities between consenting adults are sanctioned with the

139

exception of those the majority has determined threaten the general health, safety, and welfare of the people in the state.

People also have the right to express themselves as they wish. The First Amendment guarantees freedom of speech, among other rights. One can write social commentaries on how we have more freedom today than at any time or by any group in history. Others will disagree and write that we have no freedom and that we are slaves to the State, corporations, or even a shadow world government for that matter. The only limitations on speech should be those that prevent injury (yelling fire when there is not a fire is the standard cliché). Sadly, all three branches of our Federal government have combined to bring us speech restrictions by way of campaign finance reform. This is an excellent example of a combination of selfish interests in the legislative, cowardice in the executive, and activism in the judicial branches which have lead to blatantly unconstitutional restrictions on free speech.

While the right of free speech is guaranteed, it does not follow that there is a right to disseminate speech at others cost. Your right to speech does not mean you have a right to have it privately or publicly funded. That includes artists who for some unexplainable reason think that taxpayers are obligated to fund speech that is patently offensive to the taxpayers. A number of projects funded by the National Endowment for the Arts come to mind. Neither is a publisher obligated to publish the writings of those with whom they disagree, including the publishers of newspapers, books, and magazines. Last, electronic media is not obligated to give airtime to those with whom they disagree, except for stations that are publicly funded. The bottom line is that while everyone has the right to say what he or she thinks, others have the right to react to that speech as they see fit so long as the reaction is not violent. Freedom is a two way street.

Another good example of this is in the freedom to use property. I am intimately acquainted with land use law and the regulatory taking of property without just compensation. In Euclid vs. Ambler, the Supreme Court upheld the ability of governments to regulate land use even though the regulation has the effect of prohibiting a property owner from using the land as he or she sees fit. By the way, the decision was made in 1925, long before Franklin Delano Roosevelt and the evolution of the court after the New Deal. The decision validates the principle that the unrestrained use of property by one person can adversely affect the health, safety, and welfare of others.

For instance, if someone wants to put a pig farm next to one of the resort hotels on the Las Vegas Strip, that person will be politely informed that zoning law will not permit the proposed use. The property along the Strip does not allow pig farms specifically because the use would harm other property owners that have invested enormous sums of money on improvements to their property, and the value of those investments depend on compatible uses being established in proximity to them. Zoning law is designed to achieve the proper balance between the rights of individual owners and societal interests.

Profiling is another good example of the need to balance rights and responsible public policy. Profiling is a simple concept that can be an abuse of power and an infringement on the rights of those that are being profiled, but which if it is not properly used results in mind-bogglingly irrational results. The Transportation Security Administration procedures for evaluating security risks for those boarding aircraft are a good example of procedures that are so obsessed with not offending minority groups that they have the effect of undermining security and our economy. Police departments are similarly handicapped by rules that disallow them from searching those that are likely to be acting in conflict with the law but which if searched will sue for discrimination.

Another point to consider is that while exercising a right to do something that is offensive may be permissible, it does not follow that it is appropriate. For instance, protesting the war at the funerals of soldiers killed in action may be a right, but it is mind-bogglingly classless. Anyone who would stoop to this behavior deserves the contempt of all, and should be treated as the pariahs they have made of themselves. Here again, the right to act does not mean the act itself is appropriate or responsible. All thinking people have the right to express contempt for the inappropriate actions of rude, arrogant fools.

Another aspect of freedom of expression that is asserted by classless individuals is the right to use profane language. Rather than cover this subject here, I have written another chapter (see Chapter 31)

Along those same lines, anyone who makes stupid destructive decisions will inevitably be miserable. Just because one has a right to make such a decision does not mean that there will not be adverse consequences as a result of the decision. For instance, those engaged in promiscuous sexual behavior may have the right to do so, but they are not free from the emotional, social, physical, and economic consequences of their actions.

Political

Similarly, just because the Supreme Court has ruled that pornography is protected free speech and that erotic dancing is a protected freedom of expression does not mean that it is an activity that people should participate in. The right to do something does not make it right or beneficial, and certainly does not eliminate the negative consequences of the activity.

Taking into consideration that there are no absolute rights, and that not all rights should nor will be exercised by disciplined and responsible individuals, are we yet free? I think that the untold numbers of books published and available for purchase and reading demonstrates that we are. Similarly, the ongoing robust and raucous political debate between different interest groups and political parties demonstrates that we are. The internet and our instant ability to freely contribute to political, religious, and social discourse without fear of arrest also demonstrates that we are.

For that matter, complaints about the lack of freedom demonstrates that we are yet free. The day I no longer hear complaints about how oppressed we are is the day that I will begin to worry that we have lost our freedom. As a former government official tasked with enforcing land use law, when I heard these complaints, as I empathized with the individual and explained what we did, why it was justified, and what regulatory options were available to solve their specific problem, internally I was smiling and thinking to myself that our freedoms are yet secure.

Still, the perception is destructive. It leads to dissatisfaction with government, and distrust of any action taken by government no matter how well intentioned and sound the policy may be. It leads to attempts to fix laws and regulations that are not broken, often making the perceived problem worse. On the part of elected and government officials, even when there is a problem that can and should be addressed, many complaints fall on deaf ears because the complaints have become background noise to ignore.

Chapter 15

"My Vote Does Not Count"

This is the complaint of someone who either does not have a clue as to how our government works, or is too lazy, apathetic, or disillusioned to exercise the most basic right of participation in the political process. If everyone made that argument and therefore refused to participate in the elections, our democracy would fail. Each person has the ability to have an affect on their political future by simply taking the time to educate themselves about the issues and candidates of the day and then voting. Indeed, because many do have this attitude, those that do vote get to make decisions for those who do not. If only twenty five percent of eligible voters actually vote in an election, your vote has a disproportionate effect on the electoral process, and you have power four times beyond being only one person in a nation of 230 million people eligible to vote.

Those who really want to make a difference, in addition to voting, can become active in grassroots campaigns to affect the political outcome they desire. Persuading others to participate in a political cause will indeed have a much more significant effect than simply voting.

Of course, in the end a minority of the voting population will always be on the losing end of an election. Even so, those that vote and work for a cause that they believe in can sleep well at night knowing that they did what they could for that cause. In my opinion, they also earn the right to criticize those who are in power. Those that sit by and do nothing in their own political interest have no moral authority to criticize the results of their inaction.

Voting is not just a right; it is a duty. Our ability to maintain our rights and freedom depend on an informed population participating in the electoral process. If enough people sit out because they are holding their breath and throwing a tantrum because they have lost in the past, or because they are lazy or indifferent, elections can be determined by those with narrow interests, and elected officials will have little incentive to act in the interest of those from whom they can not gain support.

On a side note, it is not enough to just mindlessly vote without informing yourself about candidates, their positions, and campaign issues.

Political

Those that cast uninformed votes are at least as harmful to democracy as those who do not vote.

Once again it is appropriate to quote Edmund Burke's famous truism. "All that is necessary for evil to triumph is for good men to do nothing" accurately reflects the possibility of this nation losing its hard fought and priceless freedoms simply due to apathy, indifference, laziness, or disillusionment.

Section 2

God and Religion

Chapter 16

"Prove there is a God!"

This is easily one of the most frequently used challenges raised by secularists and atheists to discredit the belief in God and adherence to religious principles. The argument is that if the existence of God cannot be proven, He must not exist because we typically do not accept as truth or fact ideas for which we have no evidence. If the existence of God can be disproved, or even made questionable, the moral foundation that has served Western culture for millennia can be dismissed as myth and unjustified tradition.

That said, this is one of the most ridiculous challenges around. First, we cannot prove anything exists, let alone the existence of God. Second, the presumption that God does not exist if it cannot be proven that He does exist is a non-sequitur. Just because the existence of God cannot be proven does not mean that He does not exist. Third, a believer can redirect the challenge and ask the atheist to prove there is not a God.

The challenge is misdirected. The issue is not whether the existence of God can be proven, but rather if it is possible to know of the existence of God based on reasonable criteria, much the same as the criteria used to determine the truth of any other theory or fact.

In order to defend this position, I will need to lay a foundation by briefly reviewing a number of epistemological facts, especially the nature and reliability of knowledge. From there, I will explain the rationale for my assertion that the knowledge of God can be as reliable as any other fact we rely upon to guide our lives.

What is knowledge?

Before we can appreciate this discussion, we need to examine how we obtain knowledge and what it is. Is knowledge the same as truth? If so, we should be able to conclude that if we know something that it is true. If not, we need to examine the difference between the two.

All of the knowledge we have accumulated over the years is the result of the experience of individuals who have transmitted the information they obtained to others. That experience is rooted in our ability to perceive by sensory means what we trust to be real. Those senses include sight, touch, smell, taste, and hearing. Based on observations and tests, including increasingly sophisticated tests using instruments more delicate than our natural senses, natural events and processes have been observed, and a rational explanation for many observed phenomena cataloged and transmitted to others by our use of symbolic speech (a form of which you are reading now).

Generally, if the observations are not written, they are lost with the death of the observer, although in some cultures detailed oral records are transmitted from generation to generation. Even so, oral traditions depend upon the survival of the culture and the accuracy of transmission to each succeeding generation. All it takes is one generation to break the tradition and the entire record is lost. For that matter, written knowledge can be lost if the records are destroyed, or the language becomes extinct and there is no means left behind to translate the language (such as the Rosetta Stone).

Because many of these observations and their results can be repeated time and time again by persons other than the original observer, we consider them to be reliable. This is inductive reasoning; that is the theory that if something has occurred many times under the same circumstances the result will always be identical under the same circumstances. If an observation or experiment produces a different result, the assumption is that some underlying change in the conditions of the observation or experiment resulted in the different result, that the original observation or result either did not account for all possible variables, or the original premise was flawed.

We also build upon our base of knowledge using deductive reasoning. We take underlying premises or known facts, put them together and draw conclusions from the result. This is best represented by the use of a syllogism such as the following: all birds fly, a canary is a bird; therefore, all canaries fly. This process is a useful tool in explaining the world; we can take the result and test it against other known facts to see if the logic holds up. In the example above, if we substitute the word "ostrich" for "canary" we find the result is not true, so we are forced to examine the underlying premises. In this case, we are forced to conclude that not all birds fly.

Using observation, inductive and deductive reasoning, and the inventions of modern science, we have constructed a vast base of knowledge, much of which has been employed to improve lives and advance our civilization (unfortunately, this knowledge has also been used for destructive purposes, but that is another subject). We rely on this knowledge on a daily basis; indeed, without it our civilization would collapse and there would be a tremendous die-down in the world's population.

We routinely accept as fact the representation of others that we cannot observe or prove for ourselves. I have never seen a DNA molecule, but I accept the statements of the scientific community that they do exist as fact. The use of that fact has lead to many improvements in science in general and medicine in particular. I also accept as fact the representations of mathematicians that two plus two equals four, even though that fact is established within a closed, defined scheme that has been invented to create a workable mathematical system. Similarly, I have never been to London, but I accept as fact that it does exist because of the representations of others. In addition, I accept as fact that Charles Darwin spent time in the Galapagos Islands and observed natural phenomenon, which supported his conclusions about evolution in spite of the fact that he died long ago and I have only historical records to corroborate his existence and observations. If I accepted as fact only those things which I can personally observe, I would know virtually nothing in comparison to the wealth of knowledge available to me, and much of what I know would be in error because of flawed observations.

Is knowledge truth?

Having said all this, we need to go back to where we started in our analysis of knowledge and examine what knowledge is. The most important question is whether knowledge automatically equates to truth. If we define truth as the actual state of things as they are, as opposed to things as we perceive them, we are forced to conclude that they are not the same.

The foundation of our knowledge rests on the assumption that the empirical observations we make are real. I cannot tell how many times I have been told that when I "assume", I make an "ass" out of "u" and "me". Assumptions are something we try to avoid if at all possible. Therefore, our instinct is to try to prove without using assumptions that our observations are true, that is how things are regardless of our perception. However, we are left only with our empirical observations, and the observations of others, which we can only conclude is what we observe and therefore perceive to be true.

Unfortunately, it is possible that what we perceive to be true will not be accurate. For instance, as I drive down a desert highway my eyes perceive that there is water on the road in front of the car. Strangely enough, the water is receding from me at the same speed at which I am approaching it.

149

This is, of course, a mirage, a well-documented phenomenon that all recognize. It is an optical illusion that is caused by the reflection of the sun on the ground surface. While everyone recognizes a mirage, its existence forces us to ask what else our senses perceive as fact are not real, the underlying question we have before us now. We do know that a combination of senses confirming the existence of an observation is more reliable than only one sense. With a mirage, even though we can see the water in front of us, we can never touch, taste, smell, or hear it, something we can do if we actually find a lake out in the middle of the desert.

Philosophers have recognized the inherent unreliability of what we observe, and some have rejected sensory perception as a determinant of what is real. Plato's analogy of the cave is probably the best example. Plato believed that what we observed was no more real than the light and shadow reflected on the wall of a cave from real events occurring outside. He believed that to know truth, we had to metaphorically turn around and go outside to see what is true. Hindu and Buddhist theology holds that the world around us is an illusion, and that enlightenment consists of discovering what is actually real. Other philosophers have tried to reason their way out of this box and prove the reality of our observed perceptions, but inevitably came to the solipsist's conclusion that it cannot be done.

In fact, it is even worse than that. The solipsist concludes that he exists, and then reasons that he cannot know anything else. We are familiar with Descartes' premise "I think; therefore, I am" as the springboard for his failed attempt to prove the existence of the observed world. In fact, Descartes made an assumption in his premise. That he perceived that he thought is not proof of his thought, even to himself. He assumed that his thought was real. Each of us also, when faced with the same question, must also conclude that our awareness of ourselves is something that we perceive, and which cannot be proven absolutely to ourselves, let alone others. Our perception of our conscious being is no more proof of our existence than the perception of any other sensory experience.

It gets even worse though. That which we observe is often contradicted by the observations of others, especially those with a different point of view. When I say different point of view, I mean both in the literal and philosophical sense. What I see from one corner may differ from what someone else will see standing on another corner with nothing other than a different angle of view (lawyers make a lot of money exploiting these differences). What I see may be colored by my perception of the world, and I may see what I want to see regardless of the light and images that are projected into my brain. Others with a different philosophical bent could observe the same facts from the same viewpoint and come up with a different conclusion.

For that matter, frequently we completely ignore observations and results that contradict our worldview. For instance, the winners write history; the losers are marginalized and rejected even though the only reason their worldview did not prevail is that they lacked the might to prevail in the conflict. It seems that might makes right after all. Even so, often different perceptions survive conflict, and can color the future perception of what is fact and not. There are some in the Southern states that still do not believe the South lost the Civil War or insist that the South will rise again. We also use definitions to manipulate perception, and often construct circular arguments to support our worldview. For instance, if you do not carefully follow my logic to find the flaw, I can logically prove that black is white and white is black.

Beyond the difficulty we have in interpreting observations is the fact that communicating ideas to others is at best tenuous. What a person says is knowledge transmitted from the person speaking, which when heard by the listener is interpreted based on the perception and cultural filters of the listener. Our perception of language is colored by experience, and words and terms frequently have different meaning for different people and groups within our own culture.

In some cases, the transmission of knowledge is made at least more difficult and in some cases inaccurate because of linguistic differences. Translation often does not communicate the essence of the original document or stated view because often there are not words or ideas in some languages that precisely correspond to words and ideas in the language into which the work or idea is translated.

Compounding this problem even further is the intense pressure brought by the scientific community to force conformity of thought regardless of what other scientists think. Global warming is a good example of this;, in spite of many scientific studies indicating results that conflict with global warming orthodoxy, anyone who publicly disputes global warming and human causality of it are ridiculed. This is the norm; almost every revolutionary scientific advancement was initially met with ridicule from the scientific establishment of the age.

This also includes cultural pressure to conform, with respect to our observations and conclusions, to expected norms. If anyone, especially an airline pilot, claims to observe what he or she perceives to be a UFO, a significant percentage of the population, especially the scientific community, will ridicule the observer. Along the psychoanalytical spectrum used to marginalize them (and therefore their observation) will be the possibility that they 1) have misperceived reality, 2) lied, 3) sought attention, 4) lack education or 5) are delusional.

It doesn't take a rocket scientist to figure out that if you see unexplained phenomenon you should be quiet and keep it to yourself. Thus, some of what is observed is, in effect, covered up or ignored for fear of ridicule from others. This is especially true for those whose experience has been a significant milestone in their lives and who do not desire others to ridicule what they perceive to be precious to them. Many who have described out of body experiences after having been pronounced clinically dead fall into this category. Rather than have what to them is a spiritual awakening ridiculed, they take their observations with them to their eventual grave.

Then there are charlatans who deliberately assert or manipulate facts to propagate a particular belief, seek political power, or obtain economic gain. Goebbels postulated that if you repeated a lie often enough eventually a majority of the population would accept it as truth. Unfortunately, he was right, and this tactic is widely used today in the propaganda war our society is engaged in. Many keep repeating as fact that George Bush deliberately lied in order to invade Iraq. Over time, many have become convinced of the truthfulness of the lie, which makes the lie a fact for them. This is a remarkable instance of a lie that has gained wide acceptance as fact in spite of clear historic documentation that clearly demonstrates the opposite.

All of these impediments to correctly understanding the world around us do not account for the lack of capacity of our senses and our inability to comprehend all that our senses receive. Our senses do not receive more than an insignificant portion of the natural phenomenon occurring all around us, let alone what is happening across the universe. In addition, we are cognizant of only a very small percentage of the narrow spectrum of data that our senses pick up. Therefore, we are conscious of only a small portion of the available information that our senses receive, which in turn is only a miniscule portion of the actual information available to be perceived. The same holds true for the instruments that we have developed to improve our ability to measure and observe natural events and phenomenon. We are so unaware of so much of the natural universe that we do not even know how to begin to try to become cognizant of information of which we have no concept or ability to observe and measure. This does not engender much faith in our ability to perceive the actual state of nature.

To sum up what we have covered so far, our base of knowledge is founded on our very limited collective perception biased by cultural pressure and filters. In some cases, this bias borders on desperation to protect what entrenched interests want us to believe, especially if political power or economic gain is at stake. We see and hear what we want to see and hear (not to mention taste, smell, and touch). This sausage grinder is hardly the basis for us to conclude that truth is the result. Because of all these facts, it is wholly inappropriate to say our observations and the conclusions we reach are truth.

Going back to the discussion in the opening of the chapter, we concluded that all of our knowledge is based upon assumptions. As much as we dislike making assumptions, we know they are unavoidable. Without them we would be paralyzed, unable to progress or even to survive. We have become comfortable with that conclusion too. No geometry student makes a fuss about the lack of proof for the existence of a point, line, or plane. They take the teacher's word for it and use the assumptions to build one formula upon another that creates a mathematical system based on inductive and deductive reasoning. We are comfortable with assuming that our empirical observations are correct, even though we know that they are sometimes unreliable, such as when we see the aforementioned mirage receding before us when traveling the desert highway. We are even more comfortable if we can support the conclusions of one sense with the use of additional senses, such as when we can view, touch, and taste a morsel of food, which we see, pick up, put in our mouth, and chew.

When all is said and done, our observations are all we have to survive in the world, and using them to solve problems is critical. For that reason we must rely on what we perceive, and seriously question those who tell us not to trust what we observe. When someone says, "Who are you going to trust; me or your lying eyes?", we are extremely skeptical of that person.

If we have concluded that all knowledge is founded upon assumptions, we also must conclude that knowledge cannot be proven absolutely. We can prove something is consistent with the body of knowledge we have assembled, but we must always be prepared to revise that knowledge based on new observations. Facts change as collective knowledge increases. A good example is our perception of the earth's form. Before Columbus, it was a "fact" to most of western civilization that the earth was flat, and that anyone sailing too far would fall off the edge. That "fact" guided human behavior for some time. After Columbus, it became a fact that the earth was round. That fact was a considerable improvement over the former, and resulted in significant advances in knowledge and the spread of western civilization (yeah, yeah, there were negative aspects of that spread, but that is also another subject), but it too was replaced. The latest fact is that the earth has an elliptical form, bulging slightly at the equator. We must always be prepared to adjust knowledge to conform to observations that are more accurate than previous observations. The acceptance of new facts and discounting old ones is healthy if the motivation is to discover truth. If the motivation is to denigrate facts to justify behavior that is in conflict with those facts, the motivation is dishonest. It is also important to make sure the old facts are truly disproved by the new observation.

What logic justifies a belief in God?

Assuming this argument to be fact, if we are asked to prove the existence of God, we can only conclude that it is impossible to have absolute proof. The only thing we can hope to prove is whether we can know of His existence as well as we can know of our own existence, or as well as we can know any of the other facts established by any of our empirical observations. It is important to observe again that even if we cannot prove His existence, it does not mean that He does not exist. The lack of proof that something is true does not prove the opposite.

So what do we know about the existence of God? Can we observe him using empirical observation? I can tell you that I have not seen, touched, tasted, smelled, or heard God. I suspect that most if not all of those reading this would probably say the same. Again, that in and of itself is not proof of His non-existence; however, we cannot logically use that fact as justification for His existence. Those who seek to demonstrate to others that He exists have the burden of demonstrating credible evidence of His existence. As indicated in the first paragraph of this Chapter, we typically do not accept as fact premises that are not supported by evidence.

At this point, it is useful to observe that the sum of our accumulated knowledge includes written records from those who have testified that they have seen and heard God, and in some cases that they touched him also. These observations cannot simply be dismissed out of hand, as many would prefer. I propose to take one of these observations and systematically dissect it with the intent of examining all the possible reasons why it might not be an accurate account of a factual set of observations. By doing so, I believe I will demonstrate that it is just as plausible to accept this account as fact as it is to accept any other commonly accepted historical account as fact. In other words, this historical account constitutes credible evidence of the existence of God.

The resurrection of Christ

I will use the documented observations of John and others in the New Testament in describing the resurrection of Jesus Christ as the example. In the combined accounts, the authors assert variously that 1) Jesus was dead, having been crucified and his death ensured by the piercing of his body by the Roman guard, 2) a few days later the body of Jesus was not in the tomb where it had been laid, 3) Jesus' live physical body was observed after his death by numerous people, and 4) Many of those who saw him also heard Him speak, touched the wounds in His body, and observed Him eating food. It is important to note that before His death Jesus had claimed to have the ability to resurrect himself, in addition to claiming that He was God (a claim that is unique among the originators of the major religions of the world). If these accounts can be demonstrated to be inaccurate or untrue, the arguments used by Christians the world over as evidence that Jesus is God would be worthless.

Do these accounts accurately represent factual history? We must decide whether the claims made by those who ostensibly witnessed these events are plausible or not. Possible reasons that could justify disbelief in the veracity of the claims are as follows: 1) the various witnesses imagined the observation, either from the effects of hysteria, inaccurate observation, or mass delusion, 2) the account is an elaborate lie perpetuated either by the witnesses or writers, 3) recollections of the actual observations are unreliable because of the time between their occurrence and the time the experience was written, 4) Jesus misrepresented or misunderstood himself, or 5) the entire record is a myth. Let us examine each of these possibilities to evaluate the probability of the accuracy of these accounts.

The account is a result of hysteria or delusion

The witnesses may have imagined the observation, which could have been the result of inaccurate observation, hysteria, or a collective delusion Mr. Dawkins would take this position, he dismisses these types of observations as the result of collective delusion. He may be right, but does this explanation make sense given the specific circumstances?

Assuming the account to be accurate (see comments under myth below) this does not seem to be a credible explanation of the account. If only one sense, such as sight, was used in the observation, that might be a plausible

155

argument. However, all of the disciples present indicated that they saw, touched and heard the resurrected Jesus. Multiple people had the same experience corroborated by three specific senses. Remember, the reliability of our perception is substantially increased when observations are corroborated by more than one sense, and even more so by the senses of others. If we reject the actuality of the resurrection based on witness delusion, we would have a difficult time accepting as fact any observation, even when corroborated by multiple senses.

Was the observation the product of hysteria? That also seems improbable given the stated facts of the case. There is nothing remotely resembling frenzy or hysteria in the accounts, which occurred over several days. In addition, these accounts were written many years after the fact by different people, some of which were recording the testimony of the actual witnesses. Indeed, there was considerable doubt on the part of the participants in the event at the time, it is difficult to argue that there was a collective hysteria that resulted in all the observers seeing, hearing, and touching the same thing having started out as being skeptical of the evidence of their own eyes, ears, and hands.

It is possible that the witnesses perceived events that did not occur, such as an elaborate mirage that can be explained away with a rational scientific explanation. While that may be the case, it also seems improbable. Once again, the witnesses saw, heard, and touched the risen Jesus. The resurrected Jesus made a special point to have his disciples physically experience the reality of his restored body, probably as a means of ensuring that future generations would have evidence as incontrovertible as possible for the time. Again, if more than one sense perceives the same set of facts, the likelihood of that perception being accurate substantially increases. If more than two senses are involved, the probability is even greater. Those that make this argument seem to be grasping at straws; that is they would have us disbelieve the testimony of the witnesses in favor of some unexplained phenomenon which would take a greater leap of faith for anyone to accept.

Is the account a result of the collective desire on the part of the disciples to believe in the reality of Christ's resurrection to the point of perceiving events that were not real? This also does not seem to be the case. Indeed, the disciples were in mourning, and were discouraged in the fact that they no longer had their leader. There was even resistance to the idea of the resurrection demonstrated when Mary Magdalene described her encounter with the resurrected Jesus, of which the disciples were very skeptical.

Indeed, Thomas did not believe the others even when they described the event, it took a separate appearance to Thomas to convince him that Christ had resurrected.

The account is inaccurate or a lie

To the skeptic, the account is incredible. After all, the story represents that a person who had been ruthlessly executed and who had been dead for at least thirty-six hours came back to life. That story must be inaccurate, right? We don't believe in people coming back to life after death do we? Oops, oh wait, because of medical advancements maybe we do. But this is different because the person coming back to life was now immortal and at the same time could apparently adjust the atomic structure in his physical being to allow him to seemingly magically appear without entering through a door.

So what else could explain the story? Perhaps the witnesses were lying, in which case we should look for a motivation for the lie. Seldom does a person lie unless there will be personal or economic benefit to himself, including acceptance, fame, fortune, or power. If we cannot find such a motivation, we probably should give that person's story the benefit of any doubt. It may be that all those who testified of the risen Jesus were pathological liars, and would lie if the truth sounded better; however, that is also difficult to accept given what we know about them from the records of others and the culture within which they were raised. Last, if it can be demonstrated that the person suffered physical or economic harm because of his testimony, the likelihood that his testimony is a lie drops to almost nothing.

In this case, the witnesses did not receive either fame, fortune, nor power during their lifetimes. They became pariahs within their culture because of their claims, and suffered the consequences of being ostracized throughout their remaining lives, including the very real threat of death as a martyr. Indeed, most of the original witnesses were killed because of their testimony and their unwillingness to recant it. It is exceptionally unlikely that someone will support a lie to the point where they accept death rather than admit to the lie.

What if the lie was perpetuated, not by the alleged witnesses, but by the writers of the gospels? It is possible that others wrote the records long after the fact as a lie to support an ideology they wished to propagate. If this is the case, the entire story may be fabricated from whole cloth.

This seems to be at odds with both established fact and logic. First, the gospels were written either by the original witnesses, or by writers recording the recollections of the witnesses. This "lie" would have had to have been perpetuated with the knowledge of the witness, or at least with the knowledge of the believers in the area. This does not seem likely.

Second, to repeat the previous point, a lie only makes sense if it results in acceptance, fame, fortune, or power to the liar (or group of liars). Before and after the records were written Christians were persecuted and killed. Even if the accounts were lies made in an attempt to ameliorate the persecution of the Christians, which by itself does not make sense because the best way to ameliorate the persecution would have been to deny the faith they had in Jesus, it clearly did not work. It is very unlikely that anyone who would have attempted to perpetrate a lie in conflict with the original witnesses accounts would have been willing to die for it.

What if there was not a deliberate lie, but just a lengthy and complicated story written that is simply an inaccurate description of actual events. Here again, the facts discount this possibility. The level of agreement between the various accounts, each of which were written independent of the others, substantially reduces the probability of this being a figment of any one author's imagination. While these records were written many years after the fact, it is clear from the detail in the narratives that the witnesses remembered the facts of the events very well, whether they wrote the record themselves or their stories were written by others. It seems the event made a significant impression on all of the witnesses, as would be expected for such a life-changing event. This possibility seems improbable also.

Jesus misrepresented or misunderstood himself

Jesus may have either deliberately misrepresented that He is God, or He may have imagined it; that is the witnesses accounts were accurate in that what they observed was real, but that Jesus lied to all about whether He was God or that He simply misperceived who He was.

For us to accept this argument we must accept the possibility that a man who is not God can bring himself back to life. As I indicated before, Jesus was unique among the founders of all the world's major religions in that He claimed to be God, and if the account given to us by the New Testament authors is true, He demonstrated it by word and action. No other human has made that claim and subsequently demonstrated its truth by resurrecting himself, or by any other extraordinary means. In addition, if the supposition is that Jesus lied, we are back to the question of what would be His motivation to lie. He probably could have lived happily in Nazareth to the end of his days without the trials of His ministry and his eventual death (which He predicted and anticipated). The highest probability is that if the recorded events are accurate, that Jesus is also who He claimed to be.

Remarkably enough, Mr. Dawkins accuses Jesus of being a sadomasochist because of the crucifixion. Once again displaying a schizophrenic attitude, he praises Jesus for his theology then promptly denigrates his character, assuming the worst possible motivation for His acceptance of His own death.

The account is a myth, unfounded in fact

This category is somewhat redundant, the assertion is similar to the arguments listed above. However, because of the debate concerning the reliability of all scripture, I decided to cover those arguments here. There has been a concerted effort made over the last 150 years to debunk the authenticity of the Bible. I will not attempt to cover the details of the arguments; it is sufficient for me to say that there are numerous theories about who wrote what, upon what was the record based, and when it was written. So much has been written, much of which is pure speculation that does nothing more than cloud fact, that it is no wonder that there is considerable confusion on the matter.

Atheists dismiss the account of the resurrection, and indeed the entirety of the Bible, as myth perpetuated by theists. For that matter they reject all written works purported to be from God, but I am not equipped nor inclined to defend any scripture other than the Bible and supporting works. They consider the Old Testament to depict God as evil, arbitrary, vindictive, and psychotic. Some even reject the historicity of Jesus, claiming His existence to be myth also. They maintain that even if Jesus did live, He was simply another human, and the account of His resurrection was invented.

The marginalization of scripture is critical if atheists are to have a coherent defense of their beliefs. If a credible account of God communicating with humans exists, credible evidence of the existence of God also exists. After that, the only question becomes what was said and what we as humans need to do to conform to God's wishes. For that reason, scripture is attacked and ridiculed.. This is especially true of the scientific community, the leadership of which has largely been taken over by atheists (see chapter 17). It is no surprise then that so many people think religious belief is ridiculous and backward; it is because those who marginalize religious belief has defined that belief as ridiculous and backward.

God and Religion

With respect to the Bible in general and the Old Testament in particular, atheists look at its teachings, then proceed to criticize the work based on 1) the worst possible narrow selective interpretation of events and teachings, and 2) today's cultural climate. While I agree that we have advanced considerably over the past three thousand years, I don't believe it is fair to judge historical cultures by our standards. Most of the harshest criticism of biblical history comes from those who are aghast at the treatment by the protagonists of the Old Testament with other cultures and people. They fail to look at the broader world and the very real danger presented to the survival of that culture. In retrospect, given the conquest of the ten tribes by the Assyrians, the Jews by the Babylonians, and the destruction of Jerusalem and subsequent Diaspora of the Jews by the Romans it seems they may have underestimated the threat to their culture.

In addition, they fail to see the morality that is the underpinning of the morality of the present. The Ten Commandments are the basis of much of our morality and law even today. Teachings regarding the importance of obedience, sacrifice for others, and justice are extant, but the atheists do not want to concede that there is any socially redeeming value associated with the book.

The same criticism extends to God. Ostensibly God is the evil being described in the paragraph above. What they fail to see is that God, if motivated to do what is best for his creations and at the same time continue to allow free will but yet provide for future world influence on the broader population, probably had good reason to act as He did. They are looking at God, once again, through a modern cultural lens and fail to see the possible justification for His actions based on the world that existed at that time.

Much of the atheistic criticism of scripture is directed at what they perceive to be the failings of God when in fact they are critical of the actions of specific people and groups. Abraham is criticized for his attempts to pass his wife off as his sister, which for some unknown reason is used to justify criticism of God. Excuse me, but when have the mistakes of people become reason to be critical of God?

For that matter, it is useful to note that every word of the book was written by a human being, each of which had their own world view and attitude, which was in turn reflected in their writing. It is also inappropriate to blame God for the attitude demonstrated in the writing, especially if the writer was the product of the cultural conditions of the time? Only portions of the text that directly describe communication with God should be used to assess the attitude and nature of God.

Even the historicity of people and events in the Bible are doubted. The reality of Adam, Abraham, and even Moses are doubted. Indeed, the default seems to be to automatically assume any person or event described is myth unless there is either a corroborating account or physical evidence from a non-biblical source supporting the account.

I would submit that this attitude demonstrates a double standard. I am unaware of any other historical work that has been held to be completely false unless it has been proven to be fact. For instance, even though we have reason to be skeptical of the writings of Josephus because of his personal background, we accept his histories as largely accurate. Most other histories are generally accepted unless there is evidence that the history is inaccurate. This default acceptance is not accorded to the Bible.

For that matter it seems to be racist. The entire history of the Jewish people is marginalized as myth in spite of the well-documented efforts of that people to maintain their records, especially the Torah, through incredibly difficult circumstances for the past three thousand years including subjugation, persecution, and the Holocaust. In spite of the hardship and suffering, they have remained a culturally cohesive group and continue to live and educate their people according to those records. It is breathlessly arrogant to relegate Jewish scripture to the intellectual dustbin on that basis alone.

Another argument used to justify the complete disqualification of the Bible as scripture is the proposition that a believer must believe all or nothing of the book. If it is written in the Bible, it is either the word of God or myth; there can be nothing in between. This is a ridiculous argument, the equivalent of saying we have to accept every word of a history, even though ninety percent can be demonstrated to be fact and the remainder is clearly in error. It makes no difference that the book is scripture. We can still read and clearly distinguish the inspirational and instructive differences between portions of the Bible. For instance, the Songs of Solomon has a chapter that gushes about the beauty of the female breast. While female anatomy is a wonderful creation that deserves appreciation, this chapter has nowhere near the inspirational and morally instructive value of Isaiah or Proverbs. For that matter, some of the books included within the Bible have substantially less credibility than does most of the book. When the Bible was canonized, the books to be included were selected by the equivalent of a committee, and we all know how effective committees are in their work. We, as readers, are obligated to judge for ourselves what is fact and fiction within the book, and Christians have the example and instruction provided by Jesus

Christ against which to judge all things, including Old Testament writings and law.

Atheistic criticism of the New Testament is similar to the criticism of the Old Testament, although because of the revolutionary nature of the teachings of Christ they are less vociferous in their critique of the book's morality. In fact, they like much of the morality, they just dislike the source of the morality. And so the book is also dismissed as myth, and even the existence of Christ is questioned. They justify this attitude because of the lack of corroborating works independent of the New Testament and the confusion surrounding authorship of the various books within it.

With respect to authorship, what difference does it make? If someone other than the author represented in the text is the author, so what? What is important is that each of the books of the New Testament were almost surely written between 45-100 AD. They were written by Christians. Even if the specific books were not written by the person traditionally held to be the author, each of them were surely written with the input and influence of the respective early Christian leader whose words and works are described within the specific book, especially the twelve selected by Christ to be his witnesses to the world. As such, these works represent the most accurate description of early Christian history and doctrine.

With respect to a lack of corroborating evidence, the expectations for detailed histories of the time and place seem unrealistically high. This is millennia prior to the invention of the printing press that made mass publication possible. It is also prior to technical advances that resulted in long term record preservation. Because so few writings at all from that period of history describing the events occurring in present-day Israel have survived to this day, we are led to believe that we must throw out what we do have because it purports to describe God's dealings and communication with humans. This does not seem like a reasonable approach to learning and understanding history.

In addition, there are multiple corroborating sources; each of the books of the New Testament is a separate book or letter written independent of each and every other book in the New Testament. As such, the New Testament is self-corroborating. Further, the writings of Josephus at a minimum corroborates the existence of Jesus.

With respect to the details of New Testament accounts that do not match other recorded history, it is worthwhile to remember that these histories were written by the Romans, who were the victors in war over the Jews and who wrote history based on their viewpoint and interest. For example, it would not be unusual for Roman chroniclers to ignore the execution of children under the age of two if Herod the Great took steps to ensure that such an account was not written to stain his legacy. For that matter, such an atrocity to us may not have even been noteworthy to a historian of the time.

With respect to the New Testament, I believe it is instructive for us to step back and take a broad view of the historical context of the book and the claims contained within it. As I described in the sections before this section dealing with the Bible as myth, we need to look at the overall motivation of the writers of the books of the New Testament. If there is delusion or deceit involved, there should be evidence of it. What we do have is a set of independently written books that corroborate the account of the resurrection of a man who claimed to be God. Because of the number of witnesses involved, and the number of senses that were used to substantiate the observation of the resurrected Christ, I believe the account would hold up in a court of law. For that reason alone, I also believe it constitutes credible evidence of the existence of God.

After all is said and done, we have records representing that a person who claimed to be God came back to life after being killed for his beliefs. Again, this cannot be explained away as easily as some would think, or in many cases hope. The probability of it being either a lie or an elaborate delusion is relatively low, in fact lower than most historical records that we routinely accept as accurate.

Comparison with other facts

As I previously indicated in this chapter, Darwin's historical account of what he did and the results of his observations should be believed. Others have corroborated the fact of his existence, his trip to the Galapagos and of his observations; however, it is important to note that the result of Darwin's studies was fame and fortune for him. Even though he had motivation to lie, we accept his conclusions because of the records that he left. Is it any less reasonable to conclude that the New Testament records are accurate? Those who were witnesses to the events persisted in their testimony as to the truth of the accounts even though that testimony cost them their lives.

It is critical to the advancement of our civilization that we accept as fact the combined pool of knowledge that has been transmitted to us unless it can be demonstrated by some means that specific facts are erroneous. In spite of cultural pressure to reject observations that do not conform to expected norms, we cannot choose which facts we want to accept if we are intellectually honest with others and ourselves.

God and Religion

This includes facts related to God and religion. We cannot dismiss them simply because we are not comfortable with that particular subject and the observations of those who have said they have observed God. If I accept the testimony of those who have personally observed God, including witnesses who represented that they saw, heard, and touched the resurrected Jesus, I can have just as sure a knowledge of that fact as I do of Darwin's expedition to the South Pacific (you are right, the selection of this example was not accidental). Each person must judge for himself or herself whether to accept these accounts as fact, and act accordingly. However, we must account for our own desire to believe what is being represented as fact, and ask ourselves whether we believe them because they agree with our preconceived notions, as opposed to believing because we have critically evaluated what they claim.

Near death experiences.

In addition to historical records, we also have the testimony of numerous people who have had near death experiences that support the existence of God. Thanks to Dr. Raymond Moody, who wrote the seminal work Life After Life in 1975, we have detailed accounts of people who were declared clinically dead but were subsequently resuscitated. I will not reference the many other works have been written telling essentially the same story because of the attention received by Life After Life; it can be reasonably argued that subsequent testimony and written accounts may have been unduly affected by its publishing. The only written work that I am aware of before Life After Life is George Ritchie's Return From Tomorrow, which apparently provided Dr. Moody with the inspiration to research the subject but which was not widely known. The same criteria for judging whether the evidence presented is plausible or not is applicable.

The typical experience starts with the conclusion by medical professionals that a patient has died. I will treat the death as real and the individual as male for descriptive purposes. The patient later either is resuscitated or comes back to life, and gives a detailed description of an out of body experience consisting of at least some of the following elements. The individual first experiences a ringing in the ears, then finds he is outside of his body, normally looking down at his remains. He can see those in the room and what they are doing, and can give a detailed description of what is occurring, which can later be corroborated by others who are present. He then enters what is best described as a tunnel, and travels through it toward a brilliant light at the end. When he reaches the end, he finds a being of light that he perceives to be God, who asks him "What have you done with your life?" There follows a panoramic vision of his entire life, which allows him to see not only the details of his actions but also the effect of his actions on others. Last, the being of light directs him to return, indicating that he still has things to accomplish as a human being, following which the person regains consciousness.

These experiences are highly personal, and most people are not willing to discuss them if they perceive they will be treated with disrespect. More important, the experience profoundly affects the direction of their lives and the decisions that they subsequently make.

Life After Life gives us numerous accounts, independently experienced, all of which tell either the same basic story or components of it. A critical and common component is the appearance of the being of light that all interpret to be God. There is no physical evidence of the experience, only the fact that the person has been pronounced dead and subsequently revived. The accounts cannot be proven; if we are to believe them we must make a judgment for ourselves that the collective testimony of all these people who managed to come up with the same story independent of one another is true. Let us examine the possibilities as we did with the New Testament account of the resurrection of Christ.

1. Could the experience have been imagined? Certainly yes; however, considering the fact that these people can describe what was occurring around them while they are presumptively dead, that seems unlikely. If they described events that had not occurred it would be safe to say that their experience was the product of something other than real life (or death). That they accurately describe real events supports the supposition that the experience is real.

2. Could the experience be the result of hysteria? That also seems possible given the circumstances. I would imagine death to be traumatic, and the mind and body could do many extraordinary things to try to survive. However, this still does not account for the detailed descriptions of what is occurring at the place of death between the time the patient has been pronounced dead and the time of resuscitation.

3. Could the persons be lying? If so, the result is the most remarkable string of lies telling the same story that the world has ever known. These people, scattered over the world and without knowledge of the stories that others were telling, came up with consistent accounts. What is the probability of that occurring? In addition, most of these people remained anonymous, not wanting to draw attention to themselves, which reduces the possibility that they could profit from a lie.

4. Many accounts were recorded long after the fact, so it is possible that many of them could have changed over time, either because details were forgotten or because the stories were embellished when retold. However, all the independent accounts recount an experience compatible with other descriptions that are rich in detail. It seems that few forgot the details that became so ingrained in their lives. Further, these accounts were not lightly shared with others so embellishment over time is even less likely.

5. It is possible that these experiences could be the result of a natural phenomenon associated with death. There may be physical phenomenon we are unaware of which could explain the experience. However, in the end we still have the same set of facts laid out above, which is that many independently told the same story to Dr. Moody, and that their observations of what occurred while they were physically unconscious accurately describe what occurred. The argument that these experiences were not real seems contrived and more difficult to accept than taking the experiences at face value. That is a difficult sell.

Is it plausible that these experiences taken collectively be considered as evidence of the existence of God? I would say so. To be sure, others have arrived at a different conclusion; however, most of the alternative explanations I have heard seem more delusional than a literal interpretation of the experiences would suggest. Indeed, most of the alternative explanations seem to be desperate attempts to dismiss the evidence out of hand no matter how ridiculous the alternatives sound. The net effect is that they tell those who had the experience to believe their explanation rather than the evidence of their own experience. The vision of someone asking, "What are you going to believe, me or your own eyes" comes to mind.

In analyzing what the best explanation for observed phenomenon is, it is worth discussing Occam's razor. This is an analytical principle that holds the simplest explanation of a phenomenon is the most plausible. The most plausible and probable explanation is that these people did indeed have a close encounter with God that profoundly changed their lives. For those of us who have not had the experience, it should be easy to accept the many consistent testimonies of all of these independent witnesses. To use a previous example, I have not been to London but I know of many who have. They all tell a similar story and describe the same physical environment. Most have formulated their descriptions without consulting with others who made the same trip in order to coordinate their descriptions. The probability that London is out there and that I could, if I had the money, go there is in my mind as near to certainty as my ability to travel to the neighborhood grocery store. For me, the same is true of near death experiences.

What other evidence justifies a belief in God?

Apart from historical records and the testimony of those who have had near death experiences that substantiate the existence of God, are there other facts that also substantiate His existence? I believe there are. The existence of the universe and all that is in it is evidence of the existence of God. Natural laws and processes have resulted in the universe and our awareness of it. In order for the universe to form and for us to be aware of it, a remarkable chain of events occurred. I have covered this evidence in much more depth in Chapter 17 along with arguments which I believe effectively refute the notion that God is a delusion.

What argues against the existence of God?

I have covered arguments that purport to disprove the existence of God in Chapters 17 and 19 and need not repeat them here.

Summary

The accumulated knowledge we have collected over the millennia, and our progress as a society because of it, is dependant upon our acceptance of written records as largely true, especially if observations today can corroborate the same information. Historical fact in many cases cannot be corroborated, and we must evaluate the objectivity of the chronicler to accept, take with a healthy dose of skepticism, or reject the record outright. We have documented cases of direct observation of God or his messengers, and those documented cases, while marginalized by skeptics and those who have an emotional, economic, or authoritative interest in the denigration of these records, can be accepted as fact, and indeed are accepted as fact by a significant portion of the world's population. Elites denigrate the intelligence of people of faith, and ridicule religion as the opiate of the masses, but that does not disprove the existence of God. In fact, this tendency is normal; if those who denigrate religion cannot win the argument logically, they resort to ridicule regardless of the lack of merit of their argument and the strength of the argument of those who accept as fact that we have adequate evidence of the existence of God.

It stands to reason that if God does exist and that He created us that He considers us to have value to Him. This can be deduced by assuming that He would not have created us unless He thought the effort was worth it. In asking if the creation of the universe, our planet, and the life on our planet took some effort, we merely need to examine the totality of what we know to have been created. While there are indeed many spectacular phenomenon within the universe, it seems to me that nothing compares with the life we can see on this planet.

Human life and our ability to observe and somewhat comprehend the complexity of the universe is easily the most remarkable component of the universe that we know of at the moment. Given the immensity of space and the universality of natural law, it is also safe to assume that life is not restricted to this planet only. While stars, planets, solar systems, nebula, quasars, pulsars, black holes, galaxies, and other observed components of the universe are certainly interesting to look at, measure, or observe their effects, their existence in terms of God's creation only makes sense if we assume that these are vehicles for the creation of that which He values most, that is life in general and human beings in specific.

It also stands to reason that if He does value us, and has a place for us in His plans that He would communicate that purpose to us. If He did not, it would undermine His purpose in creating us. We certainly cannot by any means available communicate with Him unless He provides for it. Indeed, if we relegate the accounts we have of God's communication with us to the category of delusional fiction, we indeed create for ourselves a justification to deny His existence. If He does not care enough about us to communicate His and our purpose to us, we would be justified in denying His existence. This makes careful consideration of accounts of His dealings with humans all the more important to consider and determine whether belief in them is warranted.

168

In summary, while it is true that we cannot prove the existence of God, it is also true that we cannot prove anything else either, and we certainly cannot prove that God does not exist. We live our lives by having confidence (faith?) in the reality of our experiences and the facts that we are taught, which are as nearly as we can determine truth. The individual determines for himself what to accept as truth. There is no proof. We can have faith in facts that support the existence of God, or we can have faith in facts that can be interpreted to discount the possibility of his existence. When all is said and done, the existence of God cannot be proven to one who is unwilling to accept facts supporting His existence as evidence. However, their inability to accept these facts does not mean that they are not real.

The purpose of this chapter is simply to demonstrate that belief in God is at least as reasonable and logically justifiable as the opposite view. There will be many who will discount the logic demonstrated; if they have valid arguments against it I would like to hear from them. Others will perhaps concede the possibility of the argument, but choose not to accept it. That is fine. Everyone is entitled to his or her point of view. There will always be some who will look at a glass that is nine-tenths full of water and observe that it is one-tenth empty.

Not all knowledge is obtained through empirical observation. Much of the knowledge we rely upon in our lives is dependant on things that are not observable, except to the extent we can observe the effects of the phenomenon. Love is one example. Most people love friends, family, spouses (hopefully), and to some degree all people, but the emotion is not something that can be proven and measured empirically. There are many other emotional responses, which are often unpredictable and occur in spite of reason. Personal knowledge of the existence of God is similar; it is not something that can be learned by empirical observation, but can only be learned by the means He has provided.

Even though knowledge of these things cannot be observed, the effects of this knowledge can. We can look at the interactions between family, friends, and groups and see the effects that love (or hate for that matter) has, and conclude that there must be a rational explanation for the phenomenon. Likewise, we can examine the effects of those who believe in God and see what direction it has had on individuals, families, communities, nations, and civilizations. As demonstrated in other chapters, the foundation for civilization has been the underlying religious beliefs of the culture.

God and Religion

If we accept the existence of God as fact for any of the reasons I have stated above, we can begin to ask what God's purpose is and what His purpose for us is. If we accept as fact the representations of those who claim to have seen or heard Him give instructions for the express purpose of giving us guidance, we can understand His and our purpose. We can add to this base of knowledge by using deductive and inductive reasoning to construct a real and useful model for living that is far more beneficial to us than is available through the scientific advancements upon which we place such a high value.

Chapter 17

"God is a Delusion"

While my instinct is to avoid ridiculing the religious beliefs of others, I will make an exception for many atheists. In my opinion, many of those who call themselves atheist are either lazy, stupid, cowardly, dishonest, or some combination of the four (I can see the hate mail coming already!). I admit that this judgment seems harsh, intolerant, bigoted, and unreasonable, but when I read the mindless rants and irrational arguments of those who call themselves atheists on blogs who then go on to accuse theists of being stupid, uninformed suckers I generally have a negative reaction. My attitude in this chapter reflects that negative reaction; however, that does not mean the charge is unfounded. Read on and you will see.

There is one group of atheists with whom I somewhat sympathize, even while emphatically rejecting their logic. These are they who have been exposed to illogical and obnoxious religious doctrine and found it to be, well illogical and obnoxious. Some of these doctrines are regularly used to great effect in persuading others that God does not exist and that religion is evil, including the belief in the endless torment of Hell and an emphasis on sin instead of a focus on making decisions that will lead to happiness. If I had been taught as a child that God loved his creations but then was bent on sending the vast majority of them to a horrific place of intense everlasting physical torture after death because of one simple incorrect decision, especially if the opportunity to make the decision was not possible, I like to think I would have categorically rejected that belief. I can certainly understand why they would. So, as you read the chapter and my accusations against atheists, bear in mind this category of people whom I am excluding from much of my harshest criticism.

In 2006 Mr. Richard Dawkins (who has plausible arguments and seems to be sincerely repulsed by traditional theology)[16] wrote a book entitled The God Delusion. Plausible though his arguments are, I believe they are fatally flawed. I will analyze the principal arguments in this chapter, and in the

---

[16] The God Delusion, Richard Dawkins, Houghton Mifflin Company, A Mariner Book, 2006, p 74

process I believe I will make a stronger case that ignoring the overwhelming probability of the existence of God is much more of a delusion than is God.

Because of the complexity of the subject, I have broken the chapter into sections and subsections. First, I will clearly identify the objects of my scorn. From there I will discuss the possible nature of God. The next several sections will deal with the arguments contained in The God Delusion, including the issue of who created the creator; the probability of the formation of life, both in the whole of existence and in the universe; and natural selection. Thereafter I will cover the common arguments made against the existence of God and will finish with an analysis of the various types of atheists and the possible motivations for their beliefs.

What is an atheist?

For this discussion, it will be necessary to define atheism and agnostic, ignoring the irrelevant meanings of the words.

> "Atheism, in its broadest sense, is the absence of theism (the belief in the existence of deities). This encompasses both people who assert that there are no gods, and those who make no claim about whether gods exist or not. Narrower definitions of atheism, however, typically only label people who affirmatively assert the nonexistence of gods as atheists, classifying other nonbelievers as agnostics or simply non-theists."[17]

> ag·nos·tic 1.
>   a. One who believes that it is impossible to know whether there is a God.
>
>   b. One who is skeptical about the existence of God but does not profess true atheism.[18]

For the purpose of this discussion, I will arbitrarily use the narrow definition referred to in the definition of atheist. The atheist that I castigate as lazy, stupid, cowardly, or dishonest is one who affirmatively asserts that there is no God. A related term, "antitheist, applies to those not just affirmatively asserting that there is no God, but also is in direct opposition to the belief in God for various reasons, including the destructive effects that

---

[17] Atheism. (2007, June 2). In *Wikipedia, The Free Encyclopedia*. Retrieved 00:04, June 3, 2007, from
http://en.wikipedia.org/w/index.php?title=Atheism&oldid=135406369

religious conflict has wrought and the perceived irrational position of religious doctrine. For the purpose of this discussion, an antitheist and atheist are the same.

Agnostic is separately defined even though as indicated in Wikepedia's definition frequently the terms are used interchangeably. They really mean completely different things. For the purpose of this discussion, an agnostic is one who, while accepting the possibility that God may exist, has concluded that even if He does exist we cannot possibly know of it and therefore it is useless to concern ourselves with the matter. I will also include within my arbitrary definition of agnostic those who consider the probability that God exists to be very low and who live their lives assuming He does not.

There is a considerable range in belief, and only the most extreme antagonists of theistic belief are included in my criticism. In The God Delusion, Mr. Dawkins has an analysis that spans the spectrum between theistic and atheistic belief. This is a very useful tool, which I will cite here to clearly explain the position of those who I am so critical of. Mr. Dawkins writes:

"Let us then, take the idea of a spectrum of probabilities seriously, and place human judgments about the existence of God along it, between two extremes of opposite certainty. The spectrum is continuous, but it can be represented by the following seven milestones along the way.

1. Strong theist. 100 per cent probability of God. In the words of C. G. Jung, "I do not believe, I know".
2. Very high probability, but short of 100 percent. *De facto* theist. "I cannot know for certain, but I strongly believe in God and live my life on the assumption that he is there."
3. Higher than 50 per cent, but not very high. Technically agonistic but leaning toward theism. "I am very uncertain, but I am inclined to believe in God"
4. Exactly 50 per cent. Completely impartial agnostic. "Gods existence and non-existence are exactly equiprobable."

[18] agnostic. (n.d.). *The American Heritage® Dictionary of the English Language, Fourth Edition*. Retrieved June 02, 2007, from Dictionary.com website: http://dictionary.reference.com/browse/agnostic

5. Lower the 50 percent but not very low. Technically agnostic but leaning towards atheism. "I don't know whether God exists but I'm inclined to be sceptical."

6. Very low probability, but short of zero. *De facto* atheist. "I cannot know for certain, but I think God is very improbable and live my life on the assumption that he is not there.

7. Strong atheist. "I know there is no God, with the same conviction that Jung "knows" there is one"[19]

Anyone from one to six on this scale can justify their belief by one means or another. While I obviously disagree with those who are in the four to six range in this analysis, I can respect their position and the reasons they may have to justify what they believe. Those in the four to six range I will call agnostic for the purpose of this discussion. Those who take position seven are true atheists, and it is they to whom I refer in this chapter.

People reject or cannot accept the existence of God for various reasons. The agnostic argument is the argument with which I am most sympathetic. If we cannot know of God, why should we waste time worrying about it? Many people live their lives with this philosophy as they deem best, ironically enough, living according to the foundational religious precepts incorporated by their culture that they perceive they cannot know the truth of. Some who call themselves atheists also fall into this category.

I have a great deal of respect for anyone who lives a good upstanding life in spite of the lack of belief in that which motivates most people. Frankly, if I were not convinced of the truthfulness of Christianity I would be an agnostic. I understand why agnostics would have reached the conclusion they came to, having come close to reaching the same conclusion myself. There are agnostics whose actions mirror the behavior of atheists; but then there are many who believe in God who do the same. It is the belief and the underlying role the belief has on behavior that is relevant to this discussion.

Of all religious beliefs, the strong atheistic view is the one with which I have the least sympathy (yes it is a religious belief if it concerns God or a replacement for Him). Indeed, in my mind such a person is a fool, a point of view that receives biblical support (see Psalms 14:1). To categorically say that there is no God is not logical. It is perfectly logical to assert that the existence of God cannot be proven. It is even logical to argue that His

---

[19] Ibid, p 73.

existence is improbable, although (as you will see) I believe these arguments are fatally flawed. It is entirely different to cite the fact that His existence cannot be proven or is improbable as proof that He does not exist. To such I would ask, "what proof do you have of His non-existence?" There is none. Zippo. Nada. Absolutely nothing. The arguments used by atheists emphasize that the existence of God cannot be proven or is improbable; therefore, there is no God. This is a non sequitur. It does not follow (I know I am repeating myself, but I do not want there to be any confusion about this). As demonstrated in Chapter 16, I have credible arguments and evidence supporting His existence.

In spite of the fact there is no evidence whatsoever that there is no God, yet atheists affirmatively assert He does not exist. Many ridicule those that do believe, calling them suckers or intellectually inferior. To support their argument they point to theoretical possibilities, which they cite as evidence, even though the possibilities they cite are generally desperate attempts to justify their beliefs, or are misconstrued interpretations of facts that really support the opposite of their belief.

The next few sections of the chapter will cover the various arguments both for and against the existence of God. As previously indicated, I will carefully cover the objections and arguments presented by Mr. Dawkins in The God Delusion. The responses are my own, although I will readily admit that very few of my arguments are entirely my own. I have had a lifetime of learning, reading, listening and thinking, and incorporating learned facts into my personal philosophy. I should also mention that I am a believing member of the Church of Jesus Christ of Latter-Day Saints (Mormon), and therefore my theological background and belief is different from most other Christian churches. That said, I am not a spokesperson for the Church and have no right to speak on Church doctrine. Further, many of my arguments go well beyond what the Church teaches. The reader should in no way construe my opinion to be the doctrine or position of the LDS Church.

What are the possible attributes of God?

Mr. Dawkins discusses various theistic belief systems, which includes a range of possibilities as to the existence and nature of God. What follows is my analysis of the possibilities drawn from Mr. Dawkins's description:

1. There is(are) no God(s) and the universe as we know it came about by undirected natural means.
2. There is one or multiple Gods that started a creative process but then ceased His(Her/Its/Their) creative acts.

3. There is one or multiple Gods with malevolent intent whose purpose is to torment His(Her/Its/Their) creations.
4. There is one or multiple Gods who are indifferent to His(Her/Its/Their) creations.
5. There is one or multiple Gods concerned with the welfare of His(Her/Its/Their) creations.

In the following discussion, I will drop the differences between theistic and polytheistic possibilities and differing gender pronouns, as the resulting grammar would be convoluted. I will simply use the traditional male pronoun to describe God or Gods. I also freely acknowledge that the summary below is biased toward human interest. After all, I am a human and am interested in my own welfare. It does not necessarily follow that God's interest will be the same. I also will make some deductions that are based on human reasoning, which may or may not be reasonable to God. But our rational and observational abilities are all we have to attempt to make sense of the universe, so that is what I have to use. Further, I believe God gave us brains and therefore expects us to use them. That said, let us look at the consequences of the possible nature of God.

- If possibility one is true, it is safe to say that the universe is a product of nature and that life is a result of increasing biological complexity by the means of random chance and natural selection.
- It is fairly easy to dismiss as irrelevant to human interest possibilities two and four, for all practical purposes these possibilities explain nothing with respect to human existence. There may as well not be a God. Further, any creator should have a purpose for any action He undertakes. If the purpose is simply to start a process then either lose interest or to roll the dice and see what happens, I don't see much of anything to justify calling such a being God. He certainly would not have my respect or worship. While not generating the antipathy that a malevolent being would, He would still be detached and irrelevant to humans. Indeed, the real question is why such a God would bother to create life, including intelligent life. What would have been the point?
- Possibility three seems to be self-defeating as to purpose. If God is malevolent and His purpose is to inflict suffering for no good purpose, why would any intelligent being worship Him, even if they were created by Him? I would suggest that such a God would be met with antipathy, rebellion, and hostility by His creations,

assuming these creations have free will. We know from the course of human history that humans invariably rebel whenever free will, or freedom, is taken from them. There is even the question about whether such a being could be omnipotent.

- Possibility five offers the most plausible explanation of the nature of God. It provides a purpose for creation other than a malevolent one, and gives such a God the means to omnipotence by virtue of the respect and worship of intelligent life. It would also explain why direction would be given to His creations; if God has the welfare of His creations at heart, He will direct them with the purpose of maximizing their opportunity for happiness.

The remainder of the comparative sections will be a comparison between possibilities one and five. God, if He exists, is assumed to be an omnipotent being who has created the universe and the life within it, and who values and has a purpose for those creations.

What are the arguments supporting the atheistic view?

Mr. Dawkins spends a whole chapter ostensibly covering arguments that support the existence of God. In Chapter 2 of The God Delusion, he covers a number of traditional theological and theoretical arguments made over the centuries. Unfortunately, most of the arguments he cites can and have been refuted and subsequently dismissed as evidence for the existence of God, which he in turn proceeds to do himself. He then uses this ostensible lack of proof as a springboard for his argument that God almost certainly does not exist. In effect, he creates a straw man, which he can easily knock down and thereby seem to increase the rationality of his argument. What he does not do is list any of the empirical evidence and arguments that support the existence of God, for the most part because he either rejects the evidence or views the evidence as supporting his point of view.

Mr. Dawkins goes on to make a number of arguments supporting his supposition, which are as follows:

- God almost certainly does not exist because a complex God would need a creator.
- The origin of life in our universe is statistically probable because all possible universes which may not contain life make the occurrence of life somewhere in reality probable, and that somewhere could be here in this universe.
- The origin of life on earth is statistically probable because all possible planets in the universe which may not contain life make the

177

occurrence of life somewhere in the universe probable, and that somewhere could be here on earth.

• Once life has originated, the diversity of life on earth can be explained by the process of natural selection.

Each of these arguments are used to dismiss the need for a creative intelligence manipulating matter, energy, and natural laws to bring about a purposeful creation. I will cover each of these points in turn.

Who created the Creator?

Mr. Dawkins's central argument is that God is highly improbable because He is a complex being that cannot have come to be without being created. There are at least three assumptions that he makes which I can see, all of which can be challenged, although some better than others. These assumptions are as follows;

1 God is a complex being or intelligence.
2 Complex beings, or highly developed intelligence, are a result of evolutionary processes.
3 If a complex creator is to exist, it must be the result of the creation of a different complex being.

Is God complex compared to the simplest component of the universe?

Let us examine each of these assumptions in turn. First, are we certain that God is a complex being? Mr. Dawkins holds that if He exists He must be, but I'm not quite so sure. I can easily imagine a God not nearly as complex as the being Mr. Dawkins describes.

Let us think back to the beginning of our universe and speculate. Imagine a pre-big bang existence where in the pre-time both pre-matter and/or pre-energy somehow existed in the pre-space as a point of singularity smaller that an atom that was infinitely hot. (Note for future reference: the matter, energy, time, and space in the cosmos originating from such a point seems to conflict with the First Law of Thermodynamics). At the same time it is possible that conscious entities also existed. To those wondering what possible justification I can find to suppose that these entities existed, I would argue from the same logic that theoretical physicists use to justify speculation about theoretical universes, multiverses, and megaverses, including those with different physical laws that make life impossible. That is, it offers one possible explanation to the origin of the universe and life. And please don't throw up the canard that because we can't see or measure them (yet), we can't speculate as to their possibility. We can't see or measure multiple universes either (also yet), but that has not stopped the speculation about them. While I am sure some will accuse me of supporting the existence of the equivalent of Bertrand Russell's teapot orbiting the sun somewhere in the solar system, the teapot offers no plausible explanation for anything, while the existence of pre-universal conscious beings would explain a lot.

For ease of discussion, let's call these entities intelligences. It is easy to imagine that if there was one intelligence, that there may have been many. If there is one thing our universe teaches us, it is that whatever type of object we discover in the universe, we invariably find many more of them. Indeed, there could have been untold numbers of intelligences. For all we know, they could be the fundamental component of pre-universal existence.

Because we are accustomed to a wide difference in ability on earth from one intelligent being to another, it is easy to imagine that of all the intelligences that existed, there was a variety of ability among these intelligences. If so, it is also easy to imagine that one intelligence was more intelligent than all the rest.

If that intelligence knew everything there was to know, He would be omniscient. Further, if He had the interest of all of the other intelligences at heart, He would have the allegiance and support of all of them. It is reasonable to assume that the cooperative intelligences would need assurance that no matter what the situation or circumstances, they would be treated justly. Accomplishing work suddenly becomes exponentially easier with untold numbers of cooperating intelligences. Further, with the full and unequivocal respect of all cooperating intelligences, it is much easier for the omniscient intelligence to become omnipotent, especially if all other intelligences in the universe follow His direction because of their implicit faith in His judgment. It is also easy to call such an intelligence God.

This theory of God's nature, in stark contrast to traditional religious belief, could place limitations on God's behavior. For instance, if God chose to usurp the free will of other intelligences, or perform evil acts, He would lose the respect of the other intelligences. Without the unified support of intelligences in favor of the common interests of all, He could cease to be omnipotent and could therefore cease to be God. In addition, He could be subject to natural law, even if He designed and implemented the law. This would answer the inane and sophomoric questions such as "How many angels can God fit on the head of a pin?", or "Can God make a rock so heavy that He can't pick it up?". "A house divided against itself cannot stand" may apply to more than human existence.

Even if God were constrained by natural law, it does not follow that He cannot accomplish what would seem to us to be miracles. In this regard, I am of the same opinion as Mr. Dawkins, which is that if we accurately observe what we consider to be a miracle it is merely an operation of natural law that we do not yet understand. If an omniscient God understands all natural laws and how to use and manipulate them to accomplish His purposes, such activities would not be miraculous to Him.

By the way, some of the attributes we associate with God seem to be much more plausible as we improve technology and our understanding of natural law. For instance, it is not hard to imagine a God with excellent communicative abilities when we see radio waves crossing the observable universe, including passing through dense matter. Computers and our ability to blast emails to millions of people at a time by wireless means also make it easier to believe that God may be able to widely communicate with anyone with whom He wishes to communicate. Indeed, we know that our brains function with electromagnetic impulses, and we are getting close to being able to decipher and perhaps even communicate with the brain electronically. Last, we speculate as to the nature of space-time and how it works, including the theoretical possibility that time can be warped and manipulated. If we suppose that man can do this, it is at least as easy to suppose that God can do the same.

It is also possible that such a God could act to improve His own situation. For instance, if the universe was created to eventually create life, the ultimate form of which intelligences could inhabit and thereby have the benefit of a tangible material body, it stands to reason that He could provide the same benefit for Himself. In other words, in some ways God may have changed over time. This conflicts with traditional theology, which holds that God is the same yesterday, today, and forever; however, it is possible to surmise that God's purpose, intellect, and character are unchanging while His physical attributes are not. Indeed, if the foundational tenet of Christianity is true, God came to earth and inhabited a body, which was then resurrected to an immortal state. In any case, it is difficult to argue that God cannot possibly change in any way when one considers that anyone who enters Heaven automatically changes God by increasing His power and influence.

I will concede that such an intelligence could be more complex than most of what we find in the universe, but is that perception necessarily accurate? Such an intelligence could have started out as a simple form of energy, just another energy form that is yet unobserved. Even if it were

180

complex, does it follow that it would be more complex than any other simple component or property of the pre-universe or early universe? It seems to me that we find a lot of complexity in the basic composition of our universe, including natural law, and the nature of energy and matter.

For instance, there is considerable complexity in the basic laws governing matter and energy in our universe, much of which we are yet at a loss to fully explain. Theories come and go, but over time we have been able to explain more and more of what we observe and can measure. This research is lead by astronomers, physicists, and cosmologists. In terms of the possibility of life, life exists on this planet so it is clear that universal law has created an environment in which life is possible in this universe. However, it may well be that minor changes in natural laws could result in a universe in which life is not possible, given the requirements of life as we know it. Last I heard, quantum mechanics, physics, astronomy, and the mathematics attendant to these fields of study is not simple.

And speaking of complexity, what about the concept of infinity? Can we even conceive of a time when time did not exist or space in which space does not exist? We believe that our universe will continue to expand into infinity and this expansion is accelerating over time. Into what is it expanding? Even if that model is not correct and the Big Bang, expansion, contraction, and Big Crunch cyclical theory is valid, we still have what we perceive to be a vacuum left after the big crunch, and a vacuum occupies space. Further, if we theorize that multiple universes exist, or even megaverses in which untold numbers of universes simultaneously and/or serially exist which either occupy different space, occupy the same space as our universe, or are created in black holes in our and other universes with wormholes that could enable transport to and from these universes, we still have the question of what exists beyond the megaverse. This is not simple.

In addition to the complexity of simple natural law, (sounds like an oxymoron, doesn't it?), we can look at energy and find complexity within a simple framework (or is it simplicity within a complex framework?). In any case, energy permeates the universe. Each form of energy is a simple frequency range along the electromagnetic spectrum, ranging from gamma rays for the most compact frequencies to radio for the longest. Along the way there are x-rays, ultraviolet light, visible light, infrared, and microwaves. In theory, the spectrum is infinite and continuous, although the short range may be limited by atomic particle size and the long range may be limited by the size of the universe. This does not seem that simple to me.

Matter is similarly complex. For instance, the hydrogen atom seems pretty simple until you look at the fundamentals of atomic structure. It was originally thought to be a simple electron particle circling a proton. But then we discovered that protons are composed of subatomic particles. Then there is the space within the atom to consider, which is wildly disproportionate to the size of the particles that compose it. Even with all the unoccupied space within the atom, it still acts as a solid mass that other atoms with just as much unoccupied space cannot pass through. Even worse, an electron particle circling a proton turned out to be a particle for part of the orbit but which is then somehow transformed into energy for the remainder of the orbit. Or it could be that the electron is not circling the proton, but is going through it in a figure eight configuration, again partially as a particle and partially as energy. Or it could be that the electron jumps from one location to another in the orbit or figure eight without existing in the space between its jump. Last, electrons may be in multiple places at the same time, which theory is used to justify the conjecture that multiple parallel universes can exist. (In this theory, atheistic physicists seem to demonstrate a double standard; nature can create parallel universes with infinite possible outcomes for parallel earths, but it is ridiculous to suggest that God exists in a parallel dimension.) It is clear that the simplest and most abundant element in the universe is anything but simple.

Last, the pre-universal state seems to be anything but simple. The theory is that all time, space, matter and energy in our universe originated from a "point of singularity". This point was ostensibly infinitely small and hot, but at the same time had the mass of the universe that resulted from the Big Bang. (Once again, atheistic physicists demonstrate a double standard; in that it is okay for nature to create a universe from a point of singularity smaller than a subatomic particle, but if God is the creator it is ludicrous and contradicts the First Law of Thermodynamics.) In any case, it is not simple.

I will admit that each naturally occurring element on the periodic table is more complex than hydrogen, that combinations of different elements (molecules) are more complex than elements, and that molecules that are so complex that they result in life are more complex than any of the prior elements and molecules. However, that each of these is more complex than the previous does not arbitrarily mean that intelligence is more complex than a hydrogen atom. Similarly, it does not follow that natural law or energy are any more complex than intelligence, including the intelligence of God.

Are complex beings, or intelligences, necessarily a result of the evolutionary processes?

Mr. Dawkins would have us believe that we are intelligent because we have evolved through natural selection to be more intelligent. Therefore, any intelligent God must have evolved or have been created. Is this true? This seems to be a circular argument to me. It does not follow that because intelligent life evolved on this planet that intelligence could not originate by any other process or means.

Could it be that his argument should be reversed and that we are intelligent beings because we started out as intelligent beings? If any of the people who describe out of body experiences upon being pronounced dead are an indication, it certainly is a possibility that our body is energized by something other than chemical energy generated by the conversion of carbon, sugar, and oxygen through the Krebs citric acid cycle. While these experiences are dismissed as delusions in a mind traumatized by its impending death by those who desperately want to assure the public that out of body existence is impossible, they could easily be real experiences of what I will here call an intelligence (is that a coincidence?) that inhabits the physical body. I discussed this at length in Chapter 16.

Speaking of evolving intelligences, would it not stand to reason that if Mr. Dawkins's premise is valid that over time intellectual ability would increase? The only way this premise is possible given the wide range of intellectual ability within the general population and specific groups is if the human population has hit a plateau of general intellectual ability which will not improve until we see mutations that result in superior intellectual ability.

Wait a minute. Haven't we seen these superior intellects, which are presumably the result of mutations if natural selection is the only factor? Newton, Einstein, Teller, and possibly even Mr. Dawkins himself demonstrate that if superior intelligence is the result of genetic mutation, the mutations were not immediately passed on to succeeding generations. Brilliant minds come from unpredictable genetic backgrounds and the offspring of geniuses do not often have the same ability. This is evidence that intelligence may be a result not of evolution, but of the original intelligence of the person.

Essentially, Mr. Dawkins has taken the natural selection model, assumed that increasing intelligence is the result of natural selection, then concluded that God can only be the result of a similar process. The argument is based on unfounded assumptions.

A much more troubling question naturally follows any discussion of intellectual ability, genetics, evolution, and the assumption that natural selection results in a more intelligent, and therefore more fit, organism. If mutations that result in increased intelligence are desirable and belief in God does not exist to constrain group behavior, why would not society take steps to restrict the procreation of those with less intelligence and encourage (or even force) the propagation of children by the superior intellects? Indeed, why would we not choose to systematically exterminate those who are intellectually inferior? If this is frightening, it should be. These policies describe Germany under Adolph Hitler.

If a complex creator exists, must it be the result of the creation of a different complex being?

Let's assume that my intelligence theory propounded above is proven to be nonfactual for one reason or another. We can then take the model of God accepted by the majority of Christians and evaluate whether its existence is improbable, as Mr. Dawkins asserts. In this model, God is unquestionably complex. He is omnipotent, omniscient, and omnipresent and unchanging.

Even so, does it follow that God must have been created, which then creates a need for other creators on into infinity? Well, no. Why can't a complex being exist within the unknown complexity that preceded our universe? First, we have no idea how complex our pre-universe was; indeed it seems to have been very complex. Even if it were not, it still does not follow that a complex God could not have always existed. We can look at the First Law of Thermodynamics and suppose this to be a possibility.

On another level, Mr. Dawkins seems to want to argue both sides of the issue. He points to natural selection as an ideal model to explain the diversity of life on earth, but then cannot accept the possibility that God could result from natural processes that we are unaware of at the present time. In other words, he sees God as complex, but then proceeds to argue that natural selection explains increasing complexity of life without allowing for the possibility that a creative God could have evolved on a universal level. He wants to have it both ways; that is complexity can arise from natural processes unless that complexity is God.

I admit that I am not nearly as comfortable with this argument as I am with my original intelligence theory, but the logic is still sound. In addition, traditional Christian theology may not accept my argument that God could be the result of unknown natural processes. However, there may be important nuances that I have not seen. Remember that I am a person of average intelligence with only a Bachelor's degree in Geography. I'm sure that others could do a better job in fine-tuning this argument.

To summarize, if we can assume the existence of pre-universal precursors to time, space, matter, and energy and an environment in which the Big Bang and the universe's subsequent expansion into whatever it expanded into became possible, we can also assume that the existence of God is at least as probable as the non-existence of God.

It is also important to note that Mr. Dawkins's argument is only a theoretical possibility unsubstantiated by evidence. Any evidence he cites can be easily interpreted to support the opposite of his premise. There is nothing other than logic that demonstrates that his argument is a valid possibility. As such, there is no reason to accept his logic in favor of any other plausible logical explanation. Further, his logic makes assumptions that I have shown to be arbitrary. Therefore, his premise that God is almost certainly impossible because of the lack of a creator of the creator is no more probable than any other theory, including theories that neither Mr. Dawkins nor I have thought of. With that, we will proceed to cosmological and biological considerations, which demonstrate the premise that life is a result of nothing more than statistical averages and natural selection to be significantly less probable than Mr. Dawkins argues.

Origin of life in the universe

The best theory we have at this time to explain the origin of the universe is the Big Bang theory, which is supported by observation and mathematical calculations. The theory postulates that the universe began at a finite time (about 13.7 billion years ago) and formed from the expansion very hot and dense "stuff" (for want of a better word; matter, material, or energy do not seem to be accurate descriptions of whatever it was). Indeed, this "stuff" may have been infinitely hot and dense (just try to conceive that complexity, it seems to have mass and energy). The initial expansion propelled this "stuff" away from the point of the explosion at incredible speeds, and the universe expanded exponentially. The subsequent formation of energy, hydrogen, and helium atoms resulted in the underlying conditions that allowed for star formation in spite of this outward exponential expansion, which then led to the production of the other elements in the periodic table through fusion. Galaxies and super clusters of galaxies formed. In turn, dying and exploding stars spewed elements heavier than hydrogen and helium into space, where they were incorporated into other stars or condensed into planets. Eventually (very important to us) our own solar system formed. Thereafter, life originated on earth.

Central to our focus is the origination of life, the process that resulted in the diversity and complexity of life, and therefore our consciousness of the universe. (Sorry, I can't resist the urge; would the universe exist if there were no life to be aware of it?) The salient question for us to answer is whether the universe and its complexity are the result of random chance, statistical probability, or a creator who directed a creative process.

The existence of life on this planet forces scientists to accept that life is possible in our universe. Because life has formed on this planet, they have been forced to admit that life is possible elsewhere in the universe. This was originally only grudgingly admitted, although the resistance to the concept may have traditional religious doctrine to blame. In any case, humans are left with life here and potential life elsewhere in the universe to explain.

Much study has been put into explaining the underlying conditions in the universe that allowed the formation of life. One example cited by Mr. Dawkins is the work of Sir Martin Rees. Mr. Rees convincingly argues that the formation of energy, matter, stars, galaxies, superclusters, elements, molecules, and life is governed by six numbers, each of which must be at a specific value range to allow the formation of the observable universe, including life. If the values vary from the observed and measured values, the universe would have developed in a way that made life incompatible.

That being the case, is the universe and the underlying conditions that allowed life to form the result of random chance, statistical probability, or a Creator? Given the overwhelming odds against random chance, no one, including atheists, supports this as a plausible explanation. The argument is ostensibly between statistical probability and God.

The argument in favor of statistical probability is based on two suppositions, which are that there are multiple universes and that these multiple universes have underlying physical laws that differ from the laws of this universe. The speculation is that there are perhaps an infinite number of parallel and serial universes, each of which has its own set of physical laws. If these suppositions are correct, because we know life exists in this universe, we can suppose that there is a statistical probability that life exists or does not exist in the untold numbers of universes. For instance, if only one universe in one billion had the correct physical laws that allows life (Rees six numbers), the odds against any other universe having life is one billion to one against life containing universes. Therefore, because there are so many universes without life, statistically speaking the odds are that eventually one universe out of one billion will allow life, and we are that (or one of those) universe(s). Therefore, statistically speaking, this universe with life is not a product of random chance, but a product of statistical averages and is therefore probable without the need for a creator.

Where to begin? In the first place, multiple universes are hypothetical theories that have no empirical evidence whatsoever to substantiate them. If I were making the same argument in support of God, I would be accused of the equivalent of hypothesizing that a teapot orbits the sun, which while ridiculous cannot be disproved. I repeat, there is no evidence supporting the existence of any universe other than our own. I could argue that the fantasy universes that theoretical physicists advance are nothing more than a desperate attempt to create a plausible explanation, any plausible explanation, which will allow them to dismiss the unbelievable odds against the formation of life without a creator.

The only possible empirical evidence of another universe is the existence of a supervoid in our universe that seems improbable given the relatively even distribution of matter in space. One scientist has speculated the supervoid could be the effect of a nearby universe on our own. Note the word speculate; there is no evidence.

Next, even if there are multiple universes, the assumption that each universe would have physical laws different from this universe is unsubstantiated by evidence. Do we have any evidence that Mr. Rees's six numbers would differ from ours in a parallel universe? I don't think so. Even if the observed supervoid demonstrated the effect of a parallel universe, there is no evidence that the other universe would have physical laws different from our own. For all we know, if a megaverse exists, each and every universe in it could not just allow life, but in fact contain life. What does that do to their odds? It means that the ostensibly improbable universe with life is the norm rather than the anomaly, and therefore universes with life are ridiculously more probable than can be predicted statistically. In this scenario, the choice is back to random chance or God.

Even if there are multiple universes with physical laws which preclude the origin of life, it also does not follow that statistical probability is any more plausible an explanation than God. In other words, the existence of a plausible excuse to dismiss the existence of God does not automatically mean that the excuse is any more likely to be valid than the alternative.

The whole argument can be condensed into the following sentence. We guess that life is possible in only one in one billion universes, and if there is life in only one in one billion universes, statistically speaking life supporting universes are likely to occur; therefore life supporting universes, including ours, are just as probable if there is no God as they are if there is a God; therefore, there is no God. Not one single clause of that sentence is substantiated by fact or even follows if the basic assumptions are valid. In fact the whole argument seems to be a desperate attempt to get around the random chance argument by any means possible.

In short, the scientific community has developed an intricate theoretical model that allows them to implausibly argue that our universe with life is not a product of random chance or God. However, this model, even if valid, still does not make the explanation of God any less plausible. In the end, we are left with the conclusion that our universe with its life is either the result of random chance, unsupported statistical wishful thinking, or God.

Origin of life on earth

About 4.54 billion years ago, only 9.2 billion years after the universe began, the earth began to form. Initially the planet was nothing more than a mass of cosmic debris, including heavy elements ejected from exploding stars. In the beginning, the earth was as inhospitable to life as it is possible for a planet to be, basically a molten mass under constant bombardment from asteroids, ultraviolet light, radiation, and solar winds.

Between then and now, the earth has been transformed by natural processes into a very different place indeed. By the way, anyone who has a philosophical problem with God using natural processes to accomplish His purposes has not been paying much attention to the natural world. The question before us now is the same as for the previous section; did this planet and life on it result from random chance, statistical probability, or was it created by God?

This transformation came about by a remarkable chain of events. I will not attempt to write the multi-volume work needed to detail every step and how each step resulted in an environment that allowed for the formation of life. I will highlight important points which emphasize the improbability of the process when the extreme and hostile to life conditions of the universe and solar system are considered.

The molten mass that existed when the earth was first formed continued to grow as it accreted additional material. It accumulated other elements, some of which were then incorporated into molecules, which then formed increasingly more complex molecules. Remarkably enough, a stable atmosphere could form because hot heavy metals, especially iron, sank to the inner core of the earth and became very hot due to radioactive decay and began rotating at a speed different from the surface after the surface cooled and hardened. This effect created the magnetosphere, which shielded the planet from solar winds and radiation.

In terms of composition, just the right types and amounts of elements were in the mix that allowed the formation of molecules so complex that life as we know it resulted. Remember that all these elements and molecules are combining and forming increasingly more complex molecules over vast periods of time on a small speck of material (from a universal standpoint) that is just the right distance from a powerful energy source (the Sun), is tilted on its axis and spinning sufficient to ensure the circulation of heat and the distribution of elements within its sphere, and has just the right materials to support these life forming processes. Furthermore, sufficient heat is present to support the process, but not so much that the entire speck of material and the life forming on it is either fried, blown away into space, or enveloped within an obliterating ball of fire. The speck of material and the life forming on it is shielded throughout the process by the magnetosphere, which prevents solar winds from blowing our atmosphere into space and radiation from annihilating every life form on this speck of material that we call Earth.

As in the previous section dealing with the universe as a whole, this result described above can only have occurred by one of three means. It is either the result of random chance, statistical probability, or it is the result of a deliberate design by a creator or creative force.

There is a fourth alternative which is not really an alternative in terms of explaining how life came to be. There is some speculation that life on earth was seeded, that is transported to earth by a comet or asteroid. That seems unlikely given the distances involved. That would mean another planet containing life existed in close enough proximity to earth (no more than 1,000 light years distant given the 9.2 billion years the universe existed before Earth's formation and the speed of comets) for a comet or asteroid seeded with life from the other planet to hit earth. If the odds against the formation of life are as speculated, such a planet would so far away from earth that transport would be less likely than its original formation in earth's primordial state, especially given the slow speed of this debris when compared with the size of the universe. However, even if seeding did occur, we would still be left with the question of how life formed on the original planet, which takes us right back to the three choices listed above.

Is it possible that our planet which provided the conditions for the formation of life is the result of random chance? Certainly, it is possible. It

189

could be that the universe and life within it is the result of a remarkable set of circumstances coming together and occurring at just the right times to have the result we observe. However, what is the probability of its occurrence? If we accept the Second Law of Thermodynamics as an accurate description of what happens in the physical world, we have to conclude that the probability of our existence and the results we observe being the result of random chance is ridiculously low. This law holds that matter and energy over time becomes less concentrated, with entropy the eventual result. Indeed, even atheists reject random chance as an explanation (sort of, as you shall see). Mr. Dawkins concedes that "We therefore can imagine it (the origin of life) to be an extremely improbable event, many orders of magnitude more improbable than most people realize, as I shall show."[20] In theory, random chance is an argument rejected by all.

Instead of random chance an argument of statistical probability is made, not unlike the argument made in the previous section in favor of multiple universes making the probability of life supporting universes likely because so few theoretical universes contain life. In this argument, the only difference is the argument is made based on the theoretical possibility of life on other planets in our universe.

Their reasoning is thus. In spite of the overwhelming odds against the spontaneous formation of life, it exists on this planet so we know life is possible, therefore, it is also possible that life exists elsewhere in the universe. If we suppose that the formation of life occurs only rarely, for instance only in one in one billion star systems, there should be 100 billion planets with life scattered throughout the universe. In spite of this high number, given the total number of stars (10 to the 20th power) statistically speaking the formation of life would be probable. Therefore, because there is a high statistical probability that life will occur given the number of possibilities, life is not unusual, nor need it be the result of random chance or have been created by God.

Where have we heard this before? It is the same argument posited in the previous section, and its logic is just as flawed, though on a different level:

- There is not yet evidence that life exists elsewhere in the universe. While it is easy to assume, until extra-terrestrial life is discovered we cannot conclude that life exists elsewhere. Having said that, I am the last person that will rely on this argument.

---

[20] Ibid, p. 162

- Assuming life exists elsewhere in the universe, we have no evidence that life is as rare as is speculated. Instead of the assumed one to one billion odds against life in any given star system, why wouldn't we conclude that life is common, indeed earth-like planets could easily have formed or be forming in every stable star system in the universe. Given our tendency to view ourselves as unique in spite of repeated lessons about how conditions seem to repeat themselves throughout the universe, it would not be surprising if the odds were much closer to one in one million.

- Assuming life is as rare as is speculated, we still are faced with the fact that wherever life exists, it started at each location by either random chance or God. Statistical probability only applies to the number of life supporting star systems that come into being. We are still left with the conclusion that life on each of the planets must have formed as a result of random chance if there is no Creator.

- Even taking the statistical probability argument at face value, it still does not preclude the existence of God. It does not follow that just because life is probable throughout the universe because life, given opportune conditions will form, that God did not create this life.

Mr. Dawkins further argues that life only has to form once for it to come into being. Even if that argument is true, that it only has to form once does not make its occurrence any less likely. The odds are still overwhelmingly against it, as he readily admits. Even worse, his argument that life only had to come into being once is also an unsupported assumption, given the hostile environment and any early life form's inability to significantly evolve under those conditions. It may well be that life had to form more than once, or even many times.

In effect, the statistical argument is actually an argument in favor of random chance flipped to favor an arbitrary choice. Ultimately, the argument is still for random chance. If the odds quoted above are correct, the argument is that life originated on 100 billion planets in our universe and each single occurrence was a result of random chance. In other words, the statistical probability argument is nothing more than an argument in favor of random chance resulting in life as a common occurrence (or at least as common as other astronomical objects) on a universal scale. Once again, this argument is made in spite of the Second Law of Thermodynamics and what should be a devolving environment for life.

Skeptics argue that the formation of life on earth is not inconsistent with the Second Law because of the insertion of energy from the Sun into the system, and they may be right. As I argued in Chapter 16, there is no proof. These are natural processes that have as their result the universe and all its complexity, and one may rationally argue that the result could have been simply a product of random chance that just happened to occur on our planet because the odds of life occurring somewhere favored its occurrence.

A fact that makes random chance or statistical probability even more difficult to accept as the basis for how life came into existence is the fact that without a creator life could only have originated with what Mr. Dawkins calls a "self-bootstrapping crane".[21] This is an argument unsupported by evidence or logic. How do raw elements and chemicals intelligently self-bootstrap themselves? Remember he has previously argued that life is extremely unlikely to have been a result of random chance; however, to get around random chance he argues that atoms and molecules are organizing themselves by some unknown cause as if they could themselves act intelligently. He also argues that the lessons of natural selection should teach us to be suspicious of evidence of design in non-biological fields, without explaining how complex non-biological objects could possibly result from some process equivalent to natural selection. Is there a theory of inorganic evolution out there that nobody is telling us about? Without God, life is the only agent that could do anything akin to "self-bootstrapping" which cannot explain the origination of life.

To accept this argument means that we must accept that a group of atoms somehow came together with just the right conditions that resulted in an unbelievably complex molecular combination that spontaneously came to life. The supposition on the part of atheists that the energy from the Sun ameliorates the seeming conflict with the Second Law of Thermodynamics does not explain how this energy provided the mechanism for all these atoms spontaneously coming together with life as the result. Further, attempts to replicate the process in the laboratory have been unsuccessful.

It is much more rational to believe that there is a creator behind the process that resulted in life. Here again, Occam's razor is instructive. What are the odds against enough of the right elements coming together with just the right amount of energy needed to produce the interaction between them required to form basic molecules without frying the whole planet? Even more difficult is concluding that random chance on this specific planet

---

[21] Ibid, p185

resulted in life, because conditions had to be perfect for this life to occur and survive long enough to adapt to hostile conditions. This includes everything from the precise location of our planet in relation to the sun, its exact tilt on its axis, and the protection afforded by the magnetosphere. The simplest explanation is God.

One who believes life is the result of random chance demonstrates a faith in chance that is much more of a leap than the acceptance of a guiding creative force. To use Fred Hoyle's example, if I were to allege that a large commercial aircraft came together by random chance without any human intervention in the process, you would justifiably say that I am clueless as to how our world works. You would be right. However, in the same breath many would say that the formation of life, exponentially more complex than the construction of an airplane, is the product of random chance.

Over the past fifty-seven years scientists have been trying to create life after amino acids were created in an experiment that combined water, carbon dioxide, methane, and ammonia. To date all attempts have been met with abject failure. Having said that, if in the future humans are able to create life, it does not follow that life could have been created without a creator. It will be difficult to argue that intelligent human efforts and experiments which succeed in answering how life can be created proves that life can be the result of random chance (I know some will question human intelligence, but that is another discussion).

Natural selection and the diversity of life

Once life comes into existence, it is much easier for the atheist to argue that the complexity and diversity of life is the result of natural selection. To summarize the argument, mutations in the DNA of all life forms affect the ability of the life form to survive. Mutations that improve the ability of the organism to survive would result in that specific organism's ability to survive over a similar organism without the mutation. Similarly, a mutation that decreases the organism's ability to survive would have the opposite effect. Mutations that improve the chances of survival would result in a strain of descendents that would proliferate more than the original non-mutated organism and even more than the negative mutation. Over vast periods of time, a series of mutations could result in the diversity of species we see on this planet having originated from a single simple life form. Natural selection replaces God as the designer in this argument.

This section assumes that natural selection is in fact how the various species came to be. I know that there are those who disagree; however, with what I know at this point in time I have accepted Darwinist evolution as fact. If eventually another explanation is advanced that is better than what we have now, I believe I will be prepared to accept it also.

Much has been written about the probability of this process resulting in the wide variety of life. Mr. Dawkins argues that natural selection without God is a more probable explanation than a creator, ostensibly because the creation model, to use his analogy, wants to climb "Mount Improbable" by leaping to the top of an insurmountable precipice without taking the slow gradual steps used by natural selection on the opposite side of the mountain. He goes on to argue that with the natural selection model God is completely unnecessary. He may be right.

That said, as usual Mr. Dawkins and other atheists confuse a plausible argument with a probable one, or in this case a significantly more probable one. The fact that the diversity of species is possible by natural selection does not preclude the possibility that God used natural law, including natural selection, to create all the life forms we see on this planet. In the "Mount Improbable" argument, Dawkins fails to see that no matter how plausible his natural selection model can be speculated to be, if God exists then the same process with God directing it is, by definition, more probable. Mr. Dawkins jumps to the conclusion that the choice is between the slow incremental advances made by natural selection and the giant step of God creating something from nothing. This is a false choice. If God is the designer using natural selection to get life up the gentle slope of Mount Improbable and uses His knowledge of nature to work around the grinding force of gravity (Second Law), the end result is unquestionably more probable than nature alone and unaided especially when the enemy of life (time) is factored into the equation.

With respect to probability, many of the adaptations made by organisms do not seem to follow the model provided by natural selection. The atheist will argue that extremely complex adaptations are probable over time because each mutation gives the organism a better chance at survival. If each and every mutation in a long chain of mutations resulted in an improved ability to survive, that argument makes sense. However, what about mutations that incrementally move an organism toward better survivability but alone do not give the organism a competitive advantage? In the natural selection model, these mutations would not be fit, and natural selection would not favor their survival. Indeed Mr. Dawkins asserts

"Darwinian selection habitually targets and eliminates waste".[22] Mutations that did not result in a material advantage to the organism would have been a waste and would probably not have survived even if a future series of mutations eventually could result in a material advantage. In spite of this, non-advantageous mutation upon non-advantageous mutation occurred with the cumulative result of a complex adaptation and competitive advantage. To be sure, these mutations and their result could be natural selection doing its thing, but probability still favors intelligent direction.

Ironically enough, even though natural selection is deemed to result in the survival of the species in the most efficient manner possible without waste, Mr. Dawkins goes on to assert later in the book that natural selection has given the human species a bonus.[23] It has refined our brains and given us the ability to be inspired by nature, music, speech, and the cosmos. Excuse me? What happened to the ruthlessly efficient natural selection process that eliminated waste? We don't need inspiration to survive any more than a pack of wolves need inspiration to survive. All we need is food, water, air, and possibly shelter. Inspiration is a "bonus" that is not justified by natural selection.

By the way, what about this ability to mutate? Just how did the original life form acquire this ability? It seems to me that this ability is as much of a "self-bootstrapping" event as the creation of life itself. Just because life somehow formed does not mean the life form would automatically have had the ability to mutate (or even reproduce for that matter). The atheist will point to the miracle of DNA, its ability to replicate itself, and its ability to make mistakes in that replication that do not result in the death of the organism as a miracle of nature and natural selection. It can at least as easily be the miraculous product of a designer.

To draw another analogy, let us suppose that the earth is a large life producing factory. We can see the result of the production process; the only question is whether it is the result of natural selection unaided by any force other than itself, that is random mutation after untold mutation resulting in ever more complex organisms over eons of time and evolving in spite of what should be a devolving or destructive environment for life, or whether the factory has a designer and production manager that keeps the process working to achieve a specific end, including injecting just enough energy (but not too much) into the process to make the system work.

---

[22] Ibid, p. 190
[23] Ibid. p. 405

God and Religion

In the first choice, the factory is on its own, and must survive over time in spite of all the hazards common in the universe. Time is the natural enemy of life. All it takes is one annihilating event to destroy it, which could easily occur over the billions of years that natural selection has ostensibly been working its magic. Time also works against life because of the Second Law of Thermodynamics; over the billions of years it has taken to develop the species, the process of life becoming exponentially more complex has been occurring in spite of the Second Law.

The second choice is considerably more probable. The factory seems to be highly automated and very efficiently designed, to the point of protecting it from destruction with minimal effort on the part of the Creator. Indeed, hazards seem to have had the effect of accomplishing the designer's purpose if human life was the ultimate goal. In any case, just as it is highly improbable that a factory in the Midwest, no matter how efficiently designed and how many robots are on the assembly line, could continue producing without intelligent direction, it is also true that the earth's ability to produce life is considerably less probable without God.

The earth is a planet containing a diversity of life that staggers the imagination, with multi-cellular life forms having specialized cells that support the survival of the life form in an interaction so complex that even the most sophisticated scientist among us cannot replicate. Even more staggering in their complexity are life forms so large and complex that differentiated cells with specific functions spontaneously form from the original cell within the growing organism. Most amazing, the senses necessary for perceiving the environment in which the life forms lived developed and enabled the life forms to significantly increase their chances of survival. What is more, each of these single species is a component of a sophisticated web that complements and sustains other life on the planet in symbiotic relationships that also defies replication by human action. This web is sustained by the energy provided by the Sun, and can adjust to changing circumstances because of the interactions of species and elements. For instance, carbon dioxide, while detrimental to the fauna that depends on oxygen for survival and produces carbon dioxide as a byproduct, is the essential molecule needed for flora to flourish. Over time, a balance that has the toxic byproducts of one group sustaining the other has come into being.

The atheist looks at this miracle and marvels at the ability of nature to produce it. The theist looks at it and marvels at the ability and goodness of God for the same reason. It is such a simple flip of perception that makes such a dramatic difference. Part of this bias against God on the part of

196

atheists seems to be that the intelligent designer argument is too easy and that it discourages scientific inquiry and advancement. Say what? This argument confuses what is plausible and probable with what is easy. By this logic we should ignore Occam's Razor and seek the most complex and convoluted solution to every problem or question we encounter. It also assumes that scientists who believe in God (including the closet believers who would be laughed out of their profession if they admitted belief) are not interested in discovering how God works His magic. I don't think so.

Without any rational reason to justify the leap of logic, atheists use natural selection as an excuse to deny the existence of God. The whole exercise seems to be another desperate attempt to dismiss the simplest, and therefore most plausible cause of the rich diversity of life on earth. The scientific community dismisses the need for God even though God is a much more plausible explanation than natural processes only. This attitude smacks of desperation; that is it demonstrates that scientists are more interested in dismissing God than they are in discovering what is the simplest and best explanation for the diversity of life on earth.

Other arguments as evidence of God's non-existence

The most common excuse cited as "proof" that God does not exist is the prevalence of suffering in the world, especially as caused by man's inhumanity to man. This is an intellectually lazy argument, especially if humans have free will, which the atheist must accept if there is no God. The logic presumes that 1) suffering is bad, 2) if God did exist, He would never allow anything bad to occur, 3) suffering exists, 4) therefore there is no God. The atheist has constructed a simple syllogism that supports their belief that God does not exist because there is suffering. However, if we critically analyze this logic, we can easily see that none of the premises on which the conclusion rests can be proven (remember that the burden of proof is on the person proposing the line of reasoning).This syllogism is no more valid than the argument that all birds fly that was disproved in a previous chapter.

Is suffering always bad? I would suggest that most (if not all) of the knowledge and technology that we have developed over the millennia is a direct response to suffering and our efforts to mitigate its effects. Our reaction to suffering is to develop the means to avoid or ameliorate it. Would we have genetically engineered crops over the millennia to increase harvests without the specter of starvation hanging over our heads? I don't think so. Suffering is a prime motivation for the progress we make, both as a people and as individuals.

Is it possible that God would deliberately inflict pain and suffering? Although many do not like the answer, if the records we have that purport to document God's dealings with man are accurate, it is clearly yes. Numerous instances where God has used suffering as a means of achieving a specific objective are described in scripture. It is rational to assume that there are still good reasons for God to inflict suffering as a means to an end. Atheists use this line of logic to then claim that God is either bad because He allows these "bad" events to occur, or is uncaring, either of which disqualify Him as being suitable as God. This logic presumes that suffering is bad and that a God who is interested in the progression of His creations would not use suffering as the most effective tool to advance that progression. As discussed above, we can ourselves think of good reasons why this would be the case, let alone reasons known only to God. We tend to overemphasize the short-term negative effects of suffering, when in fact suffering has been the impetus for most of human progress through time.

Much of the suffering that occurs is a direct result of man's inhumanity toward man. Is it possible that God would allow others to inflict suffering? If there is such a thing as free will, the answer is clearly yes. If humans are free to choose for themselves, it only makes sense that the actions we take, individually and collectively, are our own and not the responsibility of God. If God did not allow us to make unwise decisions that inevitably bring suffering on others and ourselves, we would not have free will.

Free will is an integral part of the atheistic belief system; if there is no God then human action is controlled only by individual humans and whatever influence society as a whole imposes on individual actions. Free will then is either a gift from God given for a specific purpose, or the result of the fact that we humans have randomly occurred and our self-interests are the only determining factor in the decisions we make. It is clear that we can have free will and still be subject to a God who has communicated precepts to us that proscribe our behavior to our benefit. It is also clear that atheists believe in free will and therefore the argument that God does not exist because He allows people to inflict suffering on others is moot.

The argument that God does not exist because of the existence of suffering then is simply a theoretical possibility that cannot be supported by fact. It is illogical to argue that suffering, especially suffering that is either self-inflicted or inflicted by the bad choices of others, demonstrates that God is evil because He allows bad things to occur or that He does not exist because He would not allow bad things to occur. For atheists to whine about it betrays a fundamental misunderstanding about the role of suffering in our lives and throughout history.

It is worth noting here that harboring ill will toward God because of suffering is not atheism. If one resents God's lack of action to protect someone from pain and suffering and withholds worship or respect as a result (much as a small child will throw a temper tantrum when disciplined by a parent), the underlying belief is still that God exists.

This point illustrates the basic attitude of atheists and the fundamental intellectual weakness of their arguments. They think that the mere ability to think of theories and possibilities that could justify their belief is evidence or proof of their position. The leap from theoretical possibility to citation of proof is made without any of the physical proof they demand from those who believe in God. For example, atheists love to equate belief in God with belief in a Flying Spaghetti Monster, inferring that there is no evidence of either, that it is illogical to speculate on the existence of an entity that obviously has almost zero probability of existence, and ridiculing belief in either as equally improbable. What they fail so see is their own arguments dismissing the existence of God is just another Flying Spaghetti Monster argument from the opposite point of view. In short, they grasp at any straw that they can conceive to justify their logically weak belief.

The conclusions they reach are made using the knowledge that we humans have accumulated. While I agree that we have a lot of knowledge (not to be confused with truth), I would also argue that there is much that we do not know. I think most people, including those in the scientific community, will agree. Indeed, normally the discovery of one fact alone results in the generation of many dozens of associated questions. And yet the atheist points to our limited base of knowledge and proclaims that because proof of God's existence is not obvious in that body of knowledge we are justified in saying conclusively that He does not exist.

This is the equivalent of someone who, looking at the night sky, fails to see God and then proclaims conclusively that He does not exist. Even with sophisticated tools that look deep into space and back through time to observe events that occurred not long after the creation of the universe, we still have many more questions than answers, and certainly do not know of everything in the universe. The atheistic who uses this argument is colossally arrogant and breathtakingly closed minded. Indeed, this is the same attitude that religious zealots had when they persecuted scientific methods in pursuing truth during the Dark Ages.

199

God and Religion

What other justification can be used as "proof" that God does not exist? The most common is the lack of physical evidence of God's existence, but as I described in Chapter 16, that argument is wholly dependant on how one looks at the evidence. The atheist looks at the evidence from their theoretical viewpoint and refuses to allow the possibility that another viewpoint or that abundant evidence supporting the existence of God is plausible. They take facts that support the existence of God and construct alternative explanations that support their belief, even if their explanation is far more implausible to the rational mind than the acceptance of the facts as supporting God's existence.

Even worse, they ridicule those who do believe in God, and publish written works and internet blogs that hold that those who believe are dupes, suckers, stupid, or leeches on the productivity of others. What motivation is there for one to come to this conclusion? As I said at the beginning of this chapter, I believe it is a result of the person being lazy, stupid, cowardly, dishonest, or some combination of the four, exactly the opposite of what they suppose to be their enlightened position.

Types of atheists

Some do not want to make the effort needed to rigorously think through the scientific, philosophical, and theological questions that we are forced to deal with when trying to determine whether there is a God or not. It is much easier to have someone else think for them. Incidentally, this harsh judgment also applies to one who blindly accepts the existence of God solely because of the thoughts or teachings of others. Each person must think through the arguments for themselves, and make a decision about important theological questions based on their own good judgment, not the judgment of someone else whose interests, obvious or ulterior, may be in conflict with their own. The person who blindly accepts that there is no God because that is the easiest way out of the confusion surrounding the argument is simply lazy.

Many cite the lack of believing scientists as support for their intellectually lazy conclusion. If God exists, why don't scientists believe in Him? Of course, many atheist scientists fuel this trend, openly arguing that the lack of believing scientists is evidence that religion is only the province of the uneducated and unenlightened.

This is a circular argument. While in the past many scientists openly expressed belief in God, since the 19th century fewer and fewer are willing to acknowledge belief. This could be the result of 1) there is less social and legal pressure to express a belief in something not really believed, or 2) since the evolutionist's assertion that natural selection ostensibly accounts for the diversity of life without the need for God, those who choose to believe in God have been subject to ridicule by the majority of intellectuals and scientists. I would argue the latter is accurate. Indeed, the more prestigious the scientific organization or award, the more likely it is that the members of the organization or beneficiaries of the award are atheist, or at least agnostic. Fewer and fewer are willing to commit professional suicide by expressing a belief in God. The net result is that there are very few believers, not because it is the intellectually unenlightened position, but because believers are effectively excluded or forced to conform. The circular argument then is that all believers are unenlightened; therefore, they cannot be included in this exclusive body of enlightened individuals, therefore, no unenlightened individuals who believe in God belong to this prestigious group, therefore all believers are unenlightened.

This condition is the reverse of the intellectual climate of the Dark Ages when the Catholic Church mandated faith. Now professional organizations effectively mandate non-belief. A good example may be Fred Hoyle, who was somehow denied a deserved share of the Nobel Prize in 1983, remarkably enough shortly after he made a presentation in support of intelligent design. Ben Stein, in a remarkably good documentary entitled Expelled, No Intelligence Allowed interviewed a number of scientists who have suffered the wrath of the scientific establishment. Their sin was not to advocate in behalf of intelligent design, but to simply write or speak the words in anything other than a critical manner. The discussion of the subject is forbidden in current science.

By the way, I highly recommend the documentary, it is enlightening. In addition, I visited a website that ostensibly refuted Mr. Stein's work and found their arguments to be circular. They insist they won't take intelligent design seriously because there has been no satisfactory research or empirical evidence to support it, therefore there will be no research effort or evidence developed because it is unworthy of investigation.

Incidentally, it is not just religion where professionals are required to tow the official line. Any scientist who strays from the global warming reservation is quickly slapped down if they don't knuckle under. Or just try to find a psychiatrist that believes that homosexuality is aberrant behavior regardless of the misuse of digestive and reproductive organs associated with that lifestyle. Indeed, it is with considerable irony that the scientific community often seems to be the least open to alternative explanations and solutions to problems. Their orthodoxy is much more dogmatic than the Catholics ever were during the Dark Ages. And if a scientist deviates from that orthodoxy, watch out. To paraphrase another cliché, hell hath no fury like a scientist whose orthodoxy is scorned.

I suspect that there are many closet believers among scientific ranks who value their professional reputation more than their faith. For that matter, there are likely large numbers of people of every profession who choose to avoid personal and professional ridicule and scorn heaped upon religious believers, especially Christians. It has been open season on Christian beliefs for a long time, and many choose to remove themselves from the fight. These are the cowards that I describe, those who are afraid to intellectually defend their faith.

Others who assert there is no God are not the brightest people in the world. They conclude there is no God without thinking out the complexity of the question based on a narrow experience or exposure to ideas. They reach conclusions without understanding the evidence and facts. If these people were in a class setting presenting this argument, the professor would appropriately give them a failing grade and note that they are intellectually challenged. If you are going to have a worldview, you should be able to defend it coherently.

Then there is the dishonest group, those who reach their conclusions because it gives them the perceived freedom to act as they wish without restraint. They have come to their conclusion based on the outcome they desired, not the result of where an examination of the facts would lead them. Their beliefs generally support a lifestyle in opposition to the Judeo-Christian values held by the majority in the United States, and by all the major religions of the world for that matter. For instance, much of their behavior would result in execution in most Islamic societies. They convince themselves that they are free to engage in whatever hedonistic pursuit they desire, and that there will be no consequences unless society as a whole has proscribed the behavior. Even then, they are engaged in a wholesale assault on the laws that support these values, and seek to allow behavior that is anathema to most people. The North American Man-Boy Love Association (NAMBLA) is perhaps the best example of this trend. The organization lobbies legislatures to allow consensual sexual relations between male children and male adults. I recall a boast several decades ago at a gay rally, at which an enthusiastic participant proclaimed, "We will sodomize your children!" Unfortunately, many predators are doing this now, but it will be much worse if NAMBLA achieves their political goals.

A principle motivation of the dishonest is to avoid guilt. They believe that by asserting there is no God they then can act as they wish without feeling guilty about their actions. Unfortunately for them (and everyone else), it is evident that they still feel guilt. This is demonstrated by their antipathy toward religion and those who believe in it. They decry in the most vociferous terms the laws that unfairly restrict their behavior, and rail at the effect of religion on those laws. Listening to these diatribes, the thought "methinks thou doest protest too much" comes to mind. The depth of the hate they demonstrate betrays the guilt that they cannot escape.

Ironically enough, if we were to use their logic against them, they would be enraged even more. If there is no God, and therefore no right or wrong and that society does not have the right to proscribe their actions based on Judeo-Christian ideals, it follows that the same ideals that have resulted in freedom and tolerance are also groundless values that can be discarded and ignored. We the majority can make whatever decisions we wish without thought for the rights of the minority. The supposition made within the Declaration of Independence, that "all men are created equal, and they are endowed by their creator with unalienable rights, including life, liberty, and the pursuit of happiness" can be disregarded and we no longer need to treat others as equal nor afford them life, liberty, or the pursuit of happiness. We can exercise our power as the majority to dismiss them, shout them down, prevent them from expressing their viewpoints, and be rude and arrogant in our attitude (this reminds me of something that I just can't put my finger on). We can even incarcerate or execute them. If there is not a God, what difference would it make? The immediate interests of the majority would be satisfied. Fortunately for them, and us, because of our belief in God we value freedom of expression and have incorporated beliefs into our law that tolerate differences in our society.

The evolution of western civilization, with the high value it places on life, liberty, happiness, freedom, equality, tolerance, and ethics, is the result of many millennia of religious teaching and its civilizing effect (as defined by our current culture) on humans whose individual tendency it is to act in opposition to these values. The atheist denigrates both the beliefs and the people who have brought us to where we are tolerant of their viewpoint. They would bite off that hand that feeds the perpetuation of their philosophy.

Chapter 18

"Freedom from Religion"

In the United States, the First Amendment of the Constitution grants individuals the freedom to worship as they see fit. This basic right is properly coupled with other basic freedoms, including speech, assembly, press, and the ability to petition government to redress grievances. These rights are inseparably connected, that is they depend on each other for the proper perpetuation of them all. If there is no free speech, it is not possible to worship according to the dictates of our consciences. If there is no freedom of religion, there cannot possibly be free speech. A free press is free speech, and the freedom to assemble is also the freedom to worship and speak. Similar arguments can be made linking the other rights enumerated in the First Amendment.

It is important to remember that these rights, as are most of the rights enumerated in the Bill of Rights, are guaranteed to the people. The Establishment Clause of the First Amendment simply restricts government from dictating religious belief to individuals and favoring one religious group over another. It does not guarantee that religious belief will not affect government (more on this in Chapter 2), and certainly does not guarantee that there will be no religious conflict on the part of proponents of different religious beliefs. Indeed, this notion is utterly ridiculous. If there is more than one set of religious beliefs, including atheistic belief, there will be conflict between them. When this inevitable conflict occurs, it is clear the amendment requires that government not take sides in the conflict except to keep the peace, require religious organizations to conform to the law, and prohibit the imposition of religious belief on others.

When we discuss religious belief, we need to keep in mind that this includes all belief about religion. Religious belief often denote faith in God, usually a supreme supernatural being known as Allah, Jehovah, Yahweh, Christ, or Shiva to name a few of the deities worshiped depending on the specific religion; however, it also includes non-belief in those deities also. Some major religions do not believe in a Supreme Being or force, but believe that the human purpose is to find enlightenment, fulfillment, and his or her place in society. Buddhism and Confucianism are notable examples. This philosophy also applies to Atheism. If one is an atheist, one affirmatively asserts that there is no God. That is clearly a religious belief in that it is a belief related to God, not much different from the religions that do not believe in God in the same sense as the major monotheistic religions to which we are accustomed. Atheism and Agnosticism describe a set of beliefs that define the adherent's attitude and belief about God; therefore, they deal with religious beliefs and are religions in the broad sense of the term.

If there really is freedom of religion, it follows that adherents of religious groups have the ability to do what they perceive is their religious duty so long as their actions are in conformance with the law. In the case of atheists, they will proclaim that there is no God, seek to persuade others to their beliefs, and seek to reduce the influence of those who have competing religious beliefs on public policy. Fair enough. It also follows that those who believe in God have the same right; that is they can seek to persuade people to accept their beliefs and to reduce the influence of believers of competing religious principles on public policy. That is fair also. In the marketplace of ideas, everyone gets to listen to the arguments from various religious groups, choose what religion they prefer, act as they deem best for themselves, and seek to influence public policy in accordance with their beliefs.

This system works well as long as government is a neutral observer, acts only to prevent violence between groups and religious practices that are in conflict with law (such as ritual human sacrifice to use an extreme example), and adopts public policy that promotes the health, safety, and welfare of its population. By the way, good public policy that has its antecedents in religious philosophy is still good public policy. However, if government takes sides in religious conflict, it is in effect sponsoring one religious group over the other with the favored group becoming a state sponsored religion.

In this context, we have a common complaint among those whose religion does not include a belief in God that any reference to God in a public forum is offensive to them. Others who have a dramatically different perception of God will claim offense if another competing perception intrudes upon them. They claim that they are entitled to be free from exposure to religious beliefs in conflict with their religious beliefs. They certainly have the right to ignore religious speech that they deem offensive and can politely ask that advocates of religious philosophies not solicit their participation in their activities or discussions. What they definitely do not have the right to do is suppress the rights of other religious groups in freely speaking about their religious beliefs in the course of public debate. There is no right, expressed or implied, of a freedom from religion.

It certainly is true that there should be no person within the United States who is forced to accept religious belief (including atheistic belief). If there are religious groups insisting that a person convert or die, that person has recourse in civil and criminal law. Indeed, no religious organization in the United States has the authority or ability to deprive any person of life, liberty, or property, with the exception that religious organizations may enter into voluntary legal contracts just as any other organization and may legally defend those contracts. If a religious group wants to punish a member for theological apostasy or some other infraction of organization's rules, their only recourse is to deny that person the friendship and religious rights accorded to their group.

That said, being forced to accept belief is a far cry from being exposed to belief. The idea that any individual has the right to be insulated from religious ideas in conflict with their belief is preposterous at its core. Society and culture is grounded in and inextricably connected to religious belief and a healthy debate about it. It is impossible to separate religion from public speech. This is a lot like a fish saying it does not want to have anything to do with water as it swims from place to place and removes the oxygen needed for its survival from the water. The only way that someone can be free of competing religious beliefs is to completely divorce them from any other human contact.

The intensity of the feeling that many of the people who insist that they not be exposed to religious thought is remarkable to me. To paraphrase Shakespeare, methinks that those who complain bitterly about being forced to endure exposure to such dangerous and horrific beliefs as faith, tolerance, compassion, and making decisions that could possibly lead to permanent happiness (insert heavy sarcasm here) doth protest too much. It seems to me that their weak grounding in their own belief and lack of confidence in their ability to logically persuade others make it imperative that they suppress the religious rights of believers in order to have any hope of persuading weak and uniformed individuals to their cause.

This is just another argument among many seeking to reduce or eliminate religious influence on public policy. That the argument has the effect of suppressing constitutionally protected rights makes no difference. In particular, atheists and secularists, with the direct support of the American Civil Liberties Union (ACLU) use this argument in an attempt to ban traditional religious groups from the public square. They are comfortable with religious speech conducted in the privacy of the home or in places of worship, but not in any public setting. In effect, they seek to prevent those that have traditional Judeo-Christian belief from having a voice in formulating public policy based on those beliefs (see Chapter 2).

The argument is essentially the same as people from the Flat Earth Society arguing that the earth is flat and that scientists that propound the theory that the earth is round should be prevented from presenting evidence supporting the fact that the earth is a sphere to anyone except those who already believe the earth is round. Even though atheists have no empirical evidence whatsoever that there is no God, (just as the Flat Earth believers have no evidence that the earth is flat), they seek the ability to convert everyone, especially children in school, to their belief and at the same time prohibit the introduction of empirical evidence contradicting their beliefs. This is the same as holding a debate but not letting the opposition speak at the debate. This is a well-worn tactic by totalitarian regimes who do not want anyone to question their leadership. Do we really want to use this as a pattern for determining what discourse is allowed?

As previously discussed, they have succeeded in their goal to a large extent. Religious symbols have been ordered to be removed from public buildings, lands, and logos. Religious speech is stifled in public hearings. Most importantly, religious speech in public schools is harshly punished, especially if a teacher has the audacity to mention a religious belief. This is true even though the speech may be a response to a direct question. Therefore, not only are the rights of the teacher being flagrantly violated, the ability of students to enjoy a free and open discussion of competing ideas is destroyed. The ACLU has so intimidated school districts across the country with the threat of lawsuits designed to stifle speech and the interchange of ideas between people that even graduation speakers are directed to not speak of religious beliefs. If the instructions of the school district are ignored they turn off the microphone of the offender. The good news is that many are challenging these policies with some success.

In the end, everyone is obligated to deal with competing ideas as they arise, including religious ideas (or is it especially religious ideas?). Those whose religious beliefs reject the concept of God are not free to impose their religious beliefs on those who do accept the existence of God. Indeed, if a believer in a religious concept is so weak in their belief that they cannot logically deal with other beliefs, they should consider changing their belief to one that they are more comfortable in defending in a public forum. In any case, everyone will just have to learn to get along with the natural exchange of ideas that results from healthy religious debate.

Chapter 19

"Religion is Evil and Should be Banned"

This assertion seems to have become increasingly popular of late. Many think that religion is the root of all evil, and that if society did not have religion to fight about and use for evil purposes that everyone would be better off. Of course, those who believe in traditional religions worry that if this philosophy gained widespread acceptance by a majority that the majority would then attempt to ban these organizations, prohibit the exercise of free speech, prohibit the use of religious ideals in formulating legislation, and exercise thought control. Their concerns would be justified. While I suppose it is possible that this could be accomplished, I kinda doubt it.

I am not aware of any successful attempt to exercise this kind of domination over people in the history of the world, although Joseph Stalin certainly tried. The notion that religion and its effects could be banned is utterly ridiculous. Saying they should be banned because they are evil can be just as ridiculous, depending on the religion that is being evaluated.

One thing is certain. This is an unambiguous assault on the Judeo-Christian values that have shaped our culture, and as such it is one of the most obvious fronts in the culture war. If a majority of the population became convinced that religion is evil and should be banned, our culture would be transformed. Remember we already have ample precedent for banning religious practices repugnant to the majority. If all religious practice became repugnant to the majority, religious practitioners would have serious problems.

Those who advocate for a ban on religion should be careful of what they ask for; a careful evaluation of what constitutes religion may show that such a ban would affect the followers of non-traditional religions as much as it would those that believe in traditional religion. The law of Unintended Consequences is operable always (my definition - whatever action is taken will result in unanticipated outcomes that create additional problems beyond the intended solution, often worse than the original problem).

It is important to note that beliefs concerning the cause, nature, and purpose of the universe include the conviction that there is no cause of or purpose to the universe. Further, a moral code governing the conduct of human affairs can include belief in moral code based on secular values, which may value principles in opposition to traditional religion. I say this to emphasize my assertion that atheism is a religion, and will be included in this analysis as such.

Unfortunately, I have never known of anyone that proclaims religion is evil refer to any group other than those religious organizations that subscribe to traditional religious values. It is only those who have faith in God and the organizations to which they belong, or faith in a set of principles that will lead to human enlightenment or social stability that are accused of being evil. Atheists, and secularists are not included; we therefore are left to assume that these groups are not considered to be evil, even though they advocate for legislation that removes proscriptions on traditionally evil behavior. Again, NAMBLA serves as the poster example of this.

At the same time, because atheists consider themselves non-religious, they claim a special status when it comes to arguments about the separation of church and state. They argue with a straight face their belief that there is no God is not a set of beliefs dealing with belief in God. The result is that they argue, again with a straight face, that their involvement in school, government, and public forums is acceptable while other religious speech and demonstrations are not.

The beliefs of those with faith in God frequently interfere with the ability of those with polar opposite beliefs to act as they wish, especially when the majority imposes their will on the minority and restricts the behavior of those who would act against what the majority perceive to be in the public interest. Most of the time, the term is used by those who wish to be free from the social and mental constraints of religious doctrine that forms the foundation for established law (see Chapters 1 and 2).

Getting back to the subject of the chapter, just because some assert with self-serving interests that religion is evil, it does not follow that they are correct. I propose to examine the rationales used to support the allegation and see if they can be substantiated. So what are the reasons behind the accusation? I am aware of the following:

- Religion is a means of exercising power over people, making them afraid of the consequences of disobedience, which then allows those who control doctrinal issues to control the behavior of believers to the benefit of the religious leadership and the detriment of the believer.
- Religion is just another means of obtaining wealth from the gullible or obtaining other evil advantages, essentially an elaborate con game.
- Religion is the opiate of the masses.

- Religion gives those on the extreme ideological spectrum an excuse and vehicle to persuade malleable individuals to destructive practices and beliefs.
- Religion is seen as the principle cause of conflict, war, and suffering throughout human history.
- Religion is evil because it is ostensibly the root of discrimination and bias. This includes the belief that because the religious group is "chosen" by God, that others are inferior, or that because doctrines proscribe behaviors those who practice the behaviors are seen as inferior.
- Religion is a massive waste of time and resources.
- Religion divides people and sets them against each other instead of uniting them.

My goodness, those are powerful accusations. If in fact religion is guilty of them, I would change my mind and take up the crusade against it. However, these accusations are really the same old arguments that have been debunked by every previous generation. Unfortunately, unlike old facts that when disproved are relegated to the dustbin of knowledge, these ideas keep coming back as if nobody ever thought of them before and no one ever addressed the issues before. It is the same as repeatedly debunking the notions of the Flat Earth Society, except that nobody gives the Flat Earth Society's arguments any credence. However, for some reason the fallacious arguments against religion must be debunked over and over again. So here we go with my rendition of why these accusations do not hold up under critical analysis.

Before taking each justification in turn, I will stipulate that religion can be evil, just as politics, economic practices, or any other human philosophy or activity. Not all religions and religious beliefs are equal. If a religion holds beliefs in direct conflict with the values that society deems as good, it follows that relative to that culture the religion will be evil. For instance, if we have a group of Aztec wannabes that believe that dragging people to the top of a stone temple and cutting their hearts out with an obsidian knife will make God happy, in our culture we can clearly state that to be an evil religion (I know, I use this example repeatedly, but it beautifully illustrates the point). If the religion teaches love, tolerance, wisdom, and civility, most people will justifiably conclude that the religion is good because of the effect it has on society as a whole.

However, the same can be said of any other human activity. For instance, a political party that advocates the violent destruction of the representative government that we enjoy in the United States and the installation of a totalitarian regime in its place is also clearly evil from our perspective. An economic theory that advocates the forced expropriation of all goods without payment to those that produce them is also considered evil by our society (so far at least). What is evil is not whether there is religion, religious thought, political thought, economic thought, or any other field of study, thought or activity. What is evil is determined by the stance of any particular religion, political party, or other entity and whether that stance is in agreement with what the majority of society has determined to be wrong.

Exercise of Power

Is the purpose of religion to exercise control over the population? Many believe it is. Even though to a degree this is desirable (see next paragraph), those who make this accusation tend to attach sinister motives to this purpose. They perceive that the purpose of religion is to oppress the population and ensure that they do not speak up to take advantage of the opportunities they have, or to enforce standards of behavior that are unjustifiable. I beg to differ.

I will stipulate that most religions do have that end in mind as a secondary goal. The premise is that religion puts pressure on their adherents to conform to cultural norms and help maintain social stability. I also agree that religion largely succeeds in this effort. However, it is an incidental effect in most cultures. Put that way, most will see the social advantages that religion brings. For those who leap from the obvious positive stabilizing effect that religion has to conclude that social stability equals mind control or oppression, I would suggest that any social institution that has the same purpose and effect would be similarly denigrated. If we argue that religion is evil because it has this effect, we are essentially arguing that all organizations that have the same positive effects are bad. This seems just a tad counterproductive to me.

Social stability can be maintained by appeals to nationality, culture, ethnicity, economic interest, the human ties between us all, and other uniting influences. If we argue that religion is evil because it affects behavior thereby stabilizing society, would we not also need to question whether these other factors are evil because they can have the same effect? Indeed, we would be compelled to question the value of social stability. In any case, reasoning that religion is evil because it can result in social stability denigrates the value of social stability and other institutions that have the same effect.

In most cases, social stability is not the goal of the religious group. Confucianism is a notable exception. Religious organizations and individuals are principally motivated by their perception that their ideology represents truth. Those that believe this are motivated to act on their beliefs consistent with what they perceive to be true. Social stability becomes irrelevant if the ideology of the dominant culture is in conflict with those religious beliefs, and conflict, not social stability, is the result. Again, social stability is secondary to the goals of the religious group.

What of other more sinister motives on the part of religious groups? Is religion used to oppress people, forcing them to act against their interests or the interests of society? Here the answer is both yes and no. Once again, there are religions that believe in and practice evil. From our cultural standpoint, those are easy to identify and condemn. That said, it is important to distinguish between the adherents of a religion and the religion itself. We cannot judge a religion's philosophy simply because the believers in the philosophy are not perfect in its execution. Indeed, most religions look on the human condition with sympathy, and teach that progress toward whatever is the ultimate goal of the religion is accomplished incrementally.

Across the spectrum of religions, there will be some established to accomplish goals not articulated in their beliefs (in other words, they are hypocrites in that they say one thing and intend another); however an evaluation of effect of any religion should reveal this. In order to evaluate whether the purpose of a specific religion is to exert evil control, we need to look past the practices of the people in it and focus on the underlying organization and teachings. If the founder of the religion taught that the religion was to be used as an instrument for social control, it is a safe bet that is at least one of its purposes. If not, a careful evaluation of the effect of the remainder of the teachings of the founder should show the cumulative effect of those teachings. Doctrine that has evolved and which may have as its result the creation of a new religions group with distinctive teachings should be examined in the context of the new religion.

To determine whether the religion's purpose or de-facto effect is social control can be seen in the effect of the teachings on the various individuals within the group. If there are a significant number of adherents that believe they lack the freedom to make choices in their lives, a good case can be made that there is at least an element of social control in the mission of the religion. If the vast majority freely choose to follow the teachings of the organization, it is a good bet that social control is not a major factor, especially if they are free to dissociate themselves from the group for one reason or another and can do so without any consequences other than membership in the organization and fellowship with other believers. If individuals are threatened with physical or economic sanctions for apostasy, clearly there is a problem, either with improper actions by misguided people, or the organization itself may be evil.

Do religious organizations oppress those who belong to the organization? The vast majority do not, at least in western cultures. The same facts in the preceding paragraph can be cited as evidence. No one in our culture is holding a gun to the head of responsible adults and forcing them to believe, contribute, attend worship services, or anything like it. The only real control the organization can exert is to withhold membership and fellowship with the group.

Some contend that the oppression is mental and that even if there is no physical force, the organization is oppressive by virtue of the threat of spiritual punishment, social ostracization, and economic punishment by severing or withholding social or economic contacts. While there are misguided individuals who do use these intimidating and oppressive means to attempt to keep believers in spiritual line, few religious organizations do so. The evidence for this is in the fluid state of the membership of most of these organizations. In the United States people quit and join various religious organizations with relative ease and minimal social and economic disruption. This is as it should be.

Do religious organizations control government to the detriment of individuals, groups, and other religions? I think the answer is a resounding no. In the United States, as in most western cultures, no one religious group controls the legislative agenda. To be sure, they have an impact on legislation as the members of the organization exercise their First Amendment rights, as they should. But believers in non-traditional beliefs have the same opportunity, including those that are diametrically opposed to traditional values. If the goal of religion is to oppress the population by legislative means, it is doing a very poor job.

When viewed in this context, I believe the vast majority of the world's religions exist to provide guidance to those that believe in them. That social stability is the net result of a culture with compatible ideologies is an effect of that purpose, and is not a malevolent expression of an evil religion.

Certainly the predominant religious organizations in the west do not oppress their membership or non-members.

Religion is a means of extracting wealth or advantage

This is a common complaint. The logic is that swindlers prey on the emotions and faith of others in order to enrich themselves or to exert control in order to obtain personal gratification, including sexual gratification. The best example I can think of is James Bakker, and the sordid affair he literally forced on his secretary, Jessica Hahn. Of course, there will be charlatans who will twist, distort, lie, and pervert religious motivations to get gain or to abuse others. However, does that make religion evil?

If a religion, whose stated purpose is to accomplish specific goals for its membership, collects funds from its members to accomplish these goals, and then proceeds to follow through and use the funds for those stated purposes, it seems difficult to argue that the religion is guilty of this charge. If some have unlawfully utilized church funds, they can and should be prosecuted for embezzlement. Others outside the organization may hold the use of the resources to be misguided or even evil; however, it is hard to argue that the religion is betraying its believers and taking money under false pretenses. That is even harder to assert if the resources are used to meet goals that are valued by the community or culture.

Further, if those in authority within a religious organization do not use their position to gain favors, especially sexual favors in direct conflict with the teachings of the organization, it also seems unfair to call the religion evil. If those who do take advantage of others inappropriately are disciplined and removed from their position so they cannot have the chance to misuse authority again, it seems that the religion itself should not be characterized as evil. Here again we need to compare what individuals do in contrast with the religion and its mission. The intent of the religion, its use of contributions, and overall actions to benefit its adherents without any evil intent should be the measure of whether it is evil or not. Individuals acting in conflict with that mission are not an appropriate measure of the value of the group.

Religion is the opiate of the masses

Karl Marx famously asserted this to be the case. It implies that religion is a narcotic that most people take to avoid reality, and they therefore live as if in a drug-induced stupor, unthinking and unable to deal with the reality of the world. I believe the evidence debunks this popular myth.

Secularists generally think that religious believers are unthinking in their devotion to their traditional religious beliefs and that they have little or no intellectual support for their beliefs. Of course, I would argue otherwise (and did so in Chapters 16 and 17). Contrary to popular opinion, there are not that many mindless believing zombies out there that attempt to defend the indefensible. In fact, if you engage any thoughtful and informed religious believer about the justification for their beliefs you will find ample intellectual support for the belief, indeed, generally much more support than can be found for religious beliefs that deny the existence of God

To argue that those that believe in God are mindless and unthinking is to denigrate the thought and intelligence of some of the most brilliant people in the history of the world, including Sir Isaac Newton. To be sure, their belief in God does not prove His existence, but it does prove that one can believe in God and still be a functional, thoughtful, and intellectual member of society. I would argue that religious belief is a positive indicator of a strong intellect inasmuch as the believer goes with the preponderance of evidence rather than raw emotion coupled with the desire to justify unfettered personal gratification.

Religion gives fringe groups the opportunity for evil.

Sad to say, this is true to some degree; there are some religious leaders on the fringe of society who are dangerous and evil. Some religious ideas are off the charts on the spectrum of sound thinking and are so extreme in their religious beliefs that they conflict with their culture and take their adherents down with them. Religious extremists can and do perpetuate evil and give moderate and tolerant religious groups a bad name. The Jim Jones's of the world truly are a threat to the general public. Islamic fundamentalists are even more dangerous and pose a significant threat to the survival of our culture.

However, to use this fact to condemn all religion as evil is just as misguided as asserting that fringe political elements with evil intent make all political groups evil. Once again, we need to look at the effect that a religion has on the individuals within it and the society in which it exists.

In The God Delusion, Mr. Dawkins condemns religious extremists. So far, so good. But then he goes on to accuse any and all religious belief of being responsible for extremists and extremism. He concludes that moderate religion is evil because it begets extremists. How absurd. By that measure any political party or ideology, including atheism, is evil. In fact, no matter what the topic of conversation (even weather when global warming issues arise) there will be those that take a moderate approach and those that take opposing extreme positions. He is in effect arguing that we should not form political parties, join unions, form community groups, or even discuss the weather because extremism will result. To argue that moderation in any form is evil because it results in extremes is to argue that we should have no organization of any kind or opinion, belief, or preference about anything.

In addition to those whose beliefs defy rational explanation, unfortunately, there are some who believe in sound ideology so emphatically that they lose perspective and use the ideology in evil ways. Those who try to intimidate, use force, or otherwise harangue people into doing what they perceive is right do the organization or group to which they belong a tremendous disservice.

By the way, it is not just believers in God that suffer from this problem, we should remember that some atheists are so convinced of the accuracy of their claims that they fall into the same trap, some even to the point of murdering those who believe in God (as occurred in the Columbine atrocity). Mr. Dawkins entitles one of the chapters in <u>The God Delusion</u> as "What's wrong with religion? Why be so Hostile?"[24] implying that hostility is the province of theists who want to impose their religious beliefs on others. In fact, many atheists are as enthusiastic about imposing their beliefs as are theists, and some take as hostile an approach to that effort as do theists. That is understandable, they have as much missionary zeal in converting adherents to their cause as do the believers in traditional religions. However, that hostility can and does have deadly consequences. Mr. Dawkins is naïve if he thinks that religious violence originates only from theists.

Religion is the cause of conflict, war, and suffering
First, let me stipulate that differences in religious belief have indeed been the source of much conflict throughout history. Such conflict ranges the spectrum from mild disagreements between friends to intense annihilating war between cultures and nations. However, it does not follow that religion is evil just because there is conflict over religious belief. Wars have been fought, but often they have been fought to defend the values of

---

[24] Dawkins, chapter 8

the culture and the ability to live according to those values. Often, wars are the result of ideological differences and the desire on the part of extremists to force other groups to accept their ideology. Other wars are simply an attempt to defend the group against non-ideological tyrants bent on destruction out of hate, the quest for power, or the acquisition of wealth. Not all wars are evil.

By the way, the potential for conflict when people, groups, and nations have differing values, including religious and political values, is all the more reason for individuals, groups and nations to discuss these differences and learn to peacefully resolve the inevitable conflict. See Chapter 22 for more on this subject.

As emphasized before, not all religions are equal. That is, many religions have diametrically opposing beliefs, and only one set of integrated and interrelated beliefs can be true. If one set of beliefs differ from another, both of them cannot be right, that is both of them cannot reflect an accurate portrait of what actually is. At least one of them will be wrong. It also follows that if one or both of them are wrong, one or both of them can be evil. However, if the beliefs are opposing, it is unlikely that both will be wrong and evil, it is much more likely that one of them is correct and good. This logic alone is sufficient to debunk the subject of this chapter; it is difficult to argue that the opposite of evil is evil.

It also follows that conflict will result when religious groups with opposing ideas interact. This is true even when the religions believe in a monotheistic God, differing only in who they perceive that God to be. The discussion below about the series of wars between Christian and Muslim nations is perhaps the best example. It is even more likely that conflict will arise when a group, such as atheists whose religion asserts there is no God and that there is no right or wrong, interacts with groups with dramatically different and opposing views. Such conflict will be exacerbated when each of these groups try to persuade those with the opposite view that laws should be adopted that reflect their viewpoint.

Religious groups are not evil simply because they advocate for and against public policy, in spite of the statements to the contrary by unthinking individuals. Such groups only deserve to be called evil when the policy positions they promote have an evil effect, or when the methods they use to influence policy are designed to circumvent the rights of others or the legitimate will of the majority. So the assertion that religion is evil is really an assertion by the adherents of one religion that another is evil, and in the case of atheists while trying to claim that their religious beliefs are not religious beliefs.

Much of the justification used to denigrate religion as a force for evil in the world is the numerous wars that have been fought over and about religion. Generally speaking, those who wage war seek to justify their actions with the use of religion, and claim that God is on their side. Remarkably enough, those on whom war is waged also use religion to justify their defensive actions, or actions that provoked the aggressor, and also claim that God is on their side. Aside from the obvious contradiction that God is most certainly not on both sides of any conflict; do the actions of these people make religion evil? I would argue no unless the original philosophy of the founder of the religion can be directly and unambiguously cited as justification for offensive war. If that is not the case, anyone using religion in that way is misrepresenting the religion, knowingly or unknowingly.

It is important to note that I consider defensive wars, including defensive religious wars, as justified. Throughout history, religious believers have been forced to act to preserve themselves and their beliefs. War is evil; however, there are things more evil than war. What is more important; abstinence from war even as you are being attacked, or the advancement or survival of the beliefs and culture that you value while avoiding subjugation or death? The reason most people are willing to go to war and face pain, suffering, and death in the process is to preserve what they perceive to be right, including life, liberty, and the pursuit of happiness. Under some circumstances we have no choice but to go to war in order to preserve the liberty that allows us to select our values.

For example, Genghis Kahn and his successors swept through most of Asia and much of Europe before people who were willing to sacrifice to save western culture stopped their advancement. Charles Martel's defense against Islamic armies bent on the conquest of Europe prevented the Islamization of Europe, and thereby probably preserved Christianity. We have a long and glorious history in this country of being willing to defend our values to the point of going to war to do so, perhaps the most memorable being the quote of Patrick Henry, "Give me liberty or give me death". If we conclude that nothing is worth going to war, we consign ourselves to atrocities, subjugation, and death by those who desire to either destroy us or who wish to impose their values on us. If we want to remain free, sometimes the only choice is to fight. Values and freedom are worth fighting and dying for.

I will stipulate that all offensive wars are evil, including religious wars. Given that, a superficial evaluation of historic religious wars could be cited to support the assertion that religion is evil. The logic is that if offensive religious wars are evil, then a religion which supports offensive wars must also be evil. As logical as it sounds, it is not necessarily true. In some cases, that which is perceived to be a religiously inspired offensive war may not be.

First, some wars that are perceived to be offensive may have been given a bad rap. For instance, Christianity is blamed for the Crusades, and condemned for the effects of the wars and perceived attempts to impose Christianity on the cultures within the Middle East. I am not so sure this accusation is accurate. During these wars, Christians committed atrocities that did not reflect well on them or help their long-term cause; however, it is worth noting that those who instigated the Crusades perceived Islam as a threat to the survival of their religion and culture. Indeed, Muslim armies had only a few short centuries before swept across the Middle East and Northern Africa, forcing those belonging to other religions, including Christianity, to convert, die or accept 2nd class citizenship. The Iberian Peninsula had been overrun by the Moors, and only Charles Martel's victory at the Battle of Tours prevented Islamic expansion into the heart of Europe. Against this historical backdrop, at the time of the First Crusade Islamic forces threatened the Byzantine Empire. A good argument can be made that the Christian nations at the time perceived these wars as defensive. In retrospect, given the actions of Muslim nations in succeeding centuries, especially the Ottoman Empire, their fears were well founded.

The underlying conflict between these respective philosophies rages today, except that only radical jihadists use violence as a means of achieving their goal of the forcible imposition of Islam on the remainder of the world. Less certain is whether those goals are actually based on religion, politics, economics, or the quest for power.

Second, it does not follow that an offensive war instigated using religious ideology as justification for the war is actually instigated in conformance with the ideology of the religion. Sad to say, there are people who will use good ideology for evil purposes. If someone seeks to wage war for an evil end, such as the quest for power, land, resources, or wealth, it is unlikely that the person will be able to persuade enough of his group to wage war unless he can convince them that there is a moral imperative for the war. In that event, the problem is not with the religion or its ideology, but with the misuse of the religion, most often in conflict with its ideology.

It is also worth noting that the lack of faith in God is a religious belief that is just as susceptible to abuse by its adherents as is any other religion. Indeed, if recent history is any indication, it may be more susceptible to abuse. People have much more reason to be worried about atheists gaining power and abusing that power than people whose belief systems include the core values of love, charity, hope, and faith if the record of powerful atheists is considered. Some of the most famous mass murderers of our time, including Pol Pot and Joseph Stalin, were atheists who were unconstrained by belief in the values of traditional religion. For them, power was the ultimate end, and no number of bodies stacked one upon the other deterred them from their goal.

War is ultimately the result of the inability of individuals to peacefully resolve conflict. Societies consist of a mass of individuals. The ability of those individuals to cooperatively resolve their differences without resorting to violence gives the society stability. If within the society there is significant unrest which cannot be resolved through the institutions the society has developed to do so, the society will be destabilized. Here the worse case scenario is civil war.

The same holds true for groups, including nations going to war against other nations. The cause is invariably the result of individuals and interests within the two groups that have staked out opposing positions that they feel cannot be resolved, or have such wildly differing values that violent conflict seems to be the only resort.

While religion often plays a significant role in these conflicts, the fact is that the major religions of the world give incentive to peaceful conflict resolution, especially conflict resolution internal to the group. That result is far from evil.

Speaking of individual behavior and the need to cooperate in order to have a stable society, the same argument made above related to war applies to individual behavior. That is, violent offensive actions of individuals are evil, some actions that seem offensive are not, and many individuals will misuse religion for evil purposes. Just as the evil effect of these actions taken by nations does not mean that religion is evil, the same is also true for individual actions.

The charge that religion is responsible for war and evil is to ignore the values propounded by religions and the gradual acceptance of these values that now has the majority of the people on earth living in peace. This is not an accident. Whatever peace and prosperity we know now is directly affected by religious belief and conformity to that belief by a majority within the culture. Without it, we would be back in the Dark Ages, or worse. That atrocities have and are now committed for religious reasons were or are seldom because of flawed belief, but rather the inability or unwillingness of adherents to conform the underlying belief. In other words, most atrocious acts are committed in spite of religion, not because of it.

Religion is the root of discrimination and prejudice

This accusation is justified because religions and groups have used religion to identify themselves as "chosen" by God. If a religious group uses that doctrine as justification to deny human rights to others, the accusation is indeed justified. However, if the purpose of being "chosen" means that the chosen group has been chosen to provide religious purpose and direction for everyone and therefore seeks to help others outside the group, I would argue that this doctrine can and has had a positive effect on humanity, and is not evil.

Much of Mr. Dawkins criticism of religion is based on this argument. Remarkably enough, he accuses Jesus Christ of discrimination by directing his teachings only toward the Jews, of which group He was a part. Nothing could be further from the truth. This assertion betrays a lack of even a cursory knowledge of the teachings of Christ. Throughout His life Christ repeatedly emphasized the worth of all human beings. A few of His specific sayings follow.

- Ye are the light of the world. (Matthew 5:14)
- God so loved the world that He gave His only begotten son, that whomsoever would believe on him would have everlasting life. (John 3:16)
- Other sheep I have which are not of this fold, them also I must bring, and there shall be one fold and one shepherd. (John 10:16)
- Go ye unto all the world, and preach the gospel to every creature. (Luke 16:15)[25]

In addition, when Christ was asked which was the greatest of all the commandments, the second part of His answer was to "love thy neighbor as thyself (Luke 27). When asked who his neighbor was, the parable of the

---

[25] All cited scriptures are from the King James Version.

Good Samaritan was given, notable because the Samaritans were a despised ethnic group occupying land north of Jerusalem. This parable was a clear indication that the charitable Samaritan was morally superior to the "chosen" individuals who ignored the suffering traveler. Last, Peter was directly challenged because he had not followed the direction of Christ and was not proselyting to gentiles. In Peter's dream he was told "What God hath cleansed, that call thou not common (Acts 10:15). It is clear that all humans were of value to Christ and that His followers were tasked with being the means of bringing his teachings to all the world. This hardly constitutes discrimination, even by today's standard.

Another argument used to condemn religion is that it discriminates against behavior which it believes is evil. Well, duh! This is the weakest argument of all. All philosophies condemn behaviors, even those who hold that there is no right or wrong. If you ask a person who does not believe there is right or wrong if it is evil or wrong to kill them, I am willing to bet good money that the vast majority of them will answer in the affirmative. The issue is not whether the condemnation of behavior is right or wrong, but what behavior is right or wrong.

It is true that some unthinking individuals unjustifiably condemn individuals who practice behavior in conflict with their beliefs even though the behavior does not have any significant socially negative consequences. However, in our culture the predominant belief is to hate the sin and love the sinner. This is an attitude that encourages the rehabilitation of those whose behavior is in conflict with the religious values of the group but at the same time provides a tolerant climate in which all can be free to do as they please so long as the behavior is not legally prohibited. This outcome is not evil.

Religion is a waste of time and resources

Some believe that religious practices and the resources used to provide for religious buildings and materials constitute a massive waste of time and resources not needed for survival. In particular Mr. Dawkins makes this accusation. Even if his belief that there is no God is accurate, this assertion does not make sense when all the positive benefits of religious practice are considered.

First, there is demonstrable good that results from the efforts of religious groups. Churches, synagogues, and mosques are gathering places where citizens go to worship, mingle, share beliefs, commiserate with each other, help each other with the burdens they bear, and establish long lasting bonds of friendship. Even without God, these are constructive ends. In addition, religious groups contribute to various philanthropic and humanitarian causes that benefit the entire world, not just their limited group. This is not a waste of time and resources.

If the argument is that the use of precious resources for religious purposes is not warranted because the use is not needed for our survival, the argument still does not hold water. If the cathedrals that took hundreds of man years to construct during the Dark Ages were not constructed, how many of the workers would have starved without employment? Would merchant and artistic classes have formed? Would the technology needed to build these structures been possible if they had not been built? Would we have the Sistine Chapel and the unparalleled work of Michelangelo to inspire us? And would those in need of purpose in their lives have found it in their tireless struggle to survive under difficult conditions? The use of resources for constructive and contemplative worship is not a waste.

In addition, according to that rationale much of what we do, especially activities that are inspiring, is a waste of time and resources. Art is certainly not necessary for survival. Neither is music. If survival is the measure against which we decide to allocate resources or not, we would have no art museums or concert halls. Musical instruments would not have been invented. In short, we would be a species with our nose to the ground focused solely on our survival. I would hate to be trapped in such a dreary and uninspiring world.

Religion divides instead of uniting people

Some will point to differences in religious thought and argue that these differences are destructive because they divide us into competing groups. Not noted is the fact that any difference in thought or interest also divides us into competing groups; however, we do not hear very many people advocating for uniformity of all thought or economic conditions, or banning different political parties or economic systems, just to avoid having competing groups. Furthermore, just because there are different religious beliefs, it does not follow that they are divisive. As with anything else, it depends on the religious beliefs.

This is another accusation of Mr. Dawkins. He asserts that religion has the effect of labeling people and that the labels have the effect of dividing people into opposing groups. How absurd. Not the accusation, but the supposition that without religion we would not be labeled and not be divided into opposing groups. Each and every person is labeled, and most of those labels have nothing to do with religion. For instance, I am a father, grandfather, American, Nevadan, Las Vegan, Republican, conservative, planner, and so on. These labels are not destructive in their effect (although some liberals may disagree with that conclusion).

In fact, labels are essential. Leaving aside religious differences each and every individual is different, and has just as unique a personal philosophy as he or she has a unique fingerprint or genetic code. We need labels to broadly organize ourselves into coherent groups that are designed to work together and share basic common values. With or without religion, people will be divided into cooperating groups and be labeled as such.

If the argument is that the intensity of emotion of non-religious groups is not as negative as the intense emotions generated by religions differences, the argument is still ridiculous. Humans, with or without religion, have intense emotions, which can include emotions about politics, ethnic groups, family, nationality, community, and even sports. Looking at the violence associated with soccer matches across the world is stark evidence of this. The lack of religion will not change that. Religion channels emotions, and if the religion is constructive it channels emotions to constructive ends.

I would argue that since time immemorial we have recognized that our survival has depended on more than our own abilities and actions even when groups have worked together for the common good. The reliance on deity to provide the means for that survival has had a unifying and inspirational effect on human activity through time.

I am also convinced that because religious traditions and beliefs are the foundation for our society and culture that the resulting society and its strength and unity can be directly attributed to religion. We have a world in which six billion plus people live in relative peace in spite of fractured interests because we have many common religious beliefs that unify us all. Religion is much more of a unifying force than a divisive force. This is not evil.

Over the course of history, much evil has been performed in the name of God and religion, and actions on the part of individuals and groups that act in conflict with the core religious beliefs they espouse are repugnant. However, that some have abused religion to accomplish their own selfish and discriminatory objectives does not make religion or religious beliefs bad.

Quite the opposite is true. Religious belief has served as the foundation for enlightenment and social progress across the world and without the major religious philosophers and philosophies our world would be dramatically different for the worse. Religion has been the principal means of social, cultural, and economic advancements over the history of the world advocating for the interest of society and the group over narrow individual interests.

Conclusion

Is religion actually the root of the evil in the world? No, base human instinct is. Religion is not of itself evil, what people do with it can be. With or without religion there will be some who seek power and wealth, or seek to impose their will on others. There will be others who have such a warped view of God that they lead others to actions in direct conflict with the interests of society and the members of that group. The problem is not religion; for some it is just an excuse for bad behavior. Those who will take those actions will rationalize their action by one means or another. If religion is not used to justify conflict and evil, something else will be.

When evaluating whether any organization or ideology is evil, I believe the most useful tool that can be used to make that determination is what effect the organization or ideology has on society and the individual. If the net effect of the religion is to make society stronger while at the same time making the individual generally free to act within responsible limits, from our cultural standpoint not much of a case can be made for the organization or ideology being evil.

For instance, if we live in a society that has religious traditions tolerating diversity of thought and debate such that we can argue whether religion is good or evil, it seems to me that the religious tradition is anything but evil. I would argue that the cultural climate we enjoy is a direct result of the Judeo-Christian religious thought that permeates every corner of our attitude about human relations and government. In particular, the Sermon on the Mount given by Jesus Christ revolutionized over time human attitudes and behavior toward other human beings. To be sure, we as humans have not always lived up to the ideal presented in the doctrine, but the ideal is there and has profoundly affected human relations for the better. This is not what can be expected from something that is evil.

The argument that religion is evil is no more valid than the argument that politics, economics, or education is evil. It is true that extreme religious groups and ideologists that preach doctrines in direct conflict with the traditional mores of our culture can be evil, especially if they attempt to force their ideology on individuals or the group. But the same cannot be said for religions or ideologies that directly support, and indeed form the foundation for the traditional mores of the culture. The same argument can be made for politics, economics, or education. Extreme political groups can advocate for political change in direct conflict with the political system that has led to the freedoms we enjoy today. That these political extremists are evil does not make all political organizations evil. If some capitalistic companies act in conflict with law and defraud the public, including those who have invested in them, it does not follow that capitalism is bad, only that the companies who have acted against the public interest are. If a teacher in a school system teaches extreme values and thereby causes his or her students to have a warped view of society and their role in it, it does not follow that education is evil, only that the motivations of the teacher are.

Assuming that religion could somehow be banned, as is advocated by some, would the result be a utopian peace on earth? If everyone could somehow forget all the religious beliefs they have ever been taught and were left with only non-religious teachings (as if there were no connection between the two) would we have a world without conflict and war?

I think not. An attempt to ban religion, if it somehow could be enforced (which is obviously impossible) is to advocate for a climate in which we attempt to control thought, stifle discourse, and force uniformity of thought and action. This result is not exactly the utopia envisioned by those who advocate banning religion.

In addition, if there are not religious differences to fight about, something else will simply take their place, whether they are economic, philosophical, or political. Conflict is inevitable because humans have different values and interests that they care deeply about. Even if we could wave a magic wand and cause everyone to forget any religious teaching that they had ever been exposed to, we would still have conflict because the issues fundamental to regulating social conduct cannot be forgotten. Conflict, up to and including war will be the most likely result even without religion to fight over. Humans will always be in conflict with one another, and the only means of seriously mitigating the tendency toward resolving conflict by resorting to violence is to advocate for the peaceful resolution of conflict and show the cost of a resort to violence. That is what most religions do best.

Indeed, if recent history is any example, conflict may be more likely in the absence of traditional religion. The lack of a belief in God did not mean that Joseph Stalin or Pol Pot were motivated to act in the interest of those whom they governed. They had no qualms about creating a hell on earth for their subjects, ruthlessly killing millions of their countrymen without fear of religious consequences even though they believed in Communism, which should have resulted in a workers paradise if Marxist dogma is valid. The political climates of their respective countries were unquestionably not a paradise for anyone, including the highest members of their leadership.

The attitude that religion is evil has led to an increasingly intolerant cultural climate for traditional religion. The result is that those who believe in the religious traditions that have made our society the most free and open society in the history of the world are pariahs in the intellectual community and are disparaged generally. This has also led to overt hostility toward traditional religions and individual believers that have actually resulted in the recent killing of at least one courageous and outstanding person who refused to deny her faith in the Columbine massacre. Those who take the extreme position that traditional religion is evil contribute to the climate of intolerance which results in the persecution of those who believe in that which is the foundation for our society. It is also in direct conflict with the culture that allows them to so advocate.

I will take my chances on a society with traditional Judeo-Christian religious values, especially the religious doctrine taught by Christ, including the core values of faith, hope, charity, and love, and that believe in individual liberty over a non-religious ideology that values social Darwinism or the subordination of the interest of individuals and groups to the interest of the State. The former are teachings that are far more likely to result in a society that lives together in relative peace than a society that holds as its ideal the removal of religious thought and motivation because those beliefs result in categorizing behavior as right and wrong. If no behavior is right or wrong, no atrocity can be held to be evil, making the likelihood of peaceably living together ever more unlikely.

Contrary to the nonsense put forth by secularists and atheists, traditional religion is the most effective tool to avoid violent conflict. If religion could somehow be banned, it would remove the most effective deterrent to violent conflict and war that we have, or ever have had. That would be evil indeed.

Chapter 20

"Science and Religion Conflict"

Since I was a teenager, I have heard the constant refrain that science and religion are incompatible and conflict with each other. The argument that then follows is that the rational person will choose to believe in science while the irrational will believe in religion. This simple-minded notion has done incalculable damage, both to science and religion. The damage to religion comes as it is marginalized in the minds of many who do not bother to look beyond the mindless claptrap they are spoon-fed and who then perceive religion as hostile to science and reason without bothering to investigate the facts. The damage to science is the antipathy toward scientific method and results that come from those whose beliefs are ridiculed in spite of their rational basis for them.

In Chapter 16, I demonstrated that while the existence of God could not be proven, neither could it be disproved. More to the point, it is evident that there are numerous scientific facts that tend to support the existence of God and the theory that He has created this earth and the life on it. I will not repeat the argument here; suffice it to say that there is overwhelmingly more evidence that God does exist than there is evidence of His non-existence; in fact there is no evidence that contradicts the existence of God. Note that I do not consider speculative theoretical possibilities to be evidence.

In spite of this, we see a continued campaign on the part of secularists to denigrate religion and the belief in God. For the part of the secularists, their intent is clear. They wish to debunk religion as the opiate of the people (to paraphrase Marx) and the product of emotion and zeal rather than a rational and considered system of belief. Part of this motivation is just another aspect of the continued campaign to replace traditional values with those mores in keeping with the lifestyle they long to legitimize, legislate, and live. In fairness to scientists who take this approach, there is some justification for the distrust of religious proponents, for many centuries scientists were told to "shut up and believe" when they asked uncomfortable questions. The residual resentment from that experience may explain current resistance to accepting God as an answer to any problem, even if that solution is the most rational. However, for whatever expressed rational reason scientists are unwilling to accept God, historical antipathy does not justify ignoring evidence and reason in the quest for truth.

There is much honest disagreement about the relationship between these two branches of learning and knowledge. Much of the problem can be traced to a fundamental misunderstanding of what both religion and science attempt to accomplish. In general terms, they both seek truth, enlightenment, and progress for humanity; conflict results when religious philosophy and scientific knowledge reach opposing conclusions. What is most often overlooked, and which results in considerable confusion, mistrust, and conflict, is the fundamental difference in what both religion and science seek to accomplish.

As I understand it, the difference is that religion seeks to ask and understand the question "why", while science seeks to ask and understand "how". There is much overlap of course, many of the how questions cannot be answered without asking some why questions; however, the fundamental purpose of religion is to know the natural world's and our reason for being, while the fundamental purpose of science is to discover how the natural world and mankind came to be. Bitter debates ensue when one or the other branch seeks to usurp the domain of the other. When religious believers attempt to tell scientists how the creation was effected, scientists ridicule them. There is justification for scientific practitioners to take this position. Try as one might, one searches in vain for a clear "how to" set of instructions in scripture that explains how God created the earth and the life upon it. The only clear message in scripture is that He is responsible for the creation. Conversely, scientists run into trouble when they attempt to answer fundamental questions about the purpose of life when all they have are observations and accurate measurements that cannot possibly explain this fundamental question.

Mr. Dawkins argues that scientists have just as much right to ask "why" as theologians. I don't disagree; however, just because a scientist asks the question does not mean they have the means to answer it. If scientists want to obtain answers to questions such as "what is the purpose of life?", they should be prepared to be disappointed if the answer cannot be empirically demonstrated. Moreover, if they answer the question using only what they can empirically measure at this time, they are doomed to suffer the same result as every previous scientific theory that fell once better means of measurement was discovered or more knowledge was acquired. The scientist seeking to identify the purpose of life is limited solely to what can be empirically proven. Speculative theoretical possibilities are not an answer. That includes speculating that natural selection is evidence that there is no God. Drawing such a conclusion is the logical equivalent of assuming Flying Spaghetti Monsters exist without any evidence.

There are even some scientific supporters who maintain that something cannot exist if it cannot be measured, implying that all available knowledge has been discovered and that because we have not been able to physically demonstrate God's existence He must not be. This is breathtakingly arrogant and absurd. If science had adopted this attitude centuries ago, we would still be clueless about the composition of atomic elements and how they interact to form molecules (come to think of it, we are still speculating about this). That logic would also support ceasing pure scientific research as we ostensibly know of everything there is to know. It is because we know the limitations of our understanding and constantly seek to expand our knowledge base with ever more sophisticated theories and means of measuring and observing nature that we are able to learn more about that which we previously could not measure. Those that conclude that we have nothing more to measure or discover relegate themselves to insignificance in terms of scientific advancement. They can only repeat what was discovered yesterday. They will never have anything new for today or tomorrow.

Much of what appears to be in conflict is not when all aspects of scientific fact and religious belief are rigorously analyzed. The best example of this is the Theory of Evolution. Decades of discussion, disagreement, debate, dissent, denigration and dissatisfaction has resulted in what seems to be an unbridgeable gulf between the scientific and religious communities on this issue. Ironically enough, there is considerable support for how evolution could have been the means of the creation described in the Bible. Because the warring groups are so busy trying to discredit the opposite point of view, they have both ignored what could be a unifying belief supported by scientific theories and facts and scripture.

Even accounting for the differences in the approach of the two subjects, there are still conclusions and beliefs that conflict. Of course, there will always be opposing and conflicting conclusions. The same is true of internal religion and science. There are so many religions in the world because there are so many conflicting philosophies about whether there is a God, and if he does what His nature and purpose is. Not all of these philosophies can be true. The same is true for differing scientific theories as well as for conflicts between scientific fact and religious belief. Only one scientific theory in conflict with another scientific theory can be true. This means the fact that there are as yet irreconcilable differences only means that there is conflict to be resolved, not that one field is completely wrong.

Once again, it is useful to debunk the notion that there are many truths that all lead to the same conclusion, and that all belief systems have equal results I believe the popular phrase is that there are many roads to heaven. As I indicated before in Chapter 16, this is profoundly illogical. Scientific method can be used to illustrate this. In order to determine a scientific fact, the scientist will test a theory against known facts while eliminating all possible reasons and factors that could skew the results of the test. If the test provides evidence that the theory is valid, it will be accepted as fact. If the opposite is true, the theory is disproved and discarded. No scientist concludes after a failed experiment that the underlying theory that was the subject of the failed test is valid and that using the theory in the future will result in profitable knowledge based in fact. Not all scientific theories are valid; the purpose of science is to determine what is fact and what is not.

Exactly the same logic applies to religion. If there are two or more competing religious beliefs, only one can possibly be true. Indeed, they may all be untrue, which complicates the matter considerably. However, just as the scientist cannot arrive at a profitable fact by attempting to use disproved theory, religious adherents cannot find truth by blindly following whichever philosophy they choose under the assumption that the choice will not make a difference because all results will be the same.

True religion and true science do not conflict. If there is a genuine established scientific fact that is incontrovertibly true to the best of our ability to determine truth, and there is another religious belief in conflict with that truth, we must conclude that the religious belief is not true. The danger of this approach is that so much of what we have believed as scientific fact has been replaced over time as our base of knowledge, understanding of the universe, and ability to precisely measure phenomenon increases. It is difficult to say with certainty that we have incontrovertible scientific truth. However, if there is truth in religion and truth in science, it is clear that they will not disagree; what is true for religion must also be true for science.

That being the case, a calculated study of where religion and science agree and support each other will probably result in a base of scientific knowledge and religious belief that is most likely to be true. In this respect, the goal of finding truth can be mutually supported by the collaboration of these two hopelessly intertwined branches of learning.

Section 3

Culture

Chapter 21

"There is No Right or Wrong"

I touched on this in Chapter 1 and other chapters, but I would like to elaborate on the subject. There are those who claim that there is no right or wrong, and that any individual decision is justified based on the personal beliefs and feelings of the individual. I believe that this idea is categorically wrong. It is worth noting that those who hold this belief invariably believe that they are right and that anyone who disagrees with them is wrong, which you should recognize as acceptance of my argument.

Even if one does not accept the existence of God, there is still right and wrong as determined and enforced by society. If an individual claims that they are not bound by society's mores, and acts in conflict with those mores, they will soon find that their freedom to act will be severely restricted; in extreme cases (or not so extreme in many Muslim societies) they may even forfeit their life. If a group holds that they are not bound by the laws of the majority, they will also find that the weight of political and cultural institutions will force them to conform or will eventually destroy them. This includes restricting the behavior of religious organizations; for instance, no matter how important to a religious group human sacrifice may be to their theology, they will still be prevented from practicing that belief in the current cultural climate.

If one accepts the existence of God, no matter what you perceive that God to be, or the motivations and attributes of Him, Her, It or Them, there must be right and wrong. If there is a God, there is truth, at which point the only question becomes what is truth and whether or how can we know of it with reasonable certainty. There are those who claim that it does not matter what we determine as right or wrong and that God will understand in the end and justify our decisions. That argument is fundamentally illogical. Again, if there is a God there is truth, and there can only be one truth. If God by His effort informs humans of truth, we should be accountable for conformance with those truths.

If there are two beliefs in conflict with one another, with respect to the truthfulness of the ideas there are only three possibilities; the first is true and the second is false, the second is true and the first is false, or both are false. It is not possible that both can be true. For instance, if one group believes

Culture

that killing is abhorrent to God, and another group believes that God desires that those who do not accept the teachings of their group should be killed, at least one of those beliefs must be wrong. Even if you believe God to be indifferent to the life that He has created, that belief is held to be truth against which other beliefs can be measured within that theological construct.

Those who claim there is no right or wrong frequently are most vociferous in their denunciation of those who claim there is, or are hypocritical because they condemn as wrong beliefs that they disagree with. They seek an environment that will allow them to choose what is right for them and ignore what others believe to be right. The level of antipathy that many of these individuals demonstrate is remarkable.

Invariably, they denounce in the strongest terms possible the majority's imposition of rules they feel are inappropriate, unfair, and based on religious dogma that they maintain should not have a place in legislation (see Chapters 1 and 2). Also invariably, they use the very terms they seek to undermine to describe the effect these rules have; that it is wrong to impose standards based on religious beliefs. Therefore, their argument is that there is no wrong, and consequently it is wrong for the majority to establish proscriptions on their behavior. Am I the only one who perceives that this is just a tad hypocritical? How can anyone maintain with a straight face that there is no wrong and in the same breath say that there is? They follow this with overt attempts to redefine what is right and wrong, in particular advocating that standards based on traditional religious morality are wrong. They cannot have it both ways; there is either no right or wrong and there are no rules, or the majority has the right to determine right and wrong for others.

Much of the attractiveness that this idea has for many is that they perceive it gives them license to act as they see fit without suffering the adverse consequences of their actions. This is of course impossible; one cannot escape the negative consequences of ones actions. This is generally well stated in the maxim "what goes around, comes around". Eventually we suffer the consequences of our poor decisions. What is worse, most often people who are innocent of making the wrong decision will also suffer adverse consequences. Regardless of these facts, some use the belief to act recklessly, leaving a wake of misery in their path, and sowing the seeds of future misery for themselves and others, most often the people they care most about in the world.

The tendency of those who advocate this position is to denigrate constructive cultural practices that have served society well for millennia. The best example of this is marriage. They point to the fact that marriages are frequently dysfunctional and that some parents are incompetent or act with criminal intent. They also point to historical practices that are wholly out of place in our time as justification for the denigration of the institution, such as the historical practice of treating women as chattel. While it is true that such historical practices are anathema to us now, it is also true that this institution has served as the building block of society, providing for the most part a nurturing environment for children borne to the union. It has played a critical role in the gradual evolution of our society into one that values love, respect, and honor. Those who seek to undermine the effectiveness of this institution fail to see how important it is to the survival of our society and our species. Denigrating its importance is the equivalent of directly undermining the foundation of society and the freedoms we enjoy within it. Past and present problems in individual marriages are no more a justification for condemning the institution as individual imperfections are justification for condemning the entire human race.

Not all ideas are equal. In fact, many social, political, and economic ideas that seem good on paper do not work out well at all. Mein Kampf helped lead the world into a destructive war that killed about 62 million people, 37 million of whom were civilians, and nearly annihilated an ethnic group. Das Kapital was ruinous to the eastern block and Asian countries that struggled to implement its ideas; as many as 295 million people may have perished with that experiment. Pol Pot's political and economic ideas nearly wiped out an entire generation of Cambodians. On the other hand, the rise of western civilization with its emphasis and moral grounding in the Judeo-Christian ethic has resulted in the establishment of tolerant democracies the world over. Democratic institutions are noticeably absent only in those cultures where the Judeo-Christian or similar ethic has not been accepted.

I could be wrong, after all it could be argued that I have been propagandized to accept my culture as superior and that I am an ethnocentric bigot, but the fact that billions of people are living together in relative harmony convinces me that western culture is at least equal to any other culture and far superior to most. The only cultures that compete with it are those heavily influenced by Buddhist, Hindu, and Confucian thought. If our culture is among the best, and has resulted in freedom for literally

237

billions of people across the globe, it stands to reason that we should consider perpetuating it instead of undermining its traditions and values.

Our society is only as strong as the cultural glue that holds us together. That common cultural glue has been the Judeo-Christian ethic that this nation was founded upon and which provided a cultural environment within which the freedoms we cherish could be established, survive in spite of the destructive instincts of people, and eventually flourish. An integral part of that ethic is that there is right and wrong, that those who act against the interests of the majority will be punished, and that punishment is needed to preserve a stable and free society. Those who argue otherwise ignore centuries of very expensive lessons in history.

What would be the effect on society if the majority accepted this notion? If one believes there is no right or wrong and therefore each individual has the right to decide for themselves what is right and wrong, they should be willing to accept the consequences of the decisions of others against their interests. If someone thinks that it is right to discriminate based on race, color, religion, or gender, and those people who believe there is no right or wrong lose economic opportunities as a result, they still should quietly acquiesce to the discriminatory behavior. If someone else thinks that rape is a legitimate means of gratifying physical desire, that too should be acceptable to a person in that group. If a religious group believes that to obtain God's approval they need to drag helpless captives to the top of a temple and cut out their hearts with an obsidian knife, that too should be acceptable to this group. Of course, these are extreme examples, which simply cannot and will not be tolerated in our society. However, if someone is ridiculous enough to insist that the majority cannot establish standards and proscribe behavior, regardless of what those standards are based upon, then these examples clearly illustrate the potential effect of what they advocate.

Many will insist that on one level there is right and wrong, but that on another level there is not. Specifically, it is appropriate to proscribe behavior that is harmful to others, but that the majority has no business proscribing behavior between consenting parties that has no negative impact on society as a whole. In terms of arguing that there is no right or wrong, this logic is also fatally flawed in that it still holds that it is wrong to proscribe that behavior. In addition, much behavior between consenting parties has been deemed harmful enough to society that the behavior is prohibited. Actions between consenting adults do not occur in a vacuum, these actions affect others in addition to the effect they have on the persons participating in the behavior. The spread of venereal disease is a good example of the actions of consenting adults that adversely affect other people.

Ultimately, society is forced to make all sorts of judgment calls as to what should be right and what should be wrong, carefully considering whether specific behaviors are harmful enough to ban, or whether prohibiting a behavior constitutes an unwarranted intrusion on a citizen's ability to have liberty and pursue happiness. Our society believes that it is right to allow much behavior that is indeed harmful, not only to the parties that engage in the behavior, but also to society as a whole. These decisions are justified because a collective judgment is made that the benefits of allowing the behavior outweigh the negative consequences. In a representative government these decisions are legitimate, so long as the majority as represented in the legislature makes the decisions rather than un-elected judges or bureaucrats. Here it is worth remembering that the majority established the Constitution and has amended it many times, not the Supreme Court.

One effect of the idea that there is no right or wrong is that many who recognize the irrationality of it turn away from organizations that do not provide a moral foundation. If a church teaches that their doctrine is no more effective in providing eternal happiness than the doctrine of any other religion, it follows that the members of their organization may conclude that allegiance to a church that is so ambivalent about the importance of what they believe is useless. They may seek other organizations that will have less restrictive behavioral constraints, or they will seek to find an organization that gives them something to believe in.

The end result of this belief, should it be widely accepted, is anarchy; that is the complete overthrow of standard social mores and the resulting breakdown in society. The rule of law would end, social Darwinism would become the rule, freedoms would be meaningless, and our economy ruined. If everyone gets to decide what is right for him or herself, most will act according to their perceived interest. Might will make right in every sense of the term, and only the strongest will survive. In such an environment, freedom is measured in terms of one's ability to stay alive. Because our economy is based on the assumption that initiative and work will be rewarded, and that effort will not be rewarded if the strongest (defined here as the person who prevails in conflict for any reason) reaps the benefit of others efforts, there will be no motivation to produce goods beyond what is needed for individual survival.

Those who think that this is not possible should look carefully at what has occurred in the United States when the lights go out in urban centers. Further, it is worth examining just how tenuous social order is and how easy it is for a relatively small group to destroy that social order. Iraq is a case in point. Terrorism, violence, and intimidation by a violent minority, and anarchy are just a few short steps away from each other. The widespread acceptance of this pernicious assertion would be catastrophic for our nation and world.

Thankfully, the majority yet recognizes that it is indeed in their interest in every sense of the word to establish right and wrong and to enforce those standards. It is only a relatively small, unthinking minority that believes this nonsense. The best way to combat the effects of this precept is through education and discussion.

This is especially true with children. Our culture transmits the values of the preceding generation to the succeeding generation, whatever those values happen to be. In some cases the values will be accepted, in others they may not. What is certain is that if the values are not communicated and the importance of them explained and demonstrated, they cannot possibly survive. This explains why the control of education is critical. Whoever controls what is being taught in the classroom will have a profound effect on our future cultural environment. Parents have an extremely important role in inculcating the values they believe within their children. They typically expect that social and educational institutions will not undermine their efforts and will react adversely if they do. One of the most important values we can communicate to our children is a strong sense of right and wrong, and the determination to attempt to do what is right. All people and institutions should share that common goal.

Unfortunately, and to the detriment of all, many have become convinced that there is no right or wrong. While there are some who believe in the concept that yet will act in the best interest of society, many will not. Advocates of this insidious idea try to divorce the cause and effect, but causal link between this belief and many of society's ills are obvious. The effect is that we have (among other things) more crime, more sociopaths, more depression, and more suicide than we would otherwise have. With a straight face those who advocate this position denigrate traditional values, insist that there is no right or wrong, then are shocked that there are consequences that come back to bite them. Crime is the most obvious example of this.

Our individual and societal interests are well served when we recognize that there is right and wrong, teach the precept to succeeding generations, and act according to what society determines is right and wrong. Of course, we can work within institutional settings to try to alter proscriptions based on what we believe is right. If our thoughts prevail in the marketplace of ideas we will have altered the cultural environment. However, it is destructive to society for us to rebel against the authority of the majority and act against its interests. Because our individual interests are inseparably connected to our collective interests, such behavior ultimately is action against our individual interest.

Chapter 22

"Never Discuss Politics or Religion"

How many times have you been told that you should not discuss politics or religion? This is an idea that has become widely accepted over the brief period of time that I have been alive. I remember that in my youth both subjects were routinely discussed in almost all social settings. Over the decades since, the idea that these subjects are socially taboo has become popular to the point that anytime either of these subjects is brought up the immediate response is that they should not be discussed. If we analyze the idea, I think we will find that this is another concept that is truly destructive.

Since I wrote this chapter I came across a study corroborating my argument. It seems that a survey performed by Vitalsmarts showed that 77% of respondents indicated that they avoid discussing politics with friends and family. Ten percent said they avoided the subject at all costs. The researchers attribute the unwillingness on the part of the respondents to engage in political discussion to a decline in healthy discussion and an unwillingness to expose themselves to constructive debate. I would argue that the decline in our ability to engage in healthy discussion is a direct result of the lack of practice, aided and abetted by this destructive cliché.

A wise teacher once told me (and the rest of his high school chemistry class) that the second most important thing in the world was the exchange of ideas between people (Mr. Grisham indicated that people were the most important). I have thought about that assertion often over the years, and while I'm not convinced that he was exactly right about the ranking, I'm not willing to disagree either. In any case, whether it is the second most important thing or not, the exchange of ideas is unquestionably one of the most important things we do as human beings.

All of the knowledge we have accumulated over the millennia is the result of the exchange of ideas between people. Of course, individuals have independently discovered facts and observed phenomenon. Nevertheless, in order for that knowledge to be transferred to anyone else, communication must occur. Whether that communication is accomplished verbally or by written documentation matters little so long as eventually someone writes it down. If an idea or observation is not communicated to others, it dies with the originator. If those with whom it was shared and verbally discussed do

242

not eventually write it down, the idea dies with the narrow group of people with whom it was verbally shared. Sadly, even writing the idea is no guarantee it will survive, written records are subject to destruction, as illustrated by the fate of the library at Alexandria.

In addition, many ideas that sound good when they are considered internally tend to be found to be lacking in merit when exposed to rigorous scrutiny by others. Further, ideas that have merit can be refined and improved by the same type of scrutiny. Conflict over ideas is to be expected given the importance of ideology to us. Over time, we find that superior ideas triumph in conflict (this can be a circular argument because these ideas are defined as superior because the winner's ideas have prevailed). Over time, the critical analysis of ideas has lead our world to a place where the ideas of western civilization has resulted in a political, cultural, and economic climate that has benefited the entire world.

We literally live and die according to the structured knowledge and mores of our society, which has evolved as a result of continuous critical analysis of ideas. That critical analysis occurs in an environment in which the free exchange of ideas is nurtured. Cultures that have failed to nurture this environment have died, either as a result of their flawed ideas leading them to destruction when in direct conflict with other more open cultures (Hitler's Third Reich is a good example) or as a result of their gradual subversion when exposed to superior ideas of other cultures (the Soviet Union comes to mind). Other cultures stagnate, their mores stuck in an environment in which discussion about them is not only discouraged, but also penalized. Many of the most backward societies in the world today are at least an indirect result of the lack of critical analysis of the values of their culture and the refusal of the proponents of the dominant ideas to allow any discussion of dissenting views.

If the exchange of ideas is so important to our civilization and its advancement, it stands to reason that consequential discourse is a desirable thing. We should be encouraging the discussion of ideas and concepts that are important to us. Indeed, the greater the importance of the idea, the more the idea should be discussed. So the question is, what are the most important ideas for us to discuss? I submit that politics and religion are subjects that will be hard to beat in terms of being consequential.

Why are we told that we should not discuss politics or religion? If you want to have a party with pleasant conversation and good will among all those who attend, you want to avoid conflict between those who attend. Many are unskilled when it comes to peacefully resolving conflict, so the

Culture

most efficient way to avoid conflict is to avoid subjects that cause conflict. This is the direct antecedent for the axiom that we are discussing; that is that politics and religion should not be discussed. Many wanted to avoid conflict at parties and other pleasant social settings so they avoided controversial subjects. Unfortunately, this idea has since been expanded to propound that we avoid the discussion of politics and religion in any social setting. Therefore, we now have a culture in which we generally discourage any discussion of these two subjects.

Because these two topics are the only ones discouraged, it stands to reason that they are the subjects that generate the most and the highest intensity of conflict. I suggest that is the case because these two subjects are most important to us. It stands to reason that if these two subjects are the most important to us, these are the subjects that should be discussed the most if we are to continue to critically analyze the ideas behind political and religious practices. If we do not, we will find ourselves in the same position as the cultures in which the discussion of ideas is overtly penalized.

What we have done is to effectively repress the discussion of the ideas that are most important to us. Ironically, the purpose of the repression of this consequential discourse is to avoid conflict, which it does not accomplish. We clearly have conflicting ideas with respect to politics and religion, and our only hope to live peaceably together is to resolve those conflicts. We do not have to convert to a shared political or religious philosophy, but we do need to understand the political and religious ideas and motivations of others, together with the effects of those ideas. With that understanding comes acceptance and the willingness to peacefully coexist. If we do not resolve these conflicts peacefully, eventually we will resolve them by more violent means. By the way, this conflict resolution problem applies to individuals, neighborhoods, communities, states, and nations. The only difference is the scale and method of discussion.

Avoiding conflict is not the same as resolving conflict. If we refuse to discuss the political and religious differences between us, we have no hope of being able to understand the ideas and motivations of those with competing ideas. As time goes on, instead of individuals learning the deeply held beliefs of others and the inherent understanding that comes with this respectful communication because of the desire to avoid conflict, problems that exist between them will be ignored in the hope that they will eventually go away. Problems do not go away if we ignore them. In fact, they almost always get worse. Generally speaking, the longer we practice conflict avoidance the more difficult will be the eventual resolution of the conflict.

The idea that we should not discuss politics and religion guarantees that we will have non-consequential discourse. That includes consequential discourse about other subjects, because such discussion cannot be divorced from politics and religion. We are told to stick to the weather and our health. We are instructed to discuss subjects that are boring and about which we can have little affect. We dumb down our discourse, discussing intellectual pabulum that accomplishes little in the way of understanding the person with whom we are discoursing. We finish the discussion feeling as empty and unsatisfied as we would if we had eaten pabulum for dinner.

Even so, it is getting more and more difficult to avoid conflict; even the weather and our health have become controversial subjects for discussion with the debate about global warming and drug, tobacco and alcohol abuse. Ironically enough, these subjects are related to politics and religion (isn't that curious?). The net effect is that we try to avoid conflict about two subjects that are critical to our understanding of one another, but in the end still fail to avoid conflict, and often that conflict is over politics and religion. All we accomplish is to attempt to avoid understanding each other's ideas with respect to the most important concepts among us.

This practice has also fostered shallow intellect. It serves to make religious and political illiterates of the population. Many of us do not have any depth of understanding as to what constitutes sound religious and political thought, and no longer have the ability to coherently discuss political and religious ideas without digressing to unrelated topics. Instead of a focused discussion seeking to understand one another, the discussion moves to ideas that are unrelated, but which those with limited understanding can discuss because they are familiar with those limited ideas. Unfortunately, often those ideas are flawed because of the lack of critical analysis applied to them and are antagonistic toward other beliefs. They exacerbate conflict rather than ameliorate it. A good example is the shouting match over what constitutes a Christian. It is amazing that there are some "Christians" who stoutly maintain that Catholics are not Christians. What kind of logic is that? Correct me if I'm wrong, but it seems to me that if Catholics are not Christians it would be hard to call anyone Christian. Those who take these positions play semantic games to justify their beliefs. A natural consequence is that simplistic and untenable ideas flourish with the assistance of demagogies and charlatans who seek power and gain.

Culture

In addition, the unwillingness to discuss consequential matters means we need to fill the vacuum with inconsequential discourse. Instead of discussing uplifting principles and ideas that expand our mind and understanding of the universe, world, and human relations, we are stuck discussing the weather, or even worse the latest in celebrity follies, or worst of all base and demeaning subjects that are depressing and vile.

It also fosters uncivil discourse. Because we avoid conflict resolution with respect to the most important beliefs we have, the unresolved conflict leads to conflict in almost all other subjects. Many lack the skill to peacefully resolve conflict and resort to uncivil discourse or violence when conflicting ideas inevitably arise because they have not had the experience of civilly debating these important subjects. The peaceful resolution of conflict requires understanding, diplomacy, and tact, and each of these skills comes only with practice. The lack of practice has lead to a significant decline in the quality of our discourse. We need only to visit religious and political blogs to see the evidence; untold numbers of visitors to these blogs cannot post anything without being deliberately offensive.

Part of the motivation for avoiding these subjects now is the desire to remain politically correct. The discussion of politics and religion necessarily involves the discussion of traditions that have long been the foundation for the beliefs we value; however, some of these traditions are under attack. The result is we avoid discussion of them not only to avoid conflict but also to avoid having people think we adhere to politically incorrect ideas, even though we do and even though to not do so would mean undermining the very values that fostered the politically correct ideas in the first place.

Not all political and religious ideas are equal. For that matter, that is true for any subject. If we are to rationally examine the implications of ideas for us personally, or for our communities, countries, or the world as a whole, we must discuss them. Through these discussions, we and others can discover the flaws in ideas and either reject or amend them. More important, we often find that our ideas are inferior to others, and adopt new ideas for ourselves. However, if we refuse to have the discussion, we will be left with competing and conflicting ideas that will never be exposed to critical analysis and constructive criticism.

My last point is to reemphasize that we do not have anything more important to talk about than politics and religion. The first is the means by which we govern ourselves, or consent to be governed by others. If we leave the understanding of politics to professional politicians, we will soon find that we will no longer govern ourselves.   The second involves the deepest held beliefs that we cleave to, those that govern our conduct and the relationships we have with all who we love or come in contact with.   To not discuss that which is most important to us is to trivialize and betray those beliefs.

Chapter 23

"It is Only a Piece of Paper"

How many times have you heard someone say that a piece of paper is insignificant when arguing against the institution of marriage? The logic is that if two people are in love and care for each other that it does not matter if they get married; their love will exist and flourish with or without the marriage license and ceremony. Even worse is the perception of some that wonderful relationships are the norm before marriage and that getting married typically ruins that relationship, which makes the piece of paper not only insignificant from the standpoint of establishing a lasting and loving relationship, but a major hindrance to it. I beg to differ with both points of view.

First, it is worth noting that pieces of paper (or their electronic equivalents) govern our lives. The Constitution establishes our form of government and enumerates the rights of the states and individuals. State constitutions and laws, and local governmental laws prescribe certain behaviors and proscribe others. All of these are written on pieces of paper.

In addition, paper provides the means for our society to function properly. We carry money with us to pay for goods and services. We write checks to do the same. We sign and record deeds to ensure the proper conveyance of property and to establish a clear record of who the property belongs to. We write and record wills to establish inheritance rights. Most of us literally deal with a blizzard of paper each day, whether it is actual paper or the electronic equivalent. Nobody suggests that all these pieces of paper are insignificant and can be discarded or disregarded. They facilitate and document the working relationships in our society, without which we would be reduced to a barter economy and would be dependant on the individual memories of those involved in transactions. And none of these examples consider the importance of pieces of paper in transmitting knowledge to future generations. Pieces of paper are very important to us.

What good is a piece of paper denoting marriage? The underlying question is what good is marriage. The better question is what bad can possibly come from getting married. I would suggest there is little or no adverse effect from marriage that any relationship would not encounter anyway. The piece of paper, and the ceremony attendant to receiving it, forms the basis for a long-term stable relationship that provides the cultural, spiritual, and physical environment needed to advance the interests of the people involved in the relationship, especially children born to the couple.

When two people meet and are attracted to one another, they are both interested in meeting their individual needs. They typically are seeking, among other things, love, acceptance, physical intimacy, and security. If the relationship grows to a point that they both conclude that they love each other and want to establish a long-term union, they have a choice between continuing within the informal undocumented association they began with, or to get married and formalize their relationship.

Regardless of the choice they make, there will be conflict between them. Because individual needs and goals differ, conflict is inevitable in any relationship. This is true no matter what kind of association we are in, including couples, families, communities, or nations. The question is not whether conflict will arise, but whether and how those involved will resolve the conflict. They can work together to resolve their differences, they can agree to end the association, one party can acquiesce to the other, or in extreme cases, one may resort to violence against the other. This will be true whether they get married or not. Because conflict is a result of the personalities involved and the interaction between the persons involved in the association, conflict is assured regardless of the marital status of the couple.

Conflict between couples who are not married is at least as common as conflict between married couples. In some cases, the level of intensity of conflict among married couples is made worse because of the marriage, which can be attributed to the level of betrayal one spouse may feel because of the inherent commitment underlying the marriage contract. However, in other cases incidents of conflict may be more common because the lack of a formal relationship may serve to undermine the importance of the relationship in the minds of one or both parties involved in the association. I have a friend who screens criminal cases for the District Attorney of a very large political jurisdiction who has observed that approximately 75% of domestic violence cases involve unmarried cohabiting partners. At least part of the reason these people loose control and become violent toward their partner is because of the lack of a commitment to making the relationship work when times get tough.

Does this piece of paper provide a benefit that the undocumented couple does not have? The answer is a resounding yes. Marriage establishes a

Culture

documented relationship. It establishes a commitment between the two parties that is much easier for both to trust than a promise that will fade with memory. The words on the marriage certificate will not fade, and will say the same thing twenty years from the event as it does the day it is issued. It is also a binding contract, which has very real legal implications, and few will incur the obligation unless they are firm in their commitment to make the relationship work over the long term. The contract makes it less likely that either party will walk away from the relationship for trivial reasons, while there is little incentive to maintain an informal relationship once the honeymoon is over. It also provides a stable and predictable setting that enable long term plans to be realized in a trusting environment, including bringing children into the partnership and enjoying the fulfillment associated with seeing the children grow and mature as responsible adults (grandchildren are even better!).

The piece of paper that many dismiss as unimportant can be the difference between success and failure. All relationships are difficult to begin with. Those who are wise maximize the probability of success in any endeavor, and getting married is the best means of assuring to the extent possible the perpetuation of a relationship that begins with optimism and love.

Chapter 24

"He (or She) is a Do-Gooder"

Let me see if I have this straight. If a person acts in his or her best interest, or in the best interest of society, that person is doing what our society has determined to be good. However, by taking this action, he or she will be ridiculed as a do-gooder. This derisive term deliberately ridicules that person for the very beneficial decision that he or she is making. What is wrong with this picture?

The term originated as a reaction against those who thought they were morally superior and who looked down on others. The expression as it originally was used was useful; very few react well to someone who views them as inferior and the term served to properly denigrate the practice. However, since then it has evolved to where we use it to describe anyone who does good, even those who are non-judgmental about the actions of others.

What is the effect of the widespread use of this term? By accusing those who do good of being a do-gooder, are we contributing to a society that no longer values those who do good? If so, then we are creating a cultural environment where those who are bad are rewarded. If we derisively call anyone who does good a do-gooder, we penalize good behavior and encourage bad behavior. We are critical of those who set the best example for society, ridiculing their behavior as if it was destructive. We criticize public figures that are excellent role models as "too perfect" as if someone trying to follow a biblical admonition cannot relate to regular people and therefore must do something bad so he or she will be more acceptable.

This attitude has very real consequences for our society. Is it possible that the rise in drug abuse, sexual promiscuity, vandalism, assault, and even murder can be linked to the subconcious attempts of individuals to avoid being labeled a do-gooder? Even those who may be inclined to do good could be persuaded to alter their behavior, especially teenagers seeking peer approval.

If we do not value those who act in our interest, we may soon see widespread actions against our interest. It doesn't take a rocket scientist to figure out that if a majority of the population, or even a significant minority, choose to be bad instead of good, our society will soon not have enough prison space to hold all the convicted criminals. That is assuming there will be enough people who recognize that criminal activity should be penalized to convict them. More likely is a breakdown in civil authority and social chaos.

This destructive term should be relegated to the verbal dustbin, and everyone should avoid its use. My standard reaction to anyone who uses this term is to ask "Would you rather he be a do-badder? It is hard enough to get individuals to avoid destructive behavior without giving them incentive to do so.

Chapter 25

"I'm Not Going to Force My Children to . . ."

I cringe every time I hear a parent say this. Ironically enough, I agree with the technical view expressed in the statement. As a parent, one of my principal responsibilities was to teach my children to make decisions for themselves. The only way to do this is to give a child the right to make decisions, and allow them to learn from the consequences. This starts early in life with allowing them to make simple choices, such as what kind of cereal they will have for breakfast. As they grow older, they are allowed to make choices that are increasingly complex until they are making decisions that can have a profound effect on their lives. If all goes well, a parent will have children that grow to be well-rounded and responsible adults that can make wise decisions in their lives that will lead them to happiness. It is critically important to allow children the freedom to make their own choices.

The difficult part of this is to allow them the freedom to make as many choices as possible, while not allowing choices that we know will have catastrophic consequences before the child is able to handle that level of responsibility. For instance, we would never allow a toddler the choice of putting their finger into an electrical outlet. Similarly, we would not allow our children to drop out of school after they finish kindergarten. It is easy to see and teach that there are good choices that will bring safety, enlightenment, and happiness into their lives. It is also easy to see and teach that bad decisions will bring darkness, sadness, danger and even death into their lives. As we allow them the freedom to make decisions, we teach them what the consequences of their decisions will be.

For that matter, parents do not really have very much choice in the matter. We can teach children the easy way (which seems like the hard way when we are in the middle of it), or we can teach them the hard way. The easy way is to allow as much freedom of choice as possible as early in their lives as possible. The more experience they get, the better they get at making decisions and learning from them. While this seems the hardest at time, it is easier than trying to teach an adolescent that does not have the experience in making decisions but who rebels against authority and wants to make unwise or self-destructive decisions. By that time, a parent can do little but to watch the child flounder and hope that wisdom and good judgment will come before catastrophe. Unfortunately, some children make decisions that lead to destruction, misery, and pain for everyone whose life is touched by the individual. Of course, some children that have experience in making decisions will make decisions that lead to catastrophe anyway, but at least the parent who has given the child this knowledge and experience has maximized the child's potential for success.

In addition, if I believe in free will (which I do), it follows that I believe my children have free will. If that is the case, it would be extraordinarily stupid for me to establish a dictatorial regime in my home and not allow dissent or deviation from a rigid set of standards. Knowing human nature and the willingness to go to whatever length is necessary to be free from oppressive rule, a dictatorial system of family government is as doomed to failure as a similar national government would be. That is not to say standards should not be set. The lack of standards will lead to anarchy in the home as surely as a lack of predictable laws will lead to the same in our communities and nation. The key is to establish reasonable standards and consequences for breaking the standards, then allow children the freedom to make their own decision and suffer the corresponding consequence.

Going back to the idea that I am seeking to dismiss, why do I cringe when I hear this statement? While the statement expresses a worthy goal of allowing free will to the extent a child can handle it, the person expressing it is generally saying something completely different. What they are really saying is that they are not going to teach their children in accordance with traditional moral values or force them to participate in traditional value oriented organizations, otherwise known as places of worship.

There are a number of reasons for this. The first is fashion. Words cannot express the depth of my loathing of fashion. I make a special point to be unfashionable for specific reasons. But I digress. That is another subject for another chapter. Parents today want to appear to be in agreement with the intellectual trends of the day. Those trends are consistent with all the idiotic clichés that I am criticizing in this work. Therefore, parents who fall into this category are not teaching their children that there is right or wrong, or good or evil for that matter; they are just going with the flow, which happens to advance secularist thought.

Even worse than the lack of direction and understanding of these critical teachings is that some parents are actually facilitating their children's self-destructive behavior. It is appalling to read of parents who have funded parties at which alcohol is prevalent. Even worse are the stories of parents who provide strippers. In their attempts to seem "hip", these parents are teaching behavior that will drag their children down, in some cases with disastrous effect.

A related reason is the desire of the parents to be friends with their children. They perceive that if they become their friends that the children will freely talk to them and thereby maintain a close and open communication with them. Unfortunately, it does not work out that way. Parents can be friends with their children, but it is not the same relationship as a peer friend. The generation gap is real, and parents can never assume the role of a friend that the children depend upon to establish social relationships outside the family. More importantly, parents who want to be friends to the point of neglecting parental responsibility do not give the children what they need in this relationship, which is guidance and discipline. Parents that want to be long-term friends with their children will give them the reason to be friends after they become adults if they give their children the tools they need to survive the onslaught of voices trying to persuade them to make poor decisions when they are young.

Another reason is that some parents have been converted to a moral relativistic viewpoint. They have concluded that there is no right or wrong, and are teaching their children accordingly. While this is at least honest, it provides the same disservice to the child as the parent who wants to propound the latest intellectual fashion.

Last are those who are lazy. Teaching children is work, darn hard work by golly, and there are just too many good television programs to watch to be bothered by it. This group allows Hollywood to teach their children, and, remarkably enough, the same fashionable values described above are taught over the airwaves. This is downright scary. Think about children whose moral values have been formed by watching "Southpark", or "Married with Children". These programs pander to the basest instincts of humans, and can easily persuade children that these instincts are to be satisfied rather than controlled through self-discipline.

Our society is engaged in a cultural war. I will not say that this is anything new; indeed: it has been waged for millennia. However, the level of intensity has been exacerbated by the prevalence of mass communications. It is easy for those who have revolted against traditional values to reach millions with television, movies, internet, and magazines. It has been made even worse because most mass media outlets have defected to the other side and are participating in the revolt.

While critical evaluation of past practices is always a good thing, it does not follow that tradition is bad simply because it is traditional. In fact, tradition should be afforded the benefit of any doubt simply because it is a tradition, and only replaced with an alternative tradition if the original is found to have destructive tendencies, or is at least more destructive than it is constructive. Unfortunately, in the culture war being waged today many would replace constructive traditions with destructive ones.

A good example is the war being waged on marriage and the family. Women are taught that being a mother is tantamount to being a second class citizen. Elites denigrate and ridicule those who choose to be a full time mother and stay home to continuously nurture their children. Fathers are portrayed as dictatorial rapists whose only interest is gratifying themselves and maintaining power over their wife and children. The family setting is portrayed as a hopelessly dysfunctional breeding ground for maladjusted children. We are told that it takes a village to raise a child, which is designed to detract from the importance of what is being taught in the home. The institution of marriage itself is under assault, with people and groups who have only a cursory interest in it clamoring for recognition within its status, the ultimate intent of which is to further undermine its dominant role in shaping our society. This in spite of the fact that the family has been the foundation for all societies over the millennia, providing the most nurturing environment possible given the cultural and political circumstances that existed at the time. This is not a tradition that can even be remotely demonstrated to be destructive. Just because flawed individuals make up families, which lead to problems for the family and for society, it does not mean there is any other better vehicle for accomplishing all the beneficial work that is done in the home.

Why do many seek to destroy constructive traditions? As discussed in previous chapters, some want to replace any current value or vehicle for its propagation that restricts their ability to act as they see fit. In some cases this is a result of philosophical differences, in others a matter of gratifying personal passions. In others, it is motivated by a desire to gain economic gain or power. For example, there are people in the world who would sell illegal products to children that will enslave them and lead to their spiritual, emotional, and physical destruction. You know who they are, the drug dealers who prey on the malleable minds of children attempting to get them to experiment with their products for the sole purpose of getting them addicted. There are other examples. Sad to say, some products that accomplish the same objective are legal, even though the only purpose they serve is to provide profit for those who produce, distribute and sell the products. In terms of its addictive effect, tobacco may be worse than illegal drugs, it has no nutritional value whatsoever, and yet it is legally marketed and becomes a forbidden attraction to youth that is relatively easy to obtain. In each of these examples, we see that people are willing to enslave and destroy the lives of others for personal profit. While this is truly despicable, it is peripheral to this discussion. What is important is that we give children the foundation in life that will enable them to avoid falling into the traps that are laid for them by these predators.

Telling a child that there is no right or wrong implies that any choice that they make has equal value. If we want our children to avoid making self-destructive decisions, we must teach them that decisions that have destructive results are wrong and that making them will have destructive consequences for them personally. Telling ourselves that a child can learn moral values for themselves and using that as an excuse to neglect our responsibility is to cede control of our children's lives, and also the lives of the entire family, to others who often have malevolent intent.

This includes teaching religious values, and instilling the discipline in them needed to focus attention on important concepts, which can only be accomplished in religious institutions. Taking the position that we should not force our children to go to places of worship and learn these principles is analogous to trying to prepare a soldier against an enemy by ensuring he has no protective gear to withstand offensive weaponry nor offensive weapons with which he can defend himself. This is a monumentally stupid idea.

Many parents believe that their children should be given the choice of attending religious services when very young. This is a no-brainer for the kids; of course they will choose not to go to a meeting where they must sit still, be quiet, and pay attention to the person speaking while dressing in much more formal attire than is normal. A parent that gives a young child this choice is guaranteeing that the child will not attend these meetings, and never will because they will not have been given an opportunity to see the value in attending. The appreciation for religious instruction comes only after the child (or adult) acquires the self-discipline necessary to sit still and pay attention. I might add, this discipline spills over into other aspects of life, including school, work, and socialization. Learning discipline at an early age by attending places of worship gives a child a foundation for success in all future endeavors. As the child is enjoined from acting inappropriately, he or she learns respect for others in a formal setting. This

257

process is not easy, but the effort is well worth it, both for the parent and the child.

By the way, this should not be done with abject force. The child must have the choice, but parents must first encourage the child, verbally and perhaps by giving treats during times when the child is bored. If encouragement does not work, the child must understand that any decision he or she makes that is inconsistent with the rules of the home has adverse consequences. Any punishment must fit the crime; it is important that the parent not go berserk when authority is challenged. But punishment must follow bad behavior if the behavior is to be discouraged and eliminated.

Properly interpreted, the expression "It takes a village..." is correct and venerable. The fact is that parents do not raise children in a vacuum. We cannot spend every waking moment with them and we must rely on the community and nation to provide support for them and us. Critical among these support systems are schools and religious organizations, which should be teaching concepts in harmony with those we value in our families. If they do not, we must either join a different institution or reform the existing one. However, we must not cede to others the overall responsibility for teaching our children. Support systems are just that, to support the family in their goal of bringing up worthwhile and productive citizens.

In the end, maturing children will make decisions independent of parents no matter how hard the parents try to enforce their will. The only question is whether they will have been conditioned to making wise decisions. Even so, no matter how much love and training we put into a child, sometimes they will make stupid decisions. We can only hope that those decisions are not fatal and that over time they will recognize the negative consequences of them and alter their behavior. Fortunately, no matter how inadequate our teachings, most children ultimately wind up making the right choices in life, or at least enough right choices to survive adolescence (this is encouraging beyond belief). The one thing that is certain is that if we don't maximize teaching opportunities, including family and societal, the probability of our children making informed and wise decisions will be substantially reduced. While we must not force our children to make these choices, we can maximize the chances that they will by establishing standards of behavior in our homes and expecting and enforcing conformity to those standards.

Chapter 26

"I Must Stay in Fashion"

Okay, I admit that I don't really have a good cliché to rant about, but I certainly have a good target. It boggles the mind what normally sane, rational people will do for the sake of fashion.

What is the purpose of fashion and being fashionable? Is it to look good? Not really. The point of fashion is to look better. It is a competition, an attempt to look or feel better than others who are less fashionable. It really does not matter that people will look great in simple inexpensive clothes that are comfortable and modest. The point is that in order to persuade people to spend the outrageous sums of money needed to buy what will keep them from being ridiculed as "unfashionable", fashion designers need to create a demand for a product that people do not need and often do not want. Most people in this country have all the clothing they will need for a good many years if they will use it long enough to wear it out. I might add that most attractive people would look great in brown burlap bags; there is very little that they can wear that will make them look bad except maybe for the outrageous offenses that are pawned off on the public as chic fashion.

Is it just me, or does this sound a lot like extortion? If a person does not buy the latest creation from those who dictate what is currently in fashion, they are ridiculed and scorned. Remarkably, if they pay protection money, oops, err, that is if they buy the new products, then the people who make the products and collect the money for them will not incite ridicule against them any more. The people who personally benefit from the accusation get to determine when it applies. What a racket!

Fashion is also repetitive. Even though there is constant change, there is really nothing new so all we do is recycle old ideas again and again. We wear the latest creations of someone who gets paid immoral sums of money to design the same clothing and accessories that were fashionable ten to twenty years ago. We are familiar with the expression, "there is nothing new under the sun". This is certainly true when it comes to those that drive the incessant quest for something "new" that can be used to separate people from their cold hard cash.

Culture

One of the arguments advanced to persuade us to stay in fashion is that we need to distinguish ourselves from others so we will be noticed and praised. Ironically enough, the net effect is that everyone with this herd mentality blindly follows the group and winds up looking like wannabe clones of the latest supermodels, indistinguishable from everyone else in the fashion herd.

Unfortunately, no matter how hard you try and how much money you spend, you can never keep up. What is current today is an old hand-me-down tomorrow. You can't win; fashion is always changing so even if you constantly update your wardrobe, you will still be out of fashion in a few weeks or months. To try is an exercise in futility. To a lesser degree, the same is true for most of the consumer goods that we buy, even those that are major investments that we depend upon for extended periods of time, such as a car or home. There is continual pressure to buy the latest model of the most expensive luxury car so that you can tell everyone that you have "arrived", even if you have not.

If the drive to be fashionable only resulted in people wasting money on a futile attempt to get an ego boost it would not be so bad. However, fashion is destructive in many ways, one of which is that it can lead to serious financial consequences. If we are ever trying to keep up with the Jones (who are living on borrowed money I might add) and take upon ourselves needless debt, we can easily jeopardize our financial well being for nothing more than a short-lived sense of satisfaction that is meaningless.

Even worse, fashion can be and is used as a weapon by people who think they are better than others by virtue of the fact that they have successfully managed to buy the latest fashion. This is especially true of young adults in school, who are often cruel to those who are not, for one reason or another, wearing what the mindless herd of sheep are wearing. School uniforms would solve that problem, but those who need to feel good by denigrating others are adamantly opposed, and they seem to have the loudest voices.

Another destructive consequence of fashion is the inclination of gangs to use it to distinguish themselves, wearing distinctive colors and styles, and assuming that anyone who wears competing colors is a member of a rival gang that deserves to be punished. In this case, the lack of a particular knowledge of fashion can get you killed. Unfortunately, the fashion industry decided to let the gangs take over color, so for a decade or so we were forced to buy clothing and accessories that were gray. I had no idea that there were that many shades of gray. The entire nation was wearing nothing but dull, drab, dreary, depressing gray. Fortunately, that trend seems to be abating somewhat.

A particularly destructive aspect of fashion is the propensity of people to mutilate themselves, or even worse, their children. I remember as a young adult being amazed at the length that people in various cultures would go to make themselves and their offspring beautiful to the people of that culture. Some would strap boards to their heads to slope the forehead. Others would put rings around the neck, forcing the elongation of the neck by adding rings as the neck would adjust to the upward pressure. Others would pierce ears, nose, and lips to insert ridiculously large plugs and rings, which over time would stretch the body part beyond recognition and severely affect the person's ability to respectively smell, hear, or eat. The children that were forced to endure the pain were being needlessly tortured simply because of a cultural beauty preference. And the pain endured for a lifetime; the deformation of sloped heads, elongated necks and large plug holes ultimately had an adverse effect on the overall health of the person.

Unfortunately, our culture has not learned anything from the destructive practices of those we study. We routinely torture and mutilate ourselves for the sake of fashion. We pierce our bodies in almost every conceivable way risking infection and disease; we tattoo mindless and aesthetically unappealing patterns all over our bodies, again risking infection and disease not to mention the pain associated with the procedure; we wear high-healed shoes that are as unnatural for walking as anything that could possibly be designed. Once again, this is supposedly to set oneself apart from others; to establish oneself as a unique individual. In reality, all these unique individuals are putting on blinders and bleating as they follow the herd of sheep, each sheep looking remarkably similar to all the other sheep with their distinctively repetitive mutilations.

Tattoos deserve to be singled out for particular attention. Tattoos are largely permanent; when out of fashion they cannot be reversed without very expensive treatment. Remember that the fashion statement of today is the washed up trend of tomorrow. Also, many regret tattoos that link them to someone who they are not longer associated with. It is sometimes difficult for future relationships when every time the new partner looks at you he or she is reminded of a past relationship. Last, tattoos do not hold their original appearance. What appeals to friends now may not when the tattoo becomes an ugly indistinguishable blob of ink.

Culture

Some people practice extreme self-mutilation. Full body tattoos are the desperate cries of insecure people begging others to notice them. Then when they are noticed, the person lashes out at the observer for having the temerity to notice them. Others insert plastic and metal balls under the skin to draw attention to themselves, Still others insert metal clips into the skin designed to hoist the body into the air, similar to the torture scene in the old movie "A Man Called Horse". Then there are those who have metal or plastic horns surgically inserted into their heads because they want to look like how they think the Devil appears. Last, some people have even tattooed their eyes. Those that practice these extreme forms of mutilation generally place themselves on the fringes of society, but they still are following the herd of people using these barbaric procedures.

As if self-mutilation is not enough, we also have become so enamored of cosmetic surgery that there is actually pressure on people to have operations performed on them just to look younger or better. I understand the desire of people who have genuine problems with fitting into society because of blemishes, an unattractive appearance, serious weight problems, or diseases and injuries that result in deformations. I think the use of cosmetic surgery to correct these problems is wonderful. However, we have gone overboard with it. It seems that today's fashion mavens have determined that everyone is obligated to be eternally young and aesthetically perfect, so aging has become an enemy to those who think they need to look young to get ahead. In this insatiable quest for physical perfection, cosmetic surgery and Botox are over utilized, often to a point where the individual looks much worse than he or she would have otherwise looked without medical intervention. Women get their breasts augmented when there is no physiological reason to. Most of these people don't think about the risk to their long term health that surgery poses. This is a fashion trend that has gotten completely out of hand.

Speaking of health hazards, fashion is definitely a threat to the health of young girls, who are bombarded with images of supermodels that have starved themselves to a point where they have almost none of the form characteristic of beautiful females. The fashion moguls have declared that this is the desirable form, so girls wind up starving themselves to where they are anorexic, or are trapped by the practice of bulimia and all of the attendant health consequences of that practice. The saddest fact of this story is that girls are beautiful with the natural figures that they are blessed with, and that the desire to attain what fashion dictates results not just in adverse health consequences, but the girls look much worse than they otherwise would because of their attempt to be fashionable.

The constant replacement of goods that yet have useful life is in itself a waste of resources. We throw away stuff that has become outdated and unfashionable, and help to fill our landfills in the process. This is true even for buildings that no longer are in style. This practice is just another cultural practice that contributes to an unsustainable economic model in which resources, including human, materials, and energy, are consumed to produce products that are designed to be marginally utilized then discarded in favor of whatever comes next. It would not be so bad if these materials were recycled, but our landfills take in most of them because we perceive that if used once they are not longer a resource.

In some cases the desperate attempts to find something new and on the "cutting edge" leads to the general degradation of our culture. Pornography unfortunately has considerably influenced the clothing that we commonly see in public. What would have been condemned decades ago is now acceptable because of the gradual upward movement of hemlines or downward movement of blouse lines. Underwear is particularly impractical. Who in their right mind wears a string in place of comfortable panties, boxers, or briefs during the course of a normal day (I will concede they may be appealing in intimate circumstances)? I can't imagine a more uncomfortable article of clothing. It seems to me that those who wear this attire essentially give themselves a permanent wedgie. This trend is truly amazing; it is additional evidence that some people will make themselves as miserable as possible to avoid seeming unfashionable.

The preceding arguments explain why I am proud to claim to be the most unfashionable person in the United States, and I have yet to find anyone willing to disagree with me. This gives me great personal satisfaction, bordering on a confirmation that I am on the strait and narrow. That is hyperbole of course, but you certainly can count me out of the fashion parade. One of my fantasy goals was to eventually make Mr. Blackwell's worst dressed list. Unfortunately, Mr. Blackwell has passed away so that is not going to happen now.

Ironically, in order to remain unfashionable, I sometimes am required to avoid wearing clothes so old that they have once again become fashionable. I hate it when this happens, because it means that the fashion dictators are still controlling what I wear, in spite of my antipathy toward them and their influence.

Culture

Eventually, someone needs to tell the fashion emperors that the clothes they are producing are not real, or at least for the most part not for real people. Everyone can do his or her part by not falling into the trap of buying whatever the fashionmongers foist upon them. Most people's closets contain plenty to wear without the need to buy additional stuff anyway. Ultimately, the consumer has the power to dictate taste and comfort to the fashion designers; it is simply a matter of using the power of the purse to do so.

Chapter 27

"Ideologues are Dangerous Fanatics"

We hear much about how ideology in general and ideologues in particular pose a threat to the social and political fabric of our nation. Is this true? Let us evaluate what the terms mean and see.

Ideology is defined as:

"the body of doctrine, myth, belief, etc., that guides an individual, social movement, institution, class, or large group."[26]

Therefore, ideology refers to the core beliefs of a group, or in other words, the moral values of the group. This should sound familiar to those who have read the first two chapters of this book. Similarly, an ideologue is defined as:

"a person who zealously advocates an ideology,"[27]

or a person who strongly identifies with and advocates for the mores and beliefs of the group. If all ideologues are dangerous fanatics, this would mean that anyone who strongly advocates for the ideas that form the guiding principles for a group is dangerous. I think not. Similarly, if all ideologies are dangerous, then philosophical anarchy is the only safe moral and political course. This is not the most coherent argument to make if social stability is a desirable result.

First, let me emphasize that any idea, no matter how enlightened, can be taken to an extreme that is either harmful or ridiculous. For example, if I have respect for life, it stands to reason that I would avoid killing living organisms for the sake of killing. However, taken to an extreme the same concept can make it impossible for me to survive if I want to avoid killing all life. For example, I would not be able to eat to avoid killing whatever organic entity food came from. It can also render me immobile to ensure that movement on my part does not result in the crushing of any living

---

[26] ideology. (n.d.). *Dictionary.com Unabridged (v 1.1)*. Retrieved June 07, 2007, from Dictionary.com website: http://dictionary.reference.com/browse/ideology

organism. It can even mean I have to stop breathing to avoid killing the microscopic life that I cannot avoid drawing into my body with the air I need to keep me alive. People who take the generally enlightened principle that we should respect life to such an extreme do not live long enough to convince others of the correctness of their belief. Ideologies taken to an extreme are almost always bad.

This brings us to a variation of the term that is what people are really talking about when they say that ideologues are dangerous. Someone who mindlessly advocates an ideological extreme without considering the consequences of the result, or who is so blinded by ideology that he or she cannot understand or accept that others may have different beliefs that are valid to them, are unreasonable and indeed dangerous. These people are the past justification for the cliché. However, what is dangerous is the extreme positions that person will take, not the fact that the person may defend an ideology. Nevertheless, a person can believe in an ideology, be an ideologue as first defined, and even be an idealist without being dangerous. Indeed, these people keep most of us focused on and grounded in the core beliefs of our culture.

Unfortunately, as with so many other expressions that started out as constructive sentiments, the cliché has been broadly applied to anyone who takes a principled stand in favor of ideology. When all that is heard is that ideologues are dangerous and irrational, the distinction is often lost on the listener, who incorrectly assumes that anyone forcefully advocating for a cause is dangerous. By this logic, everyone is a dangerous ideological extremist. Anyone who believes that some things are right and others are wrong would be a fanatical ideologue, and that includes those who believe that it is wrong to believe there is right and wrong. When it comes right down to it, everyone lives according to an ideology that they have been taught, or which they have chosen in spite of what they have been taught. The only difference is the depth of passion brought to the ideology and resulting motivations and actions.

The perception that ideology is dangerous is a hindrance to the free expression of ideas and the logical pursuit of truth and understanding. Instead of actively advocating for what we perceive is right, we waffle and hedge our arguments to avoid the appearance of blind and unthinking devotion to flawed ideas. Blind devotion to flawed ideas happens a lot of

---

[27] ideologue. (n.d.). *Dictionary.com Unabridged (v 1.1)*. Retrieved June 07, 2007, from Dictionary.com website: http://dictionary.reference.com/browse/ideologue

course, but it does not help the pursuit of truth to avoid forcefully arguing for what you believe is right because you do not want your audience to believe you are narrow-minded. What is important is to always be ready to listen to other ideas and accept them when they are a better explanation than what was previously believed.

If extremes are almost always bad, it follows that moderation in the evaluation and implementation of an ideology is almost always good. A rational calculated evaluation of the ideology that uses common sense and reason to determine how it can be practical and beneficial to the group is the only sound means of determining its worth. Ideologues advocating forcefully for the beliefs of a group who use these principles to defend and advance their ideology are seldom dangerous or illogical.

In addition to the problem with taking good ideas to an extreme, there is the problem with extreme ideas. Not all ideas are created equal; some ideologies are indeed dangerous whether taken to an extreme or not. If a group, say the Aztecs, have a sincere heartfelt belief that they can appease an angry God by sacrificing innocent people, they may not think it is extreme to practice human sacrifice even though we would. Here, what is extreme is the ideology. No matter how moderate the priest tries to act with respect to the belief, people will die if the belief persists. An extreme system of beliefs (ideology) is at least as dangerous as the immoderate interpretation of good ideas.

So we can have bad ideas with destructive results, and we can improperly apply good ideas and have a similarly destructive result. Only by starting with good ideas and using good sense, logic, and moderation in the interpretation and implementation will we have constructive results. But there always must be a result. We cannot avoid taking an ideological stand. Everyone believes in something, even if it is the opposite of traditional belief. Therefore, the idea that an ideologue is dangerous simply because they have a belief system is profoundly illogical.

Extreme ideas are not always bad. In some cases, extreme ideologists are responsible for major cultural shifts that transform cultures for the better, and that have lead to the prosperity and liberty we currently enjoy. Examples abound. Jesus Christ transformed religious belief and practice with revolutionary ideas. Gandhi's practice of non-violent protest gave peace a much better chance than it ever had without it. The founders of this nation transformed the governments of the world with their radical (at the time) ideas. We should not be quite so quick to automatically deride extremes in ideology; it may be the path to a more enlightened and beneficial future.

What is more important than ideas to live by? Moreover, who does not live according to ideological values? While there may be a relative few who live on a subsistence level and do not have the luxury of thinking about much more than survival, the vast majority of the humans on this planet are guided by the ideology of their culture. This in itself is not bad. Problems only arise when we have bad ideas or the unreasonable application of good ideas. As previously discussed, laws are based on morality, or ideology. In this context, the terms are nearly synonymous. Those that live in this nation should be able to discern extreme and dangerous ideology and ideologues and do all they can to marginalize those people and ideas. We must also be willing to fight for the ideology we believe when confronted with those whose ideology is to destroy opposing ideologies.

Before we can fight for it, we must be convinced that our ideas are superior to those against whom we fight. So, what can we use to evaluate whether an ideology is good or bad? To discern the value of ideas and ideology, there is a very simple test. What is the result? Do freedom, happiness, satisfaction, or love result from what is propounded? On the other hand, is bondage, misery, hate, and death the end result? To paraphrase a scripture, by the fruits of the ideology you may know its worth.

If we are to prevail in the culture wars, in addition to winning the violent conflict born of that war, we must value our ideology enough to fight for it by any necessary means so long as the method is consistent with our core beliefs. We know for sure that those who oppose us believe in their ideology enough to kill themselves in order to kill innocent victims to make political statements and traumatize a population. If our culture denigrates those who forcefully argue for the ideology that has lead to the establishment and perpetuation of the liberty we have, the next generation may be less likely to defend it; indeed many may cross over and support those who seek our destruction. Sadly, we are seeing all too many instances of this. To help ensure that future generations become well grounded in the beliefs we value, we must transmit the values to them. Ideology and ideologues are the means to accomplish that end, and we must stop denigrating those who seek it if we want to succeed.

Chapter 28

"Media has no Effect on Behavior"

Let me see if I have this straight. Those that foist offensive literature, art, music, movies, television, and clothing onto the general public want us to believe that this offensive material has little or no effect on social behavior? Likewise, are we to believe that news media that does not report a story accurately or completely does not affect public opinion? This is a lot like saying the air we breathe in and out every day does not affect our health. You can put me down on the exceptionally skeptical list for this one.

We are completely immersed in our culture, and everything we think and do is affected by it. Just a simple illustration of this is that each and every day the vast majority of us wake up to music from our clock radios; turn on the television to watch news or entertainment programming during our morning routines; dress in conformance to the standards of our workplace; listen to the radio, a compact disc, or I-pod on the way to work; are exposed through the working day to the dress, entertainment, jokes, and cultural practices of customers and coworkers; listen again to our medium of choice on the way home from work; listen to news or music as we prepare dinner; socialize with family members using shared cultural experiences, watch television or recorded movies in the evening, and finally retire to the sounds of music or a movie that we can fall asleep to. The next day we repeat the same process over again. Weekends vary only to the extent that our cultural experiences do not involve work (well, for some of us anyway).

Generally speaking, this is a good thing. Our culture frames the acceptable social boundaries of our lives, keeping us homogenous and relevant to each other with shared experiences and values. It provides much of the social glue that keeps us together. I have not heard anyone argue that shared cultural characteristics and values do not affect social behavior. Indeed, what else affects social behavior beyond the basic instincts (genetics) we have as humans? Not much that I can think of.

On the other hand, we have the purveyors of smut, obscene language, music that denigrates others (especially women) and glorifies violence, and other offensive entertainment that argue with a straight face that the lyrics of the music, the pornographic scenes on television or in movies, or offensive

269

art have little or no effect on social behavior. These people are either deluding themselves, or they are deliberately lying to protect themselves from litigation (where are the litigious trial lawyers when you need them?).

Most of the time we are told that links between behavior and offensive material cannot be proven. Their standard of proof is in excess of what it would take to get a conviction in a court of law. If there is no proof beyond any doubt that offensive material inspires destructive behavior, the assumption is made that it cannot possibly be true. This is patently false; that something cannot be proven to be true does not disprove it. It must be proved that it is not true before we can completely dismiss the idea as false.

My response to someone who argues that there is no proof is "so what?" There is nothing that can be proven (see Chapter 16). The question is whether there is evidence supporting the theory that destructive media inspires destructive behavior, not whether there is ironclad proof.

In Chapter 26, I discuss fashion and how normally rational people will do irrational things to themselves in order to be thought fashionable. Entertainment is just another means of influencing human behavior in order to either achieve social, religious, political, or economic ends. Correct me if I'm wrong, but isn't the goal of commercial advertisements designed to persuade customers to buy specific products or brand names of products? What songwriter does not want every teenager to have his or her song on their lips and in their minds? The makers of movies use that medium to promote social causes that they support, and thereby seek to persuade others to their point of view. I am not implying that this is bad; to the contrary it is how our marketplace of ideas works. These ideas should be presented as they are in a free and open society.

Ironically enough, some of the same people who overtly attempt to influence public behavior through the use of media then turn around and deny any possible affect on negative behavior that could possibly be inspired by destructive media content. They want to have it both ways; to take credit for the positive consequences of positive media influence but deny any possible negative influence from blatantly destructive media. This is illogical.

Make no mistake; if we financially reward musicians when they produce music denigrating women as "bitches" and "ho's", surprise, there will be a host of musicians imitating the lyrics so they can also cash in. If enough young impressionable boys and girls listen to that garbage, eventually it will become self-fulfilling. Remember Goebbels and the principle of the repeated lie. Girls who are repeatedly told that they are only worth the sum of their anatomical parts will eventually accept as fact that they are bitches and ho's, and respond accordingly. Boys will perceive the same, and will begin to treat women accordingly. I do not need to prove this; all that is needed for adequate evidence is to look at what is occurring in society today. That the media influences behavior is a given, and that holds true for destructive media content just as much as it is true for constructive content.

Even worse is when artists expect taxpayers to fund offensive media that they cannot persuade anyone else to financially support. Artists like to think that simply because they are inspired by an overwhelmingly stupid idea that they have a right to collect National Endowment for the Arts (NEA) money to financially reward themselves for the moronic idea that nobody in the marketplace would reward. A picture of a cross suspended in urine, funded by the NEA, is a really good example of "art" that took some lazy and creatively challenged artist to produce. With twenty dollars to buy a cross and glass container, a trip to the bathroom to relieve himself, and a photograph of the combination, the artist collected a huge sum of money and successfully offended the very taxpayers who he suckered into paying him to begin with. This is not about freedom of speech; the artist has every right to say and do what he wishes; however, he is not entitled to public money to do it.

Sex before marriage is a good example of how the media has influenced public behavior. For decades we have been bombarded by the entertainment industry that the notion of remaining chaste before marriage is an antiquated and even counterproductive belief. We are told that we should experience life and make sure that partners are sexually compatible before we marry in order to better guarantee the success of the marriage. This concept has been so ingrained into our culture as normal that not having premarital sex is now ridiculed, in spite of the negative individual and public consequences it has. If you don't think this is true, watch While You Were Sleeping, an otherwise pleasant, inspiring, and mainstream movie starring Sandra Bullock and Bill Pullman that unfortunately also perpetuates this belief. In it, the main character (Bullock) is regarded as abnormal by a co-worker for not having sex before marriage.

The entertainment industry routinely tries to tear down any actor who may be seen as a positive role model for those who think sex should be something special as opposed to something cheap and common. Anyone who starts out as wholesome is pressured into compromising that image by appearing nude or worse. This in turn sends a message that morality is for sale, and nothing is more important than money. Many in our culture take their cues from these messages, convinced that traditional morality is old fashioned. Two actors that I can think of off the top of my head that have fallen into this trap are Julie Andrews and Meg Ryan. Most often after doing the nude scene their image is severely damaged, and some do not come back. Fortunately for us, Julie Andrews is back with as much class as she exhibited in the <u>Sound of Music</u> with her performances in the <u>Princess Diaries</u> and other movies. It yet remains to be seen whether Meg Ryan will be able to command anywhere near the audience she had before her ill-advised attempts to please members of the film industry that did not have her personal interests at heart. If she does not it will be a tremendous loss; she is an excellent and delightful actor.

I am convinced that there is a hunger for wholesome uplifting entertainment, and that anyone producing such will be financially rewarded. Evidence of that is the fact that almost all of the highest grossing movies are rated PG-13 or better. Most people go to movies to be enlightened, encouraged, educated, and edified. The lame excuse of industry that they are only reflecting current culture doesn't mean their garbage will be financially successful, most of us have easy access to all the cultural garbage we could possibly hope to experience without shelling out cash to see it in a movie theater. Entertainment should inspire us to be better than we are, not encourage us to be worse than we want to be.

Another aspect of media influencing behavior is in the news. In an attempt to persuade the population to support liberal agendas, the major networks have for decades slanted coverage of the news to promote liberal politicians and political causes. For instance, during the first Bush Administration the mainstream media could not broadcast enough negative economic news. It was coming at us from all angles. During the Clinton Administration, there was no such thing as negative economic news, even when the economy turned south during the last eighteen months of Clinton's last term. After Bush II was elected, we were back to negative economic news, which has so influenced public perception that for the first six years of his administration people actually believed the economy to be in the tank in spite of its health and vigor.

Even when they were forced to report positive news, they would deliberately frame the report to skew the effect of the news. I remember vividly yelling at the television (yes, I'm a little psycho about this) when CBS news would report good economic news, then immediately cut to someone they had managed to find that was not immediately benefiting from the improved economy and that was suffering because of government inaction or corporate greed.. They could always find at least one person that was afflicted in the midst of prosperity. Even when the news was good, it was bad. The same is true today, although I must say I have solved my problem of yelling at the television by no longer watching network news.

The treatment of war is another means of influencing public perception and behavior. The anti-war agenda has been fueled by the media, and continues to be supported to this day. In the minds of liberals, nothing is worth going to war. If we are forced by real politics to resort to war to preserve our interests, we are immediately bombarded with the images of death and carnage associated with it, and the lobbying against it. The Vietnam War was lost because of media inspired perception of the war, even though we could have won it if we had not inspired continued resistance on the part of the North Vietnamese with civil unrest in United States.

In the past, many have perceived war to be a glorified effort in a sanitized or civilized setting because of the old media. Nothing could be further from the truth. Revulsion to war is good. As bluntly observed by William Tecumseh Sherman, war is hell. I would add that it always has been and always will be. That is why war is the option of last resort. The practice of the new media in showing war close up has resulted in both a realistic perception of and revulsion to war.

However if we must go to war we also must win whatever the cost. If revulsion to war causes us to shrink from a war that is being fought to defend our vital national interests (these would be our lives, liberties, and the ability to pursue happiness), we will be doomed to fight against all that perceive that we are weak and lack the will to defend ourselves. Our children and grandchildren will pay dearly for this mistake. Even though the images show the horror of war, and the casualties pile up and test our will, we must win. One thing is certain; if we don't win in war we will pay a much higher price in the future.

Nevertheless, the media has now gone from the practice of glossing over the horror of war to undermining our national security when faced with defensive war by emphasizing the carnage and continually telling us that nobody understands why we have to defend ourselves as if nobody recognizes the importance of national values. It is easy to ask what alternative history would have resulted if the same attitude had been promoted during other wars that made and kept this country free. If cameras had been rolling at Valley Forge, Antietam, Belleau Wood, Guadalcanal, or

273

Culture

Omaha Beach, along with editorial comments denigrating the objectives of the war effort, would we have won the respective wars we were fighting? We need to look past the carnage and keep our eyes fixed on our goals if our culture and liberty is to survive those who think we don't have the will to win.

Another of my pet peeves about how the media influences public opinion is by their lack of actual reporting. I wish I had a nickel for every time I listened to a news report which did not report the story. For some reason reporters' think they are obligated to give detailed reports about the controversy surrounding a story, but not the story itself. We will get a blow by blow account of how everybody reacted, their perception of what happened, and the potential effects of the story, but they don't bother investigating to tell us what actually happened.

Part of this is a result of simple laziness and lack of proper training. Reporting is really simple; all you need to do is tell the reader or listener the who, what, how, when, where, and why of the story. However, I believe there are also ulterior motives to the lack of reporting. It is as if media types cannot bring themselves to investigate the facts of a story for fear of eliminating the controversy they seek to create. Because the facts of a story do not lend themselves to misinterpretation, if a journalist wants controversy to be the story instead of how bogus the controversy is we often get fragments of the story, the purpose of which is to skew public opinion.

An additional complaint is the media doesn't pay attention to important stories. The general population relies on the media to report important news that will affect the people within the media market. However, they are the ones who decide what is important. For example, while working as a planner our office would issue press releases concerning planning issues to inform the community of the issues. I don't remember one press release that was actually picked up by any press outlet and reported, to the detriment of the community. The knee jerk reaction of the media was to dismiss any information provided to them as useless, no matter how useful it could be.

In some cases the media blames government entities for the lack of information when the information was presented to them. The best example I see of this is the economic devastation wrought by the failure of mortgage giants Freddie Mac and Fannie Mae. In spite of repeated warnings by the Bush Administration and the Federal Reserve, nobody, including the Congress and the media, paid attention. Now we are in the midst of a crisis, created because the media was too lazy to report what was handed to them on a platter. One news commentator, Bill O'Reilly, seems very upset that nobody gave him an engraved invitation to report the story. Unfortunately, it appears that even if the administration had grabbed him by the collar and shaken him it would not have made any difference. (To be fair to Mr. O'Reilly, he is normally an excellent reporter and I watch his show every night. He just failed us on this issue.)

Speaking of reporting on unimportant stories, yet another gripe about mainstream media is what seems to be a conscious effort to report on trivial and unimportant things. The United States is facing serious problems, but instead of reporting on actions relating to these important issues, such as the aforementioned problems of the government sponsored institutions (GSI), we instead get stories that border on ridiculous when considering the overall impact of the issue on the nation. If I hear another story about Paris Hilton I am going to become physically sick (actually, with a DVR I get to fast forward through this journalistic pablum so I don't need to worry as much about keeping an airbag next to my couch).

I am slightly sympathetic toward the mainstream media because most budgets for these operations, particularly newspapers, are being significantly downsized. The result is that there are many fewer reporters trying to cover more stories than have ever been out there before. While I understand this problem, it follows that if they report a story, they can focus on getting the facts of the story instead of spending so much time and effort on getting the reactions to the story. Even more relevant is that with so few resources to devote to investigation, it seems ridiculous to spend resources on trivial stories that mean nothing to the population at large. I also think that budgets are being cut because of a lack of accountability to the public; many (including me) get their news from alternative sources rather than listen to or read the propaganda coming from the mainstream media. In other words, many media outlets have alienated their constituencies so much of the hardship they are experiencing is self-imposed.

In summary, we as members of this society need to remember that those that entertain and inform us are often working against the interest of our society with their attempts to manipulate social behavior. The motivation may be for economic, social, or political reasons. Frankly, it really does not matter. What is crystal clear is that the media does affect social behavior.

Chapter 29

"Linear Thinking is Oppressive"

There are some who believe that linear thought is a flawed approach to evaluating the universe and determining how it functions. By the way, linear thinking is using logic and reason to arrive at solutions to problems and obtaining answers to questions. I can't help but wonder if the term "linear thought" was coined specifically for the purpose of undermining the use of logic. Rather than directly attacking logic, which most people recognize as critical, they use another term to describe the same thing to attack what they cannot discredit directly.

The logic (note the use of logic to determine that logic is an inadequate means of evaluating ideas) is that there is no truth and no right or wrong. Because there is no right or wrong, the next logical step is to conclude that all choices, ideas, and philosophies are equal. It follows then that destructive lifestyle choices are as just as valid as constructive lifestyle choices. Last, the conclusion is made that anyone who uses logic, or linear thinking, to make any judgment about perceived destructive choices and philosophies is practicing oppression and is closed minded about life and the fact (according to this philosophy) that there are many roads that lead to happiness.

It is difficult to refute this illogical logic, especially because logic used to discredit the idea is immediately condemned as oppressive linear thinking. Ultimately, each person will decide for himself or herself what decisions to make, or in other words, which road through life they will take. If a person accepts this nonsense, it is likely that he or she will conclude that if all choices are equal and eventually lead to happiness, it stands to reason that choices that result in hardship are not necessary, and that choices that are easy or self-satisfying are better.

So, what is wrong with this picture? It can be demonstrated that unwise choices, using linear thinking to determine that the choice is unwise, results in unhappiness. A simple example is the case of a person who decides to use illegal drugs to get high. In the short term there will be pleasure and euphoria. Soon thereafter, there will be dependence, misery, loss of job, loss of family, degradation, and eventual death unless the person makes an extremely difficult and painful effort to overcome the addiction. The path has been clearly marked by the wrecked lives of those who allow themselves to become addicted. The logic of those who want to be free of social constraint and who dismisses the value of linear thought in order to claim to be free would have us believe that the end result of the drug addict is equal to the end result of the person who does not become addicted and who lives productive self-satisfying lives as a result. No matter how badly these people want to dismiss linear thinking, they are trapped by the harsh reality of the physical world and the unmistakable consequences of decisions made without respect for that reality.

As a civilization, how did we get to where we are? To what do we attribute the fact that we are not living on a subsistence diet in caves with a lifespan of less than thirty years? The answer is in our ability to use logic to solve problems in combination with our ability to fabricate tools and use fire, all of which has allowed our species to affect our environment in a way that no other species has ever been able to do. In addition, we have invented symbolic speech, which we use to transmit accumulated knowledge to succeeding generations. The net result is that we have the accumulated knowledge of people who have solved problems that had the effect of diminishing our lifespan and forcing us to live hand to mouth. Problems that came about as a result of previous solutions were in turn solved, and so built on the knowledge of past problem solvers. The problems were all solved by some combination of inductive or deductive reasoning together with environmental modifications to affect the desired result. In other words, we owe all the progress we have made since leaving the caves to linear thinking.

Some will cite the above logic to condemn our species and its manipulation of our environment. Environmentalists advocate a minimalist lifestyle, trying to persuade others to decrease their impact on the environment and their squandering of resources. Some extreme elements of that cause advocate a return to nature and a repudiation of the technology that has resulted in the remarkable transformation of our environment.

This is impossible without a massive reduction in the human population. If all humans decided to pursue an idyllic dream of returning to a Walden-like existence by getting rid of the technology that is our only present means of survival in the numbers currently in existence, the human catastrophe would be staggering. The world's population did not rise to much more than 400 million people until the industrial revolution, when technology allowed increased food production and preservation, and economic diversification. If we were to return to a pre-industrial revolution economy, it is likely that the world population would drop back to those levels, if not lower. That would be a reduction from 6.5 billion to 400 million people (or less given the inevitable resource wars), a stunning loss of life and the potential associated with it.

Frankly, even if it were possible to return to a pre-industrial revolution existence, such a life would not be idyllic by any measure. Far from a thoughtful peaceful life of contemplating the wonders of nature, we would be spending every waking moment trying to figure out how to feed ourselves in the face of disease, crop failure, pestilence, crushing labor, and, yes, war waged by those who also want to eat and will not graciously lie down and die just because they were not able to grow enough food for themselves. A subsistence existence is not all that it is cracked up to be by those who decry linear thought and its effect on the environment.

I agree with the philosophy that we should try to minimize our environmental impact. This is really a no-brainer. We have a substantially cleaner environment than what existed during the height of the industrial revolution, and we should continue to reduce pollution (toxic wastes that jeopardize our health and welfare). Living in the squalor and filth of our waste is neither appealing nor healthy for anyone. This is true whether we are talking about our home, community, nation, or world. Even if the current accusation that global warming is a threat to our survival cause by human action is a myth, it does not follow that we should not try to minimize our impact on the environment. We should reduce our environmental impact as much as we can so long as we also preserve our ability to provide the physical and economic means necessary for people to survive and flourish. In other words, we should use logic and technology to improve our environment while at the same time increasing our prosperity.

There will be some who will accuse me of ignoring the hand of God in this progress; such is not the case. I believe in God and that He is ultimately responsible for the overall progress we have seen; however, I also believe that He has given us the mind and ability we need to think for ourselves and solve the problems we need to solve to survive, grow, and become productive. I don't believe He wants us to sit around on our collective derrieres and expect Him to solve our problems for us. I believe history bears me out in this regard.

However, even for those agnostics and atheists who dismiss the role of God in human affairs, assuming that humans are left to their own devices makes the argument for the importance of linear thought all that much more important. We simply could not have accomplished what we have without using logic as the means of making choices that increased our odds of survival and of achieving prosperity.

In fact, linear thought is what has brought us the most technologically advanced, culturally diverse, yet tolerant and most free society in the history of the world. Remarkably enough, all this has been accomplished with an improvement in our environment, especially when compared with conditions at the beginning of the Industrial Revolution. If we abandon this approach, we undermine the traditions that serve as the vehicle for our society's existence. Essentially, we would go from a society that makes decisions based on logic to decisions based on some other means of determining what is best.

What would the result be? I suspect it would be a society that does not make any judgment about anything; scientific inquiry of any sort determining any fact would be unacceptable because fact would be different for each person as determined by what the person wants to believe to justify lifestyle choices. Do we reinvent the scientific method in the hope that throwing away logic and the scientific systems we have used to progress will have a more effective result? Those that argue against reason prefer the justification of illogical arguments leading to irreconcilable results over logic. They certainly don't want anybody feeling that his or her contribution, no matter how incompatible with what science tells us, is not valued.

Our ability to communicate effectively would also be affected. Do we create a Babel where nothing spoken is understood because each person gets to determine for him or herself what they want words to mean? (Oh wait, we are doing that already). Similarly, we would have the same attitude about religion, culture, or morals. In the world of non-linear thought, everything has equal value, so no idea is dismissed no matter how illogical.

How far down this road do we go before we remember that linear thought is the best means of ordering our world? If all results have equal value, eventually any value that is difficult will be lost. The result will eventually be chaos and anarchy, with a return to Dark Ages and even possibly a return to human sacrifice. It is not such a ridiculous result given that there are actually some Aztec wannabes out there. Wouldn't that be a fun society to live in?

Oddly enough, there will be some who argue both sides of this debate, using linear thought when it matches their ideology and dismissing it as irrelevant when it contradicts the same. I would argue that you can't have it both ways. Logic is either a useful means of problem solving or it is not. If it is, it is just as useful in deducing philosophical, religious, and moral solutions as it is in deducing math or physical science problems.

As it is with so many of the irrational arguments made these days, this is another example of those who want to live guilt free lives while acting in destructive ways seeking to rationalize the result their actions. Those who advocate this are the same people who are fighting against traditional values and whose lifestyle desires are adversely affected by those traditions.

Another tool some use to obtain a predetermined result is to ignore facts that discredit the result that is sought. Ignoring facts to achieve a desired result is just as flawed an approach as ignoring logic.

We know our logic and knowledge is flawed and incomplete; however, it is the best we have. We should carefully consider the trend toward non-linear thought just to allow some people the freedom of mind they think they will have to do things that are illogical and destructive to themselves, others, and society as a whole. Of course we can't prove the value of what we have categorically, but then again we can't prove anything. One thing is sure; we can evaluate the differences between the "good old days" when logic was completely subservient to passion, greed, ignorance, and politics. We all remember the Dark Ages fondly, don't we?

Chapter 30

"Homosexuality is Just Another Lifestyle Choice"

This chapter will almost certainly be the most controversial I write, and will be cited as proof that I am a homophobic bigot. While I suppose that is possible, I do not believe I am. Frankly, whether I am or not does not change the logic and reason about the disadvantages of a homosexual lifestyle or the advisability of choosing that lifestyle. Also, be warned. This chapter contains an analysis of the health risks associated with homosexual sex. While I have attempted to use clinical and inoffensive terms, some may be offended by the description.

Stipulations

First, let me say that there is no excuse for the maltreatment of others, including homosexuals, in any way unless their actions merit punishment as prescribed by law. This is true whether we are talking about race, religion, gender, sexual orientation, how they part their hair, or whatever. It simply does not matter. No one for any reason should take the law into their own hands and act as judge and jury in matters where they have no authority.

Second, this chapter is an attempt to explain why I believe that homosexual conduct should be legally tolerated and not punished; however, the conduct not be legally protected and encouraged. I am not advocating the mass arrest and incarceration of homosexuals; that would be profoundly stupid, counterproductive, and expensive. Those who have chosen this lifestyle should be allowed to live it so long as they act within the law. However, I am strenuously opposed to the glorification and encouragement of this behavioral choice. This distinction will be ignored by those who will vilify me as a homophobe, but it is important that I make it anyway.

Third, although it may seem otherwise to many who do not carefully read what I say, I am not trying to tell other people how to live their lives. Each person gets to pursue what they perceive to be happiness in their own way, and I will not presume to tell many committed homosexuals that the lifestyle they have chosen is not going to give them what they want in life. However, I will make it clear that I do not perceive this lifestyle to be one that maximizes the chances for happiness for its practitioners. I simply feel that it is important that individuals who are considering the choice of a lifestyle carefully consider the repercussions of their decisions and make those decisions fully aware of what they are getting themselves into.

Let me also concede that there are some homosexuals in committed relationships that seem to emulate the basic relationship of heterosexual couples (sans children). Most of those who are in those relationships live their lives constructively as fully functional contributing members of society. These constructive associations are cited as proof that homosexual behavior is just one lifestyle choice equal to heterosexual behavior.

In particular, some lesbian relationships seem to be a response to the abuse and irresponsible behavior of men. Here I will concede that I may be sexist; my experience has taught me that many men use and abuse women sexually. As a result, some women turn to their own gender for the affection and nurturing that they should be getting from responsible males. For this reason, I can easily sympathize with those in such relationships. In addition, many of the adverse effects of homosexual relationships cited later in this chapter affect men much more than women.

That said I do not share the gay community's enthusiasm for this lifestyle choice; not all lifestyles have equal value, both for society and for the individual. My intent is to present an objective evaluation of whether the lifestyle is in fact constructive or destructive for the majority of those who practice it. Leaving aside religious belief, we should be able to objectively evaluate whether the homosexual lifestyle makes the practitioners of it happy. If the lifestyle is destructive, it stands to reason that anyone choosing this lifestyle is much more likely to be unhappy than another who does not engage in these behaviors, no matter how sincere his or her conviction that the homosexual lifestyle is best for him or her.

Marriage

This subject is slightly off-topic in that it is not specific to addressing the advantages or disadvantages of homosexual relationships. However, because so much effort is being put into trying to convince the population and judiciary that denying homosexuals the right to marry is discriminatory, I need to address it.

In every culture that has ever existed (for longer than one or two generations anyway), formalized relationships between heterosexual couples have been the norm. Over the millennia the institution of marriage has been the foundation of culture and the principal means of transmitting knowledge from one generation to another in addition to the perpetuation of our species.

Marriage and the resulting family performs a vital role in the maintenance of a civilized society.

The institution of marriage has been so ingrained in every culture across the world that until just a few years ago there was no thought about legally defining the institution as being between a man and a woman. That would have been tantamount to us being required to define homosexuality as being a sexual relationship between members of the same sex in spite of the clearly understood definition that exists. The term has always been self-defining. Indeed, in the nineteenth century the Mormon Church attempted to establish an alternative marriage system, and was promptly shown by the majority of non-Mormons that polygamy was not going to be legally permitted through the actions of Congress and the President which were finally upheld by the Supreme Court in 1890. It cannot be argued with a straight face by anyone that there was any ambiguity about what constituted a marriage until the last ten or fifteen years.

Over the past few decades, marriage has been reviled as a mechanism for the oppression of women and children. The demonization of this institution has had some effect; we actually see people who are convinced that they can be happier living together outside of marriage than they can by getting married in spite of the objective empirical evidence demonstrating that marriage is the most satisfying lifestyle choice an individual can make.

The news media feeds this perception. We are exposed to a barrage of reports telling us about abuse, incest, rape, and murder perpetrated by family members on other members of the family. These accounts are true, but the reason they are newsworthy is that the story is not a "dog bites man" non-newsworthy story. These events are unusual, and therefore news. However, because of the prevalence of these reports of abnormal results we have been conditioned to think that such events are normal in families.

Entertainment venues are even worse in perpetuating the myth of the dysfunctional family. Hollywood loves to portray the family as dysfunctional in every way, including showing families to be violent, stupid, prejudiced, oppressive and most of all, miserable for everyone trapped in them. Small wonder that the perception of the family has taken a one-hundred and eighty degree turn the past few decades. We have gone from "My Three Sons" and "The Donna Reed Show" to "Married With Children" and "The Simpsons" in that time, and the media and secularists do not waste any opportunity in telling us that the nuclear family of the 1950's sitcom is gone, if it was ever an accurate model of family life in America.

Fortunately for our society, most people are not that easily mislead. Most real families are more like the Huxtables than the Simpsons. As demonstrated further on in this chapter, marriage is still the best assurance of a happy life that can be found. Perception does not always equal reality.

Even though the institution of marriage has been denigrated by cultural elites within the nation, very recently, the homosexual lobby has concluded that to be accepted as mainstream members of society (which in itself is confusing because I have been laboring under the impression that they have been mainstream for decades now) they must be allowed to marry. Much of this effort is directed toward influencing legislative bodies to allow homosexual marriage. In my view, this legislative effort is a healthy process, the effect of which should end in a compromise that will allow homosexual partners to legally protect themselves, their assets, and their ability to care and nurture each other in a manner that is acceptable to both sides of the issue.

Indeed, there has been much legislation passed specifically designed to ensure equal treatment of homosexual individuals by government entities. It is worth noting that most of these legislative initiatives have been adopted without much fuss on the part of anyone, including conservative groups that are opposed to allowing homosexual marriage. It is also worth noting that homosexual partners enjoy the right to enter into contracts as they desire which can legally accomplish most if not all of the benefits associated with marriage. Last, nothing stops individuals from freely associating with those whom they choose to associate for any length of time.

Unfortunately, there has recently been a disturbing but familiar trend which threatens to circumvent the legislative process and dictate a solution by judicial fiat. Remarkably enough, there are many people now arguing (with straight faces I wonder?) that homosexual relationships are required to be sanctioned and protected by existing clauses within both the Constitution of the United States and the various state constitutions. Even more remarkable is that there was found a majority of judges in a liberal northeastern state that discovered that homosexuals had a right to be married under a constitution written centuries ago. The judiciaries in California and Connecticut have also followed Massachusetts in ruling that homosexual marriage is protected by their state constitutions, even though in California a majority of its citizens passed constitutional amendment prohibiting the practice. Incredibly enough, California's court may void the vote, in which case California voters will be told that they do not have the right to amend their own Constitution. Once again, judicial bodies threaten the peace and stability of our democracy by decreeing that the majority has no authority to restrict behavior in spite of the fact that homosexual marriages cannot, except only under the very limited number of circumstances when homosexuals have children, function to perpetuate the species and transmit knowledge and culture to succeeding generations.

I understand that if a state chooses to allow homosexual marriages that those marriages will be of legal effect because of the "full faith and credit" clause of the Constitution. Indeed, all of the legislative efforts of the Congress, including the Defense of Marriage Act, passed by overwhelming majorities in both the house and Senate and signed by President Clinton, will most likely fail under that test. If that does happen, I am prepared to live with homosexual marriage unless a constitutional amendment can be adopted. What I really resent, and I suspect that most others also resent, is that a majority of justices in Massachusetts, California, and Connecticut are able to force every other state to allow homosexual marriage simply because they chose to ignore centuries of cultural precedent and practice and read into the respective state constitutions a right to homosexual marriage that was never intended by the originators of the document.

For those that argue that prohibiting homosexual marriage is unconstitutional, I believe the answer to that question was answered with the aforementioned decision regarding polygamy. In 1890, the Edmunds-Tucker Act that outlawed polygamy was upheld by the Supreme Court. That decision had the effect of prohibiting individuals from entering into marriage relationships that the majority deemed to be repugnant. That the relationships were voluntary and the prohibition of them had a clear discriminatory effect on the practitioners of polygamy was irrelevant. It is clear that the majority, using state and federal legislation as the vehicle, have the authority to define marriage as it pleases, and not even the First Amendment's guarantee of freedom of religion trumps that. The arguments favoring judicial intervention to allow homosexual marriage in spite of state and federal legislation does not even have the First Amendment guarantee of religious free exercise to support it. The argument is solely that a behavioral choice is a constitutional right.

The propaganda effort

Many use the image and example of homosexual couples who are committed to each other and who seek to simply live their lives in quiet peace to portray homosexual relationships in a more flattering light than

285

heterosexual relationships. Hollywood would have us believe that there are few if any committed monogamous heterosexual partnerships; entertainment produced now shows these relationships to be troubled and unstable, and that extramarital sex among those couples is the norm.

This is an excellent method of propagandizing the general population to make a homosexual lifestyle seem more appealing than a heterosexual lifestyle. Almost all humans seek to be loved, accepted, and involved in a caring and nurturing relationship, and the media attempts to convince young people preparing to enter into relationships that this lifestyle has a better chance of giving them what they want than traditional marriage. Indeed, marriage is frequently portrayed as the virtual enslavement of women and children. Unfortunately, not only does this propaganda convince malleable individuals that a homosexual relationship can be as fulfilling as a heterosexual relationship, it also has established a mythical dysfunctionality as the norm for heterosexual relationships, convincing some to betray their spouses and destroying relationships and families in the process. It is the old, "Everyone else is doing it, why can't I?" excuse.

Because of their newfound social acceptance, many homosexuals have acted in ways that have generated a considerable amount of ill will from the general population (you are right, I am one of them). A principal means of antagonism is by means of gay pride parades and events. In these, homosexuals go out of their way to flaunt their lifestyle, including overt sexual displays that should repulse anyone with any sense of shame or propriety. And yes, if heterosexual couples did the same I would be just as offended; however, they would most likely be arrested for lewd behavior. Even worse, the participants in these events take great pleasure in desecrating that which many deem to be sacred, such as portraying nuns as lesbians. Worst of all, they jeer at "breeders" and promise that they will sodomize our children (note the term breeders also contemptuously refers to their own parents). Then they are shocked! shocked! when many have an adverse reaction to these demonstrations. When these actions draw the condemnation that they are seeking, apologists for homosexuals promptly accuse the offended of being homophobic. It is remarkable that in spite of these unbelievably cynical, offensive, arrogant, and crude demonstrations, a majority of Americans yet believe that homosexuality is an acceptable lifestyle (another example of the best offense constituting the best defense). In any case, it is clear that we are a tolerant society.

The genetic argument

The gay community and other professionals would have us accept as fact that homosexuality is a genetically inherited trait and that therefore the practice is not aberrant behavior. They insist that those who have the trait have no control over their lifestyle; that is, those who have such a genetic predisposition have little or no choice over their sexual behavior. Indeed, they insist that this genetic predilection is reason to not only accept this lifestyle as we would any other sexual relationship, but to celebrate it and encourage those who perceive they have the trait to revel in their distinctive lifestyle choice and attempt to persuade others to share in their enthusiasm. Indeed, those who do not share their enthusiasm are branded as homophobic and are demonized (hmmm..., am I repeating myself?). Incidentally, this cultural phenomenon has come about since the late 1970's, a remarkably short period of time for such a dramatic shift in social values.

First, I am not convinced that homosexuality is genetically determined. It could easily be the result of environmental conditions, cultural pressure to be in the forefront of a media championed and popular social movement, or a combination of the two. Its proponents are loud and dominate much of the social discourse in this nation, and many young people have been propagandized to a point where they accept the behavior as normal and are therefore more likely to experiment with the practice. In addition, a good argument against a genetic predisposition can be made based on evolution. Over time, a genetic predisposition would not be fit from an evolutionary standpoint as it would be much less likely that the genes would be passed on by practicing homosexuals. If it is not genetically determined, homosexuality is simply a behavioral choice that is no different from any other behavioral choice. That said, I will assume for the purpose of this discussion that homosexuality is a genetically inherited trait.

A genetic predisposition does not equal a beneficial predisposition

So what? Whether homosexuality is a behavioral choice or genetically determined is irrelevant to a discussion of whether the lifestyle is beneficial for society or for any individual who practices the lifestyle. We do not normally embrace and glorify destructive behaviors simply because there is a genetic predisposition for the behavior.

In addition to identifying homosexuality as a genetically determined trait, scientists assert that other traits are also genetically determined. These include aggression and impulsive behavior. There is a growing body of

287

research supporting the theory that genetics is the major determinant influencing behavior. If this is true, a whole host of socially undesirable behaviors are genetically predisposed (as are socially desirable behaviors). These include sexual promiscuity, child molestation, and aggression, which can lead to murder, rape, battery, and similar destructive conduct.

The conventional mantra we hear repeated over and over is that homosexuality is genetically determined and therefore the behavior is inevitable and anyone who has homosexual tendencies who does not embrace the homosexual lifestyle is not being true to him or herself. If we accept this logic, where does it take us with respect to other behavior for which there is a genetic predisposition? If genetics is the sole justification for encouraging participation in this lifestyle, it follows that genetics would be justifiable grounds for encouraging other destructive behaviors as well.

Those that argue that genetics determine a behavioral pattern that cannot or should not be resisted by the person who has these impulses essentially argue that any behavior affected by genetics should be embraced and celebrated regardless of how destructive the behavior is both to the individual or society. Therefore, those who are violent should be forgiven when their violent acts harm or kill others. Those who rape women or molest and abuse children should be applauded for being true to their inner selves (NAMBLA loves this argument). Those who argue that these behaviors should not be condoned even if genetically programmed are also conceding that homosexual behavior, even if genetically predispositioned, should be encouraged or discouraged based on the effect of the lifestyle on individuals and society.

If all this is true, does it stand to reason that we should then encourage these behavioral traits? Should we accept and tolerate the behavior of such persons as inevitable because of their genetic predispositions? In the case of violent criminals, do we resign ourselves to being subject to these violent actions and allow the behavior to go unpunished? After all, no amount of punishment has resulted in the elimination of any socially undesirable practice. We are often told that punishment is not a deterrent to crime, and a genetically driven criminal supports that notion.

I think not. Every human being on the face of the planet is motivated to survive, procreate, and to experience pleasure. Almost certainly, these are genetically inherited instincts. Our instinct is to act on these impulses regardless of the impact these actions will have on others. In spite of the fact that these are extremely powerful instincts, the fact is that the vast majority of us learn at an early age to control them, and only act on them under prescribed circumstances. We live with these impulses every single day, day in and day out. Most adults suck it up, exercise a little self-discipline, and do not allow themselves to act destructively towards others or to act in contravention to convention. That some act destructively is certainly not an excuse for us to throw up our hands and surrender to those base instincts or to condone the actions of those who do regardless of genetics or any other factor that influences behavior.

Everyone can and does make choices every day of their lives that conflict with genetically programmed impulses. They do so because they are aware of the consequences that will result if they allow their actions to be determined by these impulses. Nobody is forced by genetics to engage in behavior that is destructive, it takes a conscious decision to do so.

This is yet another form of our propensity to excuse bad behavior in others by attempting to shift the responsibility to someone or something else (see Chapter 32). In the end, we either must protect the general population from those who will prey on others, or the general population will be subject to the depravations of those whose behavior is destructive. This is true whether the destructive behavior is genetically determined or not.

The question then is not whether a behavior is genetically determined, but whether a practice is to be alternatively punished, discouraged, tolerated, accepted, or encouraged. Whether any behavior is genetically determined is irrelevant.

Regulating behavior

Historically, we have never protected socially destructive behavior. Specifically, we have never legislated protection to ensure the survival of behaviors that have a generally negative impact on society and individuals. The protections built into our Constitution and law create protected classes of persons, including race, religion, gender, color, and physical abilities. Until a few decades ago, none of these specifically protected classes included people who have specific behavioral traits. Behavior has always been subject to restrictions by the majority, who should be restricting behavior based on the impact the behavior will have.

Homosexual behavior is just that, a behavior, not a right. If we create a right for this particular behavior, there will be increased pressure to allow as rights all manner of previously proscribed behavior, including prostitution and child molestation, simply because there is a genetic justification for the behavior or because it is futile to try to restrict the behavior. Indeed, the

North American Man Boy Love Association, which not only lobbies for the legalization of consensual sex between men and young boys but also enables this currently illegal practice, is a dramatic illustration of how far behavioral restrictions could be relaxed to the very real detriment to the health, safety, and welfare of our most vulnerable citizens.

In societies across the world, destructive behavior without any other redeeming quality is proscribed and punished. This certainly has been historically true in the United States. Other behavior may be tolerated even if it is destructive because 1) the destructive effect may be marginal, 2) it may be specific to individuals, 3) it is difficult if not impossible to regulate, 4) the regulation of the behavior would be more intrusive than is acceptable from a societal standpoint, 5) or any combination of the four. Historically, these behaviors are discouraged even though they are tolerated. Other behaviors are generally constructive, but may occasionally have destructive effects; for the most part those are accepted. Last, there are behaviors that are always constructive and beneficial, and these behaviors we encourage to the extent we can.

So, the question then is whether we as a society punish, discourage, tolerate, accept, or encourage homosexual behavior. As you know from the third paragraph of this chapter, I believe it should be tolerated. I believe the practice is impossible to restrict and the attempt to restrict it would be more intrusive from a societal standpoint than would be acceptable by a majority of the population. However, I am also convinced that the behavior is destructive and should be discouraged. Relying on the demonstrable effects of the practice, it is easy for others to reach the same conclusion. The rational approach is to evaluate the effect that homosexuality has on society and the individual. In other words, does homosexuality have a detrimental effect on society and the individuals who engage in the practice? I believe the overwhelming body of objective evidence demonstrates that the answer to that question is yes as will be demonstrated by the remainder of the chapter.

Worth noting is that most of the more dramatic destructive effects described are more applicable to gay relationships instead of lesbian relationships. Therefore, a better case can be made that gays are more likely to suffer from these relationships than do lesbians. This is particularly true of lifespan and disease.

Longevity of relationships

I previously discussed the fact that there are homosexual relationships that consist of constructive citizens peacefully living their lives. However, are such relationships where two homosexual partners are in a committed relationship the norm? Studies suggest otherwise. The Family Research Council, (admittedly a conservative organization, but that does not disqualify their empirically objective research) has analyzed studies that indicate homosexual relationships do not even come close when compared with heterosexual relationships, even though the opportunity for longevity in relationships is the same for both groups. Significant differences are as follows:

- Homosexual relationships do not have the longevity that approaches the longevity of married couples. 50% of heterosexual marriages survive longer than 20 years; the average length of a homosexual live-in relationship is between 1.5 to 3 years while most relationships last no more than six months.

- The percentage of married couples that have remained faithful to their spouse is very high; including over 75% of men and 85% of women. In contrast, self-reporting homosexuals indicate that the normal number of lifetime sexual relationships is anywhere from 100 to 500; many report over a 1,000. Even where there is a "committed" relationship, at the most only 25% of persons in those associations report a monogamous relationship, and, in stark contrast with heterosexual couples, all associations that have lasted over five years reported sexual relationships outside the partnership.

- Approximately 50% of the heterosexual relationships in the United States consist of married couples. On the other hand, even when given the opportunity to marry or enter into civil unions in the United States, at the most only 21% of eligible homosexual couples take advantage of the opportunity. In Europe, countries that are on the leading edge of the liberalization of marriage laws report that less than 3% of eligible couples enter into these contracts.

This information should make it clear that for the vast majority of the participants, the homosexual lifestyle is not about establishing long-term committed relationships where the partners are faithful to each other over a lifetime. Anyone choosing this lifestyle should realize that. Even if it is an individual's intention to establish such a relationship, the homosexual culture and the overwhelming proclivity on the part of those who are a part of that culture to engage in sexual relationships outside the partnership, make the likelihood of the individual's achieving that goal considerably less likely.

However, is it reasonable to conclude that homosexual relationships are destructive based on the preceding? I would answer yes. If a person is moving from partner to partner and does not know how long any relationship will last, it is less likely that he will be able to establish a long term committed relationship based on trust and mutual respect. Can he count on that person to stand by him when he gets sick or is dying? Can he confide in his partner, knowing that the confidence will be kept over a lifetime? I perceive those that maximize the probability of a long-term committed relationship lay the foundation for a healthy supportive relationship that will endure a lifetime and provide the person with an emotional base that can carry him through the many difficulties that life presents. If the only value he has to his partner is physical, the remainder of his being becomes meaningless and trivial. I cannot imagine a more depressing mental environment.

Social Effects

Are homosexual relationships destructive in other ways? Based on the social implications of the practice, the answer is again yes. By the way, promiscuous sex within the heterosexual community is also destructive and carries with it many of the same mental and health risks. That is further evidence that fidelity to a single partner is the best predictor of long-term happiness and health.

What are the societal effects of homosexuality? First, the practice limits our ability to perpetuate our species. Homosexual couples do not produce children unless they resort to surrogates or technology. That certainly is not the norm, especially considering the cost. In addition, many homosexuals do not want children, who significantly affect their ability to practice their lifestyle. If this lifestyle were dominant, our ability to sustain ourselves would be compromised. Even a significant minority not producing offspring can have a negative effect on our ability to provide workers to sustain our economy, a condition that is exacerbated by our tendency to kill many of our children before birth (see Chapter 13).

More significantly, in an era when we may be in a protracted conflict with opponents who want to destroy our culture, limiting the number of children we have could be fatal to our civilization. In any case, when we have declining birth rates and tremendous social problems resulting from a disproportionately high number of elderly, it seems clear to me that we should discourage this trend.

Violent acts against partners are also significantly higher among gay and lesbian partners than among married couples. Incidents of domestic violence between homosexual males are nearly double that of married couples[28]. Indeed, the incidents of violence among married couples are less than any other group, including heterosexual couples who cohabitate. It seems the Hollywood perpetuated stereotype of dysfunctional families is largely a myth.

Mental health is a significant concern for homosexuals, including depression. Many attempt suicide, and youth suicides exceed the norm by six hundred percent. There is also a high percentage of this population that use addictive drugs, including alcohol, tobacco, and marijuana. Some will argue that many of these mental health problems are a direct result of oppression and prejudice from the majority heterosexual population. While that may account for some of it, it certainly is no longer a plausible explanation for all of it given the widespread acceptance and outright promotion of the homosexual lifestyle over the past forty years. Even if it is true, it does not change the fact that mental health suffers when an individual chooses a homosexual lifestyle for whatever reason. Anyone choosing this lifestyle should do so with that understanding.

The social costs of the violence, addictive behavior, depression, and especially suicide is staggering. Each act of violence tends to have a ripple effect throughout the community, resulting in more violence and suffering which can continue in a downward spiral. The depression and addictions can disable the person to society; those trapped in these self-destructive behavioral cycles will likely not be a stable functional component of the community, and will require considerable community and national resources to nurture and sustain. Suicide is the worst of all; it represents the permanent loss of what could have been a contributing member of society and the loss of a person who was dear, or at least should have been, to his or

---

[28] http://www.frc.org/get.cfm?i=IS01B1

her family, friends, and community. The societal investment in that person, including birth, nurturing, schooling, and a multitude of similar investments in time and effort on the part of many caring people and institutions has as its result nothing.

Social effects include the impact of the practice on global and community organizations. Recently the Catholic Church has faced a major scandal because of priests who have disregarded their vow of celibacy and engaged in sexual relations. Often, the offending priest would coerce minor children, including alter boys (those who they should have had the greatest inclination to protect) into having sex. This scandal has significantly affected both the financial well-being of the Church and its ability to preach its message with moral authority. This is the case simply because many homosexual priests could not exercise the requisite self-discipline. This is an example of how a few weak links in an organization can have a significant effect on the whole organization, which overall seeks to do good and is a tremendously positive world wide organization.

Another affected organization is the Boy Scouts of America. Remarkably enough, this organization has taken a strong stand against homosexuality and is being demonized as a result. The most ironic part of this is the fact that the organization is acting in the best interest of the youths enrolled in its program. Decades ago, chicken hawks (adult males who prey on minor male children) surreptitiously joined the organization and were able to use scouting functions to fulfill their fantasies. This resulted in the betrayal of some boys and the parents who depended on the organization and its leaders to protect their children. The organization suffered legal and financial consequences because of the actions of these predators. To its credit, the organization has undertaken a massive effort to ensure these occurrences are rare, for which they are now being demonized and ostracized. Legal actions to force them to accept homosexual leaders has been defeated by the Supreme Court, so now those who seek entry into this fertile field of innocent children are using financial and social weapons against the organization, including the prevention of the use of public facilities for their activities.

I was a member of the Boy Scouts of America during the aforementioned period and remember well the chaos and heartbreak inflicted on the organization and members by these predators. In fact, my family was one of those affected (you are right; it is difficult for me to be objective in this matter). The net result of this campaign is that an organization which has as its core mission the teaching of children to become trustworthy and capable adults has been largely marginalized in the minds of a significant minority of the population.

Another social impact is the increasing boldness that extreme organizations have assumed because of the social acceptance of homosexuals, the best example of which is the North American Man/Boy Love Association. NAMBLA has been around since 1978 and was founded for the purpose of encouraging the liberalization of laws that prevent sexual relationships between consenting adults and minor children. Unfortunately, not only do they advocate for legislative changes (a constitutionally protected right) but they also facilitate the illegal underground practice which they advocate, a criminal act. Even worse, they show the predators that cannot get into the Boy Scouts of America how they can lure unwitting and unwilling minor children into their web. Worse still is that some have used this information to not only sexually prey on children, but to murder them also.

Physical health

What are the physically destructive effects of homosexuality? They are many, and it does not take a rocket scientist to figure out why. Homosexual men have a dramatically shorter lifespan than heterosexual men. The reason for this is simply that the lifestyle they have chosen is physically dangerous.

Homosexuality is the practice of engaging in sex with a member of the same sex. The opinion of the American Psychiatric Association notwithstanding, unprotected anal intercourse, oral to anal contact, and other sexual practices by homosexuals are in conflict with all known sanitary practices. The human digestive system is designed to ingest nutrients and then eliminate the remaining fecal material from our bodies; this waste has high levels of bacteria that will easily kill those whose circulatory system becomes infected with such waste. Unprotected genital contact with the digestive tract invariably results in fecal material within the genitals. Oral contact with the anus, or with unwashed genitals removed from the anus, has the same result. This is remarkably disgusting to most people when objectively considered; not many people deliberately ingest feces. The negative impact of such on the physical health of those who do is not hard to understand.

The propensity to engage in promiscuous sex, particularly unprotected sex, directly results in very high levels of sexually transmitted diseases (STD's). Many of these diseases can be controlled; however, as the diseases mutate in response to the drugs that are used against them it is increasingly likely that there may be future strains of STD's that may be uncontrollable, much as AIDS was uncontrollable before technological drug advances around 1996. AIDS has devastated the homosexual male population, and while the recent advances in drug technology has resulted in extended life spans and better quality of life for those infected, it still is a significant killer, and as with other STD's, there are now strains of the disease resistant to the cocktail of drugs used to treat it.

In addition, homosexual men have significantly increased incidents of anal cancer, as much as ten times the rate of the heterosexual population. Incidents of Hepatitis, including types B and C, among homosexuals account for 21% of the cases in only 1-3% of the total population. Bowel parasites and infection are also a significant health risk.

The combined effect of violence, STD's, AID's, other diseases, and suicide has resulted in homosexual men having a lifespan 20 years less than their heterosexual friends. This is a very cold and rationally objective criterion for determining that homosexuality is hazardous to its practitioners health.

In addition to health hazards, the quality of life for aging homosexuals is questionable. Leaving aside the common lack of long term relationships, the long term physical effects of the abuse of digestive organs is likely to result in the failure of critical components of organs critical to the control of digestive functions. Chronic leakage of fecal material from the anus is common where the sphincter has been abused over time.

Ironically, those who engage in this reckless behavior seem to be the loudest in denouncing government efforts to overcome these diseases. For some reason they think that scientists should be able to wave a magic test tube and come up with a cure to all the diseases that would force them to modify their behavior. If they must modify their behavior by (gasp!) using condoms, they are being oppressed, because any restriction on their ability to engage in sex as they choose constitutes oppression. Indirectly then, government's inability to control microbiological evolution equals government oppression. Thus we see demonstrations forcefully denouncing government, as if viral evolution is going to suddenly cooperate in its self-destruction in conflict with the principles of natural selection because homosexuals are on the streets making idiots of themselves.

Lesbians also experience a high percentage of STD's, remarkably enough largely because they also engage in promiscuous heterosexual sex. (Which is curious; why do lesbians participate in heterosexual sex if they are programmed to be homosexual?) Only a small percentage of lesbians are not promiscuous (7%), and those that engage in promiscuous heterosexual sex are likely to have multiple partners. This is a fertile environment for the spread of STD's.

Conclusion

The rebels who wrote and signed the Declaration of Independence believed that our Creator has endowed each person with specific rights, including the right to life, the right to be free, and the right to pursue happiness as we choose. Later, the drafters of the Constitution listed all the specific rights enumerated within the Bill of Rights as those which they apparently thought were included in the broad general right of freedom. They also believed that it was the responsibility of government to secure those rights for its citizens. Under this philosophy, in theory each person gets to choose his or her course in order to find happiness for himself or herself so long as that course does not significantly affect the choices of others. Governments within the United States have allowed those with homosexual impulses to choose that lifestyle. However, just because the ability to choose such a lifestyle is condoned, it does not follow that such a choice will make all those who choose it happy. Those who would choose a homosexual lifestyle should carefully consider whether in fact that choice will lead to long-term happiness for themselves.

Many have been convinced that following base instincts and blindly pursuing hedonistic pleasure is being true to their own nature. This argument is not limited to those arguing in favor of a homosexual lifestyle choice; promiscuous heterosexual behavior is similarly packaged. The real question that each person must answer for themselves is whether capitulating to these impulses will lead to happiness or misery for themselves or those they love. If long-term happiness can be attained by choosing this lifestyle, it follows that such a decision would be justified and appropriate. However, if all evidence points to these lifestyle choices as destructive to long-term happiness it follows that not choosing the lifestyle is in harmony with the individual's interests. That is as true for an individual with homosexual impulses who chooses a heterosexual relationship to maximize the probability of having a long-term relationship as it is for a heterosexual who chooses a monogamous relationship to do the same.

Culture

In spite of efforts to convince the general population to the contrary, homosexuality is not just another lifestyle choice which we can pick as if from a menu and think that we will be as happy with that choice as with another. It is not like choosing between a steak dinner or lobster at a restaurant. Those who choose to be homosexual (and it is a choice as to whether or not an individual will act on genetic impulses) choose a lifestyle which leads to violence, depression, disease, and death for a significant number of its practitioners. The question is whether the benefits and pleasures associated with the lifestyle outweigh the attendant consequences of the behavior for the individuals who choose this lifestyle.

Because of the hazards associated with the homosexual lifestyle, I believe we should educate individuals about these hazards and attempt to discourage the behavior. Indeed, we should treat this behavior much as we treat tobacco. There should be a warning informing people that "homosexuality may be hazardous to your health" put on any packaging associated with the promotion of the lifestyle. I wonder if the promoters of Gay Pride parades would consent to displaying the warning? Well, never mind.

Chapter 31

"Profanity is no Big Deal"

Increasingly, public discourse is peppered with profane speech. While some decry the increasing frequency and intensity of the use of profanity, others dismiss the trend as harmless. They argue that such speech is necessary to emphasize the importance of specific arguments, and because it is so common it is no big deal as it is no longer offensive to most people. In addition, women have become much more likely to use profanity because they seek to put themselves on an equal footing with men (as if the base habits and tendencies of men are worthy of emulation). Men formerly avoided profanity in the presence of women; however, when women use language that formerly would make the proverbial sailor blush that motivation to avoid profane language goes away. Call me old fashioned if you wish, but I think that profanity is a big deal. The common use of profane speech has polluted discourse, decreased the quality of language, made communication more tenuous, and debased our culture.

First let me observe that I served in the Marine Corps and worked in construction prior to my career in government. In every environment in which I have worked, profanity has been common. I say this to let you know that I am no stranger to profanity, and am accustomed to working around it. That said, however inured to it I may be, I can still recognize the effect that its widespread use has on our culture.

What is profanity? The American Heritage definition posted on Dictionary.com defines profane as:

1. Marked by contempt or irreverence for what is sacred.

2. Nonreligious in subject matter, form, or use; secular: *sacred and profane music.*

3. Not admitted into a body of secret knowledge or ritual; uninitiated.

4. Vulgar; coarse.

Profanity is subsequently defined as:

1. The condition or quality of being profane.

2.

      a. Abusive, vulgar, or irreverent language.

      b. The use of such language.

Also useful are the synonyms for profanity, which are as follows:

- Bawdiness, coarseness, curse, dirt, expletive, filth, foulness, grossness, lewdness, oath, obscenity, ribaldry, scatology, scurrility, smut, swear, vulgarity.

By definition, profanity demeans and is contemptuous of that which is sacred. It also emphasizes that which is vulgar, lewd, and gross. Most people, when they consider their speech communication goals, would be appalled if the overall effect of their speech was debasing. And yet many of those same people use words and phrases that have that effect, often without even thinking about it. It is really the intent of the majority of those who use profanity to transform sacred things into base objects (yes I know, many do this deliberately)? Or is it their intent to cause others to think of base subjects that are unappealing thoughts in any setting? I don't think so. Nevertheless, many do, either to emphasize their argument or demand, or because of habit.

Families are affected because parents, thinking that it is no big deal, routinely use profanity in the presence of children. Even worse, many berate their children or spouses using profanity, which transforms the home from a sanctuary from a profane world to a mentally and spiritually bankrupt environment. Home should be a refuge from the profane, not the incubator for it. It should also be a place where positive social values are taught, not where children or spouses are demeaned and insulted using harsh language. An individual's use of profanity against those they should most love and want to nurture, that is a child or spouse, is symptomatic of a lack of emotional control.

Even families that refrain from the use of profanity are affected by its use. It is difficult to find a social setting in which a family can take children where they are not exposed to the crudest and most vile speech. For example, my daughter took her small child to a college football game. She wanted her child to have a positive and fun experience while also giving the child some enthusiasm for her alma mater. What could be more all American than that, to take your children to cheer on your team?

Unfortunately, she had to leave the game shortly after it started because of non-stop profane shouting matches between opposing fans. She has not taken her child to another game since then. I wonder how many people have stopped taking their families to sporting or social events because of the use of profanity. I also wonder what the economic loss is to organizations that are negatively affected by such language.

Language is affected because the use of vulgar language is so common we use it to the detriment of uplifting and thought provoking speech. Instead of dwelling on positive dialogue, thoughtful musings, or inspirational speech, we instead continually have our attention called to base subjects and thoughts.

Hollywood has played a major role in the debasement of our language. While media moguls claim to merely reflect the language that is in common use, in fact entertainment media has been the driving force in the use of profanity. They started a destructive cycle by taking the language of a few and telling everyone it is common. Now that profanity is common they claim only to reflect current culture. The result is entertainment without good communication, culture, or class. Because they are the principal means of socialization outside of school, they are teaching all that view such entertainment that profanity is the norm. This is lamentable; they should be taking the lead in improving our culture, not the bastardization of it.

Entertainment media is awash in profanity, which many use as justification for their use of vulgarity. Of course, media types defend their choice of language as a mere reflection of the real world. This is a circular argument. Which is right, those who justify foul language because it is what they hear in the movies, on cable networks and while listening to music, or the media moguls who argue that they are saying what everyone else is saying. I would argue that if media did not use profanity to the extent they do, less profanity would be used by everyone. Even if that were not true, is it always the media's job to reflect reality? If I want reality, I'm not going to pay money to see a movie; I will just attend a sporting event where adults are playing. The media's insistence on including profanity is excuse enough for me to avoid such entertainment. I routinely refuse to patronize movies that have excessive profanity.

The net result is speech communication is replete with language that is pointless. Because so many profane to emphasize their arguments and demands, the net result is that the emphasis no longer exists because the speech type is so common. This leads many to try to find words more

301

objectionable to those in current use, but to no avail because they can't find words that are worse than what is in current use. Alternatively, they repeat the same word over and over, thinking that will get the attention they deserve. I would argue that it does; they get the attention they deserve, but it is not the attention they sought. In any case, most profane language has the same effect in an argument as normal speech, simply because it has lost the emphatic power if had before it became so common. In other words, we are demeaning the sacred and emphasizing the vulgar to no real practical benefit at the expense of civil and uplifting speech.

Communication is at best tenuous. What we hear others say is filtered through our cultural lens, and the person listening filters what we say through their own lens. We hear what we want or expect to hear, which may not be what the speaker intended. Profanity complicates our ability to communicate effectively. Profane speech has become ineffective as a communicative tool because it is so common that the words have lost much of their real meaning. Profanity generally replaces much more precise language with uncertain terms.

Children are picking up on profanity because adults can't control their language. Even worse, some parents, convinced that profanity is just another means of acceptable expression, condone or even encourage the use of profanity by their children. We used to wash children's mouth out with soap when they profaned, now we laugh and cheer them on as toddlers, then wonder why they use language unsuitable for polite society at a young age. This effectively handicaps the child for life if he or she cannot learn to control their language later. George Bernard Shaw makes a valid point in Pygmalion that language skills define the culture, class, and communicative ability of the speaker. An unthinking profane speaker will remove many opportunities for him or herself to obtain a responsible or professional position.

In addition, profanity is likely the source of other problems. Language is the cue that children use to evaluate the choices they are required to make. It seems the constant emphasis on the profane may be having an effect as children are sexualized at ever younger ages. For instance, we read of 5th and 6th grade students having sex in their classrooms. This does not account for the children who engage in sex in a private setting. These are just kids who are performing sex in public. We are shocked! Shocked! that children would do this, but are oblivious to the effect that our degraded speech has on children's behavior.

Further, profanity affects our attitudes about culture, including gender relationships. We are teaching young women that they are bitches and "ho's", and (surprise!) many are believing it. If we are constantly referring to sex or feces (even when it is totally irrelevant to the conversation) we should not be surprised when everyone seems obsessed with sex and feces.

Some will argue there is no proven link between language and destructive behaviors. So what? The fact is that we are what we think. If we create a cultural climate that emphasizes sex and feces, guess what? Our children will think about sex and feces, not exactly healthy subject matter for children. We are handicapping our children as to their ability to function in society. Girls who think of themselves as sexual objects will never see their full worth as humans, friends, mothers, and functional members of the workplace. Boys who see girls as sexual objects will be forever handicapped in their ability to form meaningful relationships with women. They can also develop attitudes and habits that will put them in jail for undesirable sexual contact later in life.

While on the subject of our obsession with fecal material, I am truly confused about the intent of this emphasis. I do not understand why so many people are fixated on material that is something that very few want to think about. The four letter word describing fecal material is used by so many so often that whole conversations are polluted with these references. I am amazed that anyone would want to be constantly calling this material to their own and others attention. Nevertheless, many do. Occasionally I have asked those who cannot form a sentence without this word what it is about the material that they are so enamored of. Invariably I get an apology with a response that the term is used without thinking. This is unfortunate, both for the individual who is verbally incapable of functioning in polite society, and for our society that is polluted by such thoughtless actions.

Then there are those who deliberately profane with the intent of offending everyone they can. They even go to court to defend their right to use this language, as if this is one of the inalienable rights that the creator has endowed us with. Is it just me, or is the contempt for that which is sacred seem incongruent with the rights intended to be given us by He who is most sacred?

Some are not satisfied with polluting only the speech communications they have with others; they also seek to offend everyone who sees them with profanity printed on their clothing. These people are tasteless; indeed, they are completely devoid of class. Such individuals are dysfunctional in almost all social settings. They defend the indefensible; indeed, they revel in their defense of the indefensible. I wonder what their mothers think of their behavior?

In defense of the use of some words that have historically been considered profane, I would argue that not all profanity is equally offensive. Indeed, some historically profane words do not seem to be. The image some words bring to mind does not justify calling the word profane. Profane words should be those which demean that which should be sacred or special or those that are vulgar. Two words in particular call attention to a state of eternal punishment and the other the theological place of eternal punishment. Perhaps I have been conditioned to hearing the words "damn" and "hell", but try as I might, I don't see what is offensive about these words given their meanings. Indeed, it may be beneficial for everyone to think about the meaning of these words more often. Of course, the use of these words in directed anger toward another can be offensive. However, the use of any word directed in anger can be offensive, so that should not be a defining characteristic of profane speech.

To summarize, the pollution of language leads to the decline of communication skills and quality of discourse. This is accomplished without accomplishing the stated intent of the profaner, as profanity has become so common that the intended shock value is not there. Essentially, we have profaned our language for nothing.

While I am griping about the use of profanity, another related subject is our propensity to change the meaning of perfectly useful words into something debasing or profane. It seems that we are so enamored of all things sexual that we seek to make as many words as possible mean the same thing. This results in confused discourse, a lot of snickering at those unfamiliar with recently redefined words, and a reduction in our ability to communicate along with many more words than are needed to describe anatomy and reproductive processes. Honestly, how many words do we need to describe the female breast? If we continue along this course, in a few centuries our entire spoken language will be reduced to five or six sexual or anatomical meanings.

Individuals can contribute to an improvement in the quality of speech by working to revise bad habits. They can also gently and politely encourage others to do the same. In a business or most social settings, a simple, polite, "Please will you not use profanity?" normally gets an embarrassed apology with a promise to refrain. Most people are properly mortified when attention is brought to their use of profanity. Of course, there are those devoid of class that will react adversely to such a request, in which case not much can be done other than to avoid contact with that individual when possible, not because of their use of profanity but because their tasteless and belligerent attitude demonstrates that they should be shunned.

Some will think that I am advocating in favor or laws restricting the freedom of individuals to profane. Such is not the case, although profanity in connection with other behavior certainly may justify a disorderly conduct citation. I believe that individuals have the right to profane; however, that does not mean that it is socially acceptable to use socially unacceptable language. This is another example of a right that should wither on the vine for lack of use.

I also believe that the uncontrolled use of profanity demonstrates a lack of emotional control and perhaps even and indication of decreased intelligence of the individual. I heard long ago a wise man say "Profanity is the sign of a feeble mind struggling to express itself," and I believe the saying is as true today as it was when I first heard it.

My biggest concern is that we may be replacing the language of Shakespeare and Austen with the speech of Ludacris. As is true of any other tool available to humans, language is a tool that can be used for constructive or destructive ends. Think of the intricate melodies and lyrics of Paul Simon, Enya, or any number of poets and composers that are intertwined to create something truly beautiful, and compare that with the angry rantings of musicians and rappers whose music is distinguished only by volume, a heavy beat, and offensive drivel, most often endlessly whining about something like their inability to get satisfaction (as if anyone cares). Books, music, movies, and any other media type can be debasing or inspiring. As with anything else, we, through market forces and public opinion, will determine which forms of speech will be rewarded. Those that reward artists and writers whose signature accomplishment is debasing, demeaning, and profane should not be surprised if such language, music, and art becomes the norm.

Section 4

Personal Responsibility

Chapter 32

"The Devil Made Me Do It"

It seems like for the past four decades I have seen a constant stream of excuses, some old and some new, given to minimize accountability for personal behavior and to attempt to assign guilt for destructive behavior on something other than the individual who commits the behavior. All of the excuses are different variations on the same theme. Let us count the lame arguments we have devised in attempting to ensure we live guilt free lives, which are as follows:

- The devil made me do it
- Fate (predestination) controls what I do so I have no choice
- Society (culture) made me do it
- The environment made me do it
- The actions of others made me do it
- Genetics made me do it

The devil made me do it

The title of the chapter is the perhaps the oldest excuse around. Given the widespread belief of many major religions that a malevolent being entices people to do evil, some have concluded that the responsibility for destructive personal decisions lies with the "devil", rather than the person who makes the choices. The logic is because the devil tempts them to make decisions destructive for them or others, making the bad choice that the temptation leads to is inevitable. Therefore, the negative consequences of the decisions are conveniently assigned to the devil, and the perpetrator of the behavior ostensibly goes merrily on his way toward his next destructive decision, attempting again to avoid personal responsibility for that poor decision also.

Of course, those who do not believe in such a being are not seduced by this particular excuse. Those who do believe in the Devil and blame him for destructive decisions fail to grasp the fundamental rationale for the existence of this being. Those that believe in such a supernatural malevolent being typically believe in God. If so, they typically believe that God has a purpose for humans, and has established standards of behavior for them. The devil acts as the instrument to test conformance to the behavioral standard set by God, that is he attempts to lead humans away from God by persuading us to act against the standards set by God. In this theological construct, the only thing that makes sense is that we have the choice of following the persuasions of the devil or not. If the choices we make are not our own, certainly we would not be responsible for them; however, if that is so the theological rationale for the premise of temptation is destroyed. It makes no sense for God to establish standards if He knows that we have no control over the decisions we make. Therefore, commandments, such as the ten secularists love to denigrate, would be an exercise in futility.

Fate (predestination) controls what I do so I have no choice

Next, we have the theological doctrine of predestination, or the belief that we are fated to do what we do and the result will be the same regardless of the choices we make. That is, everything we do in life has been predetermined and that nothing we do or say will affect the predetermined outcome. In other words, humans do not have free will, the decisions they make are not their own. Many use this as an excuse to argue they are just puppets on the end of a string being forced to act according to a set script.

This doctrine also ignores the rationale for commandments. If we have no choice in the ultimate outcome of our lives, what rational reason can there be for God to set standards for us to follow? With this belief, we can also proceed merrily along whatever path we perceive has been chosen for us without thought to the decisions we make or the consequences of our perceived predetermined actions. Some may argue that God, being omniscient, knows what we will do before we do it. That does not make a case for predestination; just because I know what my children will do in a given circumstance does not mean that my children do not make their own decisions.

Society (culture) made me do it

The next is a favorite of secularists who do not believe in God or the Devil. Simply replace "the Devil" with "society" and you have one of the latest means of professional guilt avoidance. This theory holds that our behavior is the result of the culture in which we live, and therefore any adverse choices we make are the fault of our culture. Secularists who propound this principle get a twofer. They not only excuse individual behavior but they also get to denigrate our culture and traditions at the same time.

310

There is a never-ending stream of excuses for all manner of unlawful and repugnant behavior. Child molesters are victims because they were molested as children. Murderers are victims because they were abused as children. People who live in a ghetto are driven by circumstances to a life of crime. The list goes on and on, a never-ending roll of societal problems (remarkably enough perpetuated by individuals within a largely law abiding society) that seems determined to handicap anyone unfortunate enough to be born.

What the proponents of this idea ignore is that regardless of common cultural conditions, there is a wide variety of results. The fact is that not all who have been abused end up as murderers, almost all who have been molested do not molest others, and that many who are raised in ghettos are able to lift themselves above the squalid conditions that surround them. This is not necessarily a relocation from their physical environment, but taking affirmative steps to improve their lives and the lives of others within that community. It is clear that individual reactions to problems do not result in a pattern that can be used to justify the argument that culture is a behavioral determinant.

The environment made me do it

The next excuse is a variant of environmental determinism. This belief holds that the physical environment we live in determines our actions. Environment determinism is an outdated theory which proposed that the physical environment determined cultural characteristics. For example, the theory held that people who lived in tropical climates who easily obtained food year around were lazy and less intelligent than those who lived in temperate climates and whose survival depended upon planning, work, and wit to survive extended periods of limited food supplies. While the theory has been thoroughly discredited, there are still some who blame the environment for the decisions they make. An example would be someone claiming that the summer heat was unbearable so they just had to rob the beer cooler at the neighborhood convenience store. This excuse can be debunked as easily as the original deterministic theory has been. If summer heat inevitably resulted in robbery, why is it that only a very limited number of knuckleheads are driven to steal the liquor? If this were valid, every summer we would have millions of people who were driven to steal because of the heat running down the street with contraband booze tucked under their arms. I don't think so.

311

Personal Responsibility

The actions of others made me do it

One more excuse is "The actions of others made me do it". We like to blame others for our mistakes, and this logic is exceptionally irrational. People try to justify the most outrageous acts by shifting the blame to someone else, who is very often the victim of the offensive behavior. A rapist will blame the victim because she had the temerity to wear suggestive clothing. The murderer will blame the deceased because he "gave me lip" or 'did not do what I told him to do". The abuser will decry the actions of the abused and insist, "I was doing it for his own good", or even worse, "she deserved it". In some cases, people leap to completely illogical conclusions and blame someone for an act that he or she had nothing to do with it. Sort of like the greens blaming President Bush for not adopting the Kyoto Treaty when the Senate voted overwhelmingly against it (95-0 which included all Democrats who voted) three years before President Bush was elected. Oops, that was slightly off-topic. Let me try that again. Sort of like the father of a beheaded victim of Abu Musab al-Zarqawi' blaming President Bush because his son voluntarily went to Iraq and ignored security recommendations given to him by coalition forces. (Hmmm, is there a pattern here?) In any case, we have just another excuse to shift personal blame away from the perpetrator of ghastly behavior. The good news is that nobody is falling for this excuse (yet).

Genetics made me do it

Last is the favorite of the scientific community; "genetics made me do it". There has been a steady stream of news releases, each breathlessly announcing that shared genetic markers have been discovered within one abnormal group or another that is different from the norm. They argue that the shared genetic code is evidence that the behavioral characteristics of the group either determines a propensity for the behavioral differences of the group, or forces them to act in a way that differs from the norm. The underlying premise is that the genetic marker makes the behavior of the group inevitable, which therefore excuses the behavior. Alcoholism, murder, sexual deviancy, drug dependency, and homosexuality are only a few of the groups singled out for this treatment. It seems that no negative behavior is trivial enough to research and identify as one caused by genetic flaws. I recently heard a broadcast that announced that those who had a propensity for road rage had a distinguishing genetic code, identified as "intermittent explosive disorder", that ostensibly was responsible for their lack of emotional control. Again, with apologies to Dave Barry, I am not making this up.

Don't misinterpret the point I am trying to make. I do not doubt that many if not all of these genetic traits are real and that they lead to a propensity for specific behaviors (just as I am convinced that temptation, the environment, culture, and the idiotic acts of others contribute to the lousy decisions we all make). However, to say that the genetic trait results in an inevitable behavior on the part of all who share the trait is just as ridiculous as saying "the Devil made me do it". If this were true we could simply test everyone at birth, or even before birth for that matter, and eliminate those who had markers that made them unfit for society. What an Orwellian nightmare that would be. The simple fact is that not everyone who has the genetic marker for drug dependency abuses drugs, not everyone who has a propensity for sexual deviancy engages in child molestation or rape, and so on.

The common objective of each of these excuses is a desire to avoid personal responsibility for individual actions. The logic is that if the responsibility for deviant behavior is shifted to someone or something else, the individual is off the hook. He can claim before a criminal court that he is not responsible for the actions that resulted in the destruction of property or life. He can make the same argument before civil court examining legal liability. He can rid himself of responsibility that he freely took upon himself at an earlier age such as maintaining a marriage and family. He can be free of guilt.

The reality is something else. For most people, the attempt is an exercise in futility, because they carry the guilt anyway, most frequently vociferously denying it while afflicting others with their displaced anger, depression, and anxiety. In addition, most attempts to avoid legal and personal responsibility using these defenses have resulted in failure. That is the good news. Most people still expect individual conformance to societal standards and do not buy these excuses. The bad news is there is such a steady drumbeat of propaganda pushing this nonsense that some people are beginning to believe the lies. Remember Goebbels? That leads to two groups that perpetuate the lie; those who think they can get away with the behavior and those who facilitate perpetrators getting away with the behavior. Most unfortunately, all too many judges subscribe to and make judgments based upon these ideas.

Remarkably enough, almost everyone in the United States has similar environmental, social, theological and genetic environments. Everyone on earth must learn to deal with adversity and learn self-discipline in its face. I can tell you that I have been tempted to do bodily harm to people that have offended me. If I gave in to all the genetic propensities that I have, I would have no wife, family, friends, or job (oh, wait; I'm retired so I guess I don't have a job). Just because I have instincts (probably genetically inherited) that tempt me to make love with every beautiful women on the face of the earth does not mean that I have license to do so (yes, I am a normal red-blooded human being). More important, if I did I would be acting against my own interests at every conceivable level. If I want to be happy, I must do that which will make me happy, and acting to please passion, indulge impulses, or accommodate anger will have the opposite effect. Everyone else has this simple choice to make, which is to choose to act in his or her and those who they love best interests, or to give in to and seek to excuse behavior that will inevitably lead to unhappiness for all concerned.

The most important thing that each of us must learn in life in order to function in society is the exercise of the requisite self-discipline needed to control ourselves. Without self-discipline, a person is at the whim of his or her environment, emotion, and heredity, living a reactionary life in which any or all of these three factors dictate their behavior and whether or not they will be happy. Each of us must recognize that very often we must "just say no!" to not just external influences that will control our lives if we let them, but also internal impulses that we recognize will harm us and those we care most about. The only way to be free of the unhappiness that giving in to the external and internal destructive forces that we must deal with on a day to day basis is to take control of our emotions and determine that we will direct our response to these forces instead of reacting to them.

Those who do not learn this fundamental lesson in life are doomed to unhappiness. Even worse, they often take their family and community down with them. The inability of an individual to learn self-control is a lose-lose proposition. The individual is forever unhappy because he or she is irresponsible, cannot be trusted, and cannot find happiness in his or her self-destructive behavior. His or her family bears the brunt of both the consequences of the behavior and the depression, anxiety, and anger (often resulting in violence) that the individual goes through at their expense. The community is left to support the emotionally incapacitated person, and often clean up the aftermath of the destructive effects the individual leaves in his or her wake.

It is critically important that our society not condone, encourage, or accept destructive behavior. We must ensure that all persons are held accountable for their actions, regardless of whatever excuse they devise to shift the responsibility for their behavior onto someone or something else. If a person repeatedly demonstrates an inability to control their actions, society must institutionalize them to ensure they cannot victimize innocent people.

Child abuse is a significant problem in our society. Why is that? One contributing factor could be because the parents have not been able to control themselves when confronted with the adverse behavior of their children. Another is that many parents have decided to be their children's friend, and therefore have not taught them self-discipline, which then leads to abusive behavior when either or both parties cannot control themselves. Disciplining children is a pay me now or pay me later situation; the cost of late payment is far beyond the work required to teach discipline early in a child's development.

Our society functions because there is an expectation among its members that they will be accorded certain rights, the most fundamental of which are, as listed in the Declaration of Independence, life, liberty and the pursuit of happiness. Jefferson goes on to say, which I will paraphrase, that governments exist to secure these rights and that a government that does not should be replaced by one that will. If government cannot act to ensure the basic rights to life, liberty, and the pursuit of happiness for its citizens, what good is it? Obviously government has the obligation to ensure punishment is just; however, most important is the health and welfare of its citizens. If judges fail in their responsibility to enforce law, evenhandedly dispense justice, and to ensure those who violate others are incarcerated until they are no longer a threat, they will find that our social structure will begin to unravel as people seek justice and protection by other means.

Let us assume that the excuses enumerated above are real and that some or all of them affect our behavior. For individuals who must live with the consequences of their decisions, so what? Nothing changes the fact that everyone is expected to conform to the law. If the devil makes you kill someone in a cruel, callous, and calculated manner, you are still going to be executed (in most states that is). Even if you are predestined to assault children, society makes you rape women, the environment makes you deal drugs, your child's behavior forces you to physically or mentally abuse him or her, or genetics makes you lose control of your emotions such that you harm others, you are still going to pay the price, which is generally social ostracization and segregation from society, and can even mean forfeiting your life. In addition, even if someone is convinced that their behavior is not their own fault, it does not alter the destruction wrought by the action.

Personal Responsibility

Homes are still destroyed, lives are shattered, and trust is broken which can almost never be fully restored, no matter who is at fault. Blaming someone or something else will not accomplish anything. Eventually we all have to suck it up, deal with, and overcome the factors that we know negatively influence our behavior.

Another outcome from this is the propensity to use drugs to control behavior. First, let me say that there are many drugs that perform wonders for many disorders. However, we tend to rely on them too much for our own good. Some conditions are treated with drugs that need not, and indeed the drug therapy can be worse than the condition that was to be relieved. A good example of this is my oldest child, who was diagnosed with attention deficit disorder many years ago. In retrospect, I recognize the symptoms in myself, and am happy that I was born before the therapy became common. In any case, a drug was prescribed which we dutifully administered. The drug had the desired effect for the school, but not for our son. Soon he was begging us to stop the treatment while describing what it was doing to him. We stopped the treatment immediately. While raising him and his brothers who had the same condition (remember genetics?) was difficult, I believe our children are much better able to function as adults without a drug dependency because they had to learn to deal with this genetic disorder with personal discipline rather than a dependence on a drug. Of course, that does not mean that we should ignore the advice of expert medical professionals. However, drugs can be abused even in a clinical setting.

On a societal level, we must discourage destructive behavior if we do not want to live with its consequences. The best means is to make the behavior illegal, and establish swift, sure, and consequential punishment for offenders. If states like Vermont refuse to punish child molesters, the residents of that state can be assured that child molesters will take note and act with impunity on their impulses because they will understand that they will not suffer significant punishment even if they are caught and convicted. Attempts to rehabilitate offenders must be balanced in favor of protecting the population from predators.

If science continues to make these breathless announcements that lead people to believe genetics are a determinant of behavior because they do not put their discovery into context, we will see further erosion of the belief in personal responsibility. If sociologists and psychologists pander to the instincts of their patients, the same will occur, as well as clergy excusing behavior in spite of theological constraints. It is in our collective interest to encourage constructive behavior rather than excuse destructive behavior.

316

Does this mean that people will be stigmatized and feel bad? Well, yes it will. At least we hope so. That is the first step toward changing bad behavior, recognizing and regretting it. Those that pretend this process is destructive forget that they use the same tactics; that is they stigmatize and make people feel bad for doing or saying something that stigmatizes and makes anyone feel bad. Feeling bad is a part of life, as with other things our only choice is what we feel bad about.

We have two simple choices. We can encourage the evasion of responsibility and thereby continue to give license to those who would victimize others. Alternatively, we can assert clearly that regardless of what influences our behavior; we will enforce standards and protect innocents from harm to the extent possible. If we do not, people will use other means to protect themselves, including resorting to private justice and anarchy.

Blaming everyone and everything else for our problems does not make us happy. Learning self-discipline and controlling destructive instincts will be the most important thing we will ever do to advance our own interests, both on an individual and a societal level. Learning to control emotions is critical to functioning in society and being at peace and happiness with oneself and others. The way to avoid guilt is to make wise decisions that lead to guilt free lives. While that is certainly easier to say than it is to do, it is still a fact.

Chapter 33

"Accept Me for Who I Am, Don't Try to Change Me"

Let me see if I understand this argument correctly. A person (a male for the purpose of discussion) who has changed every day since the day he was born, who must change in order to survive in the world we live, who voluntarily changes at the whim of the latest fashion or trend, and who will continue to change until the day he dies whether he wants to change or not, does not want the person who he ostensibly cares about the most and upon whom he depends for support, love, empathy and acceptance to try to effect change in his life? Is it just me, or does this seem just a bit ridiculous to others also?

Change in life is inevitable. We cannot walk out of our door in the morning without changing in at least some small insignificant way. In some cases, these changes do not result in significant long-term impacts to our lives; however, in some cases incremental steps result in significant effects. Everyone jokes about death and taxes being the two sure things in life; well I would add change to that list. Change is guaranteed for everyone.

Some changes are voluntary. People change according to the latest fashion or fad, spending outrageous prices for overpriced products simply because of a label. In other cases, people engage in self-mutilation because everyone else is also engaged in self-mutilation. Most people go to school for over a decade for the sole purpose of changing their lives for the better, and learning alone represents change.

Other change occurs whether we like it or not. We are forced to change by changing societal and economic circumstances. Most people entering the workplace today will have an average of five career paths through their lives. We are now constantly encouraged to think outside the box, or in other words try to find different ways to approach problems and their solutions. This is direct pressure to change. In our personal lives, we adjust to changing circumstances or we find ourselves socially ostracized if we persist in expressing ideas that the majority in our culture deem offensive. We literally change and adjust to changing circumstances or we become dysfunctional or die.

If change is inevitable, and change for the sake of change is common, it is reasonable to conclude that it is not such a big deal. We fear it of course, as we fear all unknown things, but most of us muddle through the sea of changes in our lives with comparatively little trauma. The issue then is not whether we change, but how we change, and what the result of change is.

It also is reasonable to assume that change is as common in the lives of friends and family as it is in our own. Change is common: everyone evolves to some extent, and this evolution is to be expected. Indeed, one who does not change is trapped in the past. Accordingly, it is also reasonable that we seek changes in others, especially those whom we are closest to and whose happiness we seek.

Why do we seek change in others? In some cases, we want to be in the company of those whose behavior is similar to ours because their behavior supports and validates our behavior, and helps us maintain constructive behaviors. On the other hand, if a person is engaging in destructive or self-destructive behavior, most people will encourage change beneficial to the person engaged in the behavior. In other instances, change is encouraged for what seems to be trivial reasons. Most significant are differences in beliefs. In all cases, one person has determined that something about the other bothers or frightens them, and seeks change to eliminate the source of conflict.

Because we know that we must change, why should we resist changes encouraged by those we love or who love us? Changing for the sake of change is certainly the norm. If we are engaged in self-defeating or destructive behaviors that can result in nothing other than pain, suffering, destruction, or eventual death for ourselves or others, why would we resist the changes encouraged by those who can see the end result of the behaviors? Even more important, why would we insist that the person who loves us accept and tolerate the behaviors, and therefore the ultimate consequences of them. Moreover, what person would consent to letting those engaged in the destructive behaviors do so without trying to change the inevitable outcome? The person who wants to be accepted for the person they are as they throw their life away is either deluded or has become so addicted to behaviors or substances that he feels he cannot escape and so attacks anyone who makes him feel worse because of his dependency.

Some people misinterpret the impulse to satisfy their base desires and instincts as "being true to themselves". By making this assumption and acting on it, they assure anyone who depends upon them for emotional stability and support that they cannot be trusted. When the betrayed party lashes out at them for their selfish and irresponsible behavior, the perpetrator frequently falls back on the canard that they are who they are and that the betrayed party is being unreasonable in their demand for responsible behavior. In fact, they are simply letting passion rule their actions instead of exercising the discipline needed in their lives to ensure happiness for themselves and loved ones.

There are legitimate reasons for resisting some changes that others want a person to make. Those whose behavior is self-destructive often seek the companionship of those who engage in similar behavior. I believe the adage is "misery loves company". They will attempt to get those who do not behave the way they do to copy them, which they think will make their own behavior less offensive. They reason that if everyone is doing it, the behavior must not be so bad, and even if everyone is not doing it, at least they surround themselves with those who are doing it so nobody who is close to them will make them uncomfortable while they blindly pursue misery for themselves and the people with whom they associate. Anyone pressured by this type of person to change should end the relationship if possible. Such a person is not acting in the interest of his supposed friends.

In most cases, relationships outside of family sort themselves out well; eventually either one or the other will change or the relationship will disintegrate. Most people are uncomfortable in the company of those whose behavior is offensive to them and will avoid contact with them. Family is a different matter. We cannot choose blood relatives, and no matter how offensive the behavior of a relative, the instinct is to try to help the person overcome debilitating behavior. Severing the relationship is excruciatingly painful, and is generally done as a last resort. In some cases, even that is not a viable option.

In any case, whenever a person engages in destructive behavior, it should not come as a surprise to that person that there would be pressure to change. Encouragement by friends, family and loved ones to change the direction of their life should not be seen as an attempt to turn them into a mindless robot that needs others to think for him. If the person pleads he is a natural born drug addict and that we should let him live his life in peace (as if that were possible) he or she is delusional. Society does not buy that lame excuse; it will punish offensive behavior whether or not the person thinks he is genetically obligated to be an addict. We should give no indication that such an argument is acceptable in our personal relationships either.

Not all behavioral differences are equal (hmmm...does this phrase sound familiar?). In any relationship, each party will do things that, while not significant to the overall direction the person is taking in life, are annoying to the other party for various reasons. Of course, trying to fit two or more people together and not have resulting conflict is impossible. People get annoyed beyond reason because a partner will squeeze the toothpaste from the middle instead of the end (I know, I know, there are good reasons for squeezing the tube from the end, but that is not the point). In these instances, while changing a behavior may seem unnecessary to the person who thinks the offensive behavior is so trivial that it is unreasonable to complain about it, it obviously is to the person who is annoyed. At that point, the parties have some simple choices. The offending party can stop the behavior for the sake of harmony in the relationship, the party offended can bite his or her tongue and stop complaining for the sake of harmony in the relationship, or they can turn a trivial matter into something that can cause long-term damage to or the demise of the relationship.

Some of the more difficult sources of conflict in relationships are those related to belief. Core differences in religion and philosophy are exceptionally difficult to reconcile, and lead to long-term frustration and pain in close relationships. This is perhaps the one instance where the expression may be justified. If those who love the individual are truly concerned about his welfare, and the individual has sincere heart felt beliefs that dramatically differ from friends and family, they should indeed accept him as he is and not try to force him to act against his beliefs so long as the belief does not mean engaging in illegal or destructive activity.

In most instances, people should not heed the plea of a loved one to be left alone to his destructive inclinations. If we have destructive or self-defeating behaviors, we should be encouraged to change. Good habits should be encouraged, and not held to be morally equivalent to bad habits. The people who love us the most are most concerned with our welfare, so advice from them is in most cases the best barometer of what is best for us. Indeed, those who use this lame excuse for their bad behavior most need to change.

Nobody is perfect, but that does not mean that we should not try to live up to ideals. To resign ourselves to the lowest common denominator is to resign ourselves to unhappiness, crime, death, destruction, disease, and self-loathing. Even though everyone will fall short of an ideal, it is always better to work toward the ideal, even as we suffer relapses along the way.

Chapter 34

"Right to Privacy"

You will search in vain for a clause in the Constitution that grants a right to privacy. There are none. While some of the amendments imply some privacy rights, there is nothing explicit. The rights in question enumerate the specific rights of individuals, ensuring that certain rights are guaranteed. These amendments do not guarantee a degree of privacy that would allow private illegal conduct. Even so, there has been a recent campaign to interpret into the motives of the framers intent to create such a right. I am sympathetic to the inclination to protect privacy; however, this is a path that can easily lead to an extreme that is as destructive as a total disregard for privacy on the part of the government.

As we live our lives and make our way in the world we must continually make decisions about our conduct. This includes conduct while in public view and conduct when not. Generally, we like to think that our private conduct is just that. We would be embarrassed if such conduct were made public, even if we know that every other human being on the planet has similar if not identical behaviors. Generally, such conduct is accepted as being appropriately private, for example few people or government entities are concerned about how we practice basic hygiene and even if they do it is none of their business. We engage in intimate relations in private, also generally with the expectation of privacy. These private activities on one end of a scale of behavior are accepted by our society as normal.

Other societies have differing behavioral standards. In some cultures, those standards are dramatically different. If we travel, we become subject to those standards, and are expected to conform (When in Rome...). If others come to this country, they are expected to conform to our standards, and we do not accept ignorance of our laws as an excuse for non-conformity.

Without restrictions on behavior, we would have anarchy. Therefore, we legislate against all manner of destructive behavior. Much behavior is acceptable, or at least tolerated, whether in public or private. In some cases, we proscribe certain behaviors in public that are perfectly acceptable in private, such as engaging in intimate relations. However, there are some behaviors that are prohibited in all cases, whether the behavior is performed in public or private.

Who can proscribe behavior? That is simple. In a democratic society, the majority, as established by dully-elected representatives, determines the rules regulating behavior. That ability extends to private behavior, so long as it is determined to be destructive. By the way, actions between consenting persons can be destructive to a point where legislative proscription is appropriate. Many people have a gut reaction against that notion until they consider the implications of the opposite policy.

Do we really want government to dictate what we are allowed to do in the privacy of our bedroom? Well, that would be a yes and a no. It depends on the behavior. For instance, murder is not tolerated in our society. That includes murder in the privacy of the bedroom or home. One cannot claim that a murder committed in the privacy of the home is a legally protected activity. At least such a claim would be met with extreme skepticism by law enforcement. I would hope that someone would not be allowed to murder me just because I was invited to their home and I accepted the invitation because I thought the person might be entertaining.

On the other hand, I would also hope that government would not prohibit me from having intimate relations with my spouse if I am engaging in the conduct privately. This is a constructive, nurturing activity that results in significant satisfaction for both parties. Remarkably enough, the majority feels the same way. If any legislator attempted to prohibit couples from engaging in intimate relationships, I suspect that legislator would not be re-elected. That is how the system is supposed to work; that is, the legislature adopts laws in accordance with the will of the majority. The behaviors that I have described are prohibited and permitted as I hoped. The exception is for the specific rights enumerated within the Constitution, again none of which protects private behavior generally. The issue then is not whether we have a right to privacy, but rather what behavior will be permitted as acceptable, be it public or private.

Unfortunately for those who maintain government has no business trying to control private conduct in the bedroom, it is clear that there is a public interest in restricting certain private behavior, especially if others are in the bedroom. As previously observed, very few people will say that murdering someone in the privacy of the bedroom is acceptable. Most people accept that an intimate relationship between consenting parties is acceptable; however, what if one of the consenting parties is a male adult and the other is a small child? When presented with this scenario there is almost universal agreement that this is unacceptable conduct (Of course

323

NAMBLA would disagree). What if the consenting parties have agreed to exchange remuneration for the intimate contact? In spite of persistent attempts by some to decriminalize prostitution, the majority in almost all states yet believes that prostitution is unacceptable and continues to prohibit the practice. What if the intimate conduct between two adults who do not exchange money results in one of the parties contracting a sexually transmitted disease? The party who contracts the disease will be substantially impacted, and so will society in general because of the cost of treatment and attempts to prevent the spread of infection. This holds true for a couple that produces an unwanted child. Both parties are substantially impacted, and society is also impacted if both parties do not cooperate to raise the child in a nurturing environment. Private behavior has a public impact, and it is in the public interest to minimize that impact when reasonable.

Behavioral proscriptions can and do change over time with the changing attitudes of the majority. While some of these changes I believe are not generally in the public interest, they are justified so long as the change results from a conscious decision by the legislature, who then must justify their actions to the electorate. What is not justified is when un-elected judges who invent rights because of political pressure from a vocal minority arbitrarily change the rules over the will of the majority.

The system can work because the majority (and the legislature) generally has the good sense to permit and proscribe behavior in a way that is moderate, logical, and makes good common sense. Recent history has shown that when un-elected dictatorial judges interfere with that process, social upheaval is the norm.

Chapter 35

"Do Not Judge"

In the New Testament, Jesus Christ is quoted as saying "Judge not, that ye be not judged." Many have used this scripture to argue that we, as individuals and a society, should avoid making judgments about the actions of others. This is impossible.

Just as we cannot get out of our bed in the morning without facing changes in our lives, we also must make judgments. Most of the judgments we must make, also called decisions, are simple and programmed. We decide what to wear, what to eat for breakfast, and whether or not to avoid the pain of exercising. These are simple decisions, or judgments, that we make in response to our expectations for the day. For instance, if we have an important professional meeting, we will not wear casual attire. Through the course of the day, we are literally forced to make hundreds of decisions. If we do not make these decisions we will be unable to function in our jobs, social settings, or personal lives. Any person who does not make decisions, or judgments, is socially and professionally paralyzed.

While most decisions are simple and relatively uncomplicated, often we must make difficult, weighty, or complex decisions that can literally change the course of our lives. The decision we make can lead to personal or professional happiness or misery. It is important to make a decision that will lead to happiness, or at least result in being happier than what would result from the alternative course.

Many of the more weighty decisions we face are those that involve other people and their affect on us and those we care most about. Some people may want us to take a course that may be in their best interest, or what they perceive to be in their best interest, but which may not be in our best interest. In those situations, we must make whatever decision, or judgment, we feel will be in the best interest of whoever's welfare we value most. To make such a judgment, we must weigh the costs and benefits of the alternatives, also taking into consideration the motives of those lobbying on behalf of one alternative or another.

There are many who seek to influence what we do. Advertisers and manufacturers want us to buy their products, and do not particularly care if we need them. Religious organizations seek our support and argue that our eternal happiness will be adversely affected if we make incorrect decisions. Politicians seek our support for their political ambitions and goals, which in some cases are in conflict with our personal goals and philosophies. Sadly enough, there are even those who will seek to take advantage of us, or even destroy us in a criminal manner. With each request or challenge, we are faced with making judgments that can affect our and our family's happiness and well-being, including our temporal, spiritual, and eternal welfare.

Those that argue that we should not judge are arguing that we should not make the decisions that are most important to ensuring our happiness. In some cases, they argue that our decisions have no practical effect, and that whatever decision we make the outcome will essentially be the same. This is profoundly illogical, different decisions lead to different results, often dramatically different.

Some are weighed down by the gravity of the decision that must be made, or in some situations know what judgment is best but cannot make it because of the short-term personal pain that will result. This is particularly true when we must make a decision that is in our own personal interest, but which means that someone else's predicament is made worse. Such a decision is even more painful if that someone else is a close friend or relative. Other decisions that are difficult to make are those that conflict with previous decisions that have resulted in personal or familial unhappiness. Undoing the effects of previous decisions is extremely difficult, especially when those decisions have resulted in addictions that must be overcome.

Some are so overwhelmed by the importance of the judgment they must make that they allow themselves to be paralyzed with respect to the decision. In some cases, they perceive that the lack of a decision may be in their interest, or that if they ignore the decision they must make that it will go away. The lack of a decision is a decision, which inevitably leads to a result, generally a result that will not make us happy. As I pointed out in Chapter 22, avoiding conflict does not resolve conflict, and the same principle is true for avoiding decisions. The lack of a decision can and most often does have the same effect of an unwise decision that leads to unhappiness.

Some insist that we should not play God. For those of us who believe that the Bible represents God's instruction to man, the assumption is that judgment is reserved to God, and that any judgment we make conflicts with and usurps His authority. This assumption is flawed; if one believes in the Bible as scripture it follows that he or she will also believe that God gave us

326

knowledge of good and evil and expects us to choose, that is judge, between the two. To a degree, every decision we make has that effect, and is critical to our ability to conform to His direction. Our need to make the judgments we need to make to bring us into conformance with God's will is not in conflict with His role as the ultimate Judge.

But how do we reconcile what seems to be instruction from He who many accept as God? What does the quote of Jesus in Matthew 7:1 mean? If we look at the next verse, it is clear. "For with what judgment ye judge, ye shall be judged" implies that making judgments is acceptable; what is unacceptable is making unfounded or unrighteous judgments. We must be careful about snap judgments made without all or even any facts. Things are frequently not as they seem. That said, once we have the facts about a problem that must dealt with in some manner, we must make a judgment for ourselves as to how we will react.

Those who insist that we not judge them are often people most in need of judgment, including judgment by us. Those engaged in self-destructive behavior often want friends and family to support his or her actions, and insist that we not judge them to accomplish this. If we avoid making a judgment and therefore do not warn the individual of the consequences of his or her actions, we will be complicit in the eventual fate of the individual. Indeed, we can be held legally liable for the destructive decisions of others if we do not make a judgment and act to stop or warn others of the destructive behavior. Under some circumstances we can be charged as accessories to crimes committed by others.

Some people will seek to drag others down with him or her as they self-destruct; if we avoid making judgments about their behavior and its potential affect on us we may wind up in as bad a condition as the person who is pleading with us to not judge. Worst of all are those who deliberately harm others and yet have the temerity to insist that they should not be judged. In every instance, we must make informed and rational judgments about the affect of the person's behavior on ourselves and those who we care about the most.

We are often faced with making judgments that will have profound influences on our lives. In some cases, these decisions mean making choices between competing philosophies and friendships that can make the difference between happiness and misery. Using scripture in an unjustified way to justify paralysis in our lives is not a rational approach to determining the value of competing philosophies and complex personal interactions.

Chapter 36

"You Always Think You are Right!"

Most of us have been in arguments or discussions where in the course of advocating for or against something we are hit with this accusation. The indictment is intended to shame us into immediately reversing our expressed opinion and agree with the person who is trying to convince us of the correctness of his position. I am not absolutely sure, but I kinda doubt that there has ever been an instance in which someone has immediately thrown up his or her hands and conceded that the charge was true.

This assertion is remarkably ridiculous when it is analyzed. Would anyone argue in favor of a position if they thought that position was wrong? Well duh! Of course not. It stands to reason that an individual would always think they are right! If they did not, they would not have made the argument in the first place.

Whenever someone throws this charge at me I immediately respond with "Of course I always think I'm right, do you think I argue in favor of things that I think are wrong? And do you think I should change what I think is right because you have a different opinion?" After all, only I can make the judgment as to what is right or wrong for myself. The only other alternative is to advocate or do what I think is wrong. The person who makes such a charge wants me to substitute their judgment as to what is right for my own. That is not going to happen. Unless they can persuade me otherwise, I will stick with what I think is right. This attitude holds for all those critical of my arguments throughout this book. If I am wrong in any of these chapters, show me where asserted fact or logic is flawed.

Of course, my beliefs are founded on what I have been taught as being right and what I have concluded is right based on my experience. I will concede that just because I think I am right does not mean that I am. I can be persuaded through logic and evidence of the inaccuracy of my belief, especially if the law shows me to be wrong. However, declaring that I am wrong just because I think I am right is not the way to persuade me to conduct an introspective examination of my belief. If someone thinks I am going to change my position just because he or she accuses me of always thinking I am right they will be disappointed in the result.

Throughout this book I have explained what I think is right. Although I may be wrong in these interpretations of facts and policy beliefs, if I am I don't think I'm alone. In any case, because my focus has consistently been to link the language and practices of our culture to the impact they have on our core beliefs, as expressed in the Declaration of Independence, I am confident that the use of these principles to counteract the negative impact of idiotic clichés will result in an improved cultural climate. More importantly, individuals and society will be closer to achieving an improved quality of life, a greater sense of the liberty in which we flourish, and will be closer to achieving happiness than we would otherwise be. And those so affected will be able to assist others in counteracting the effects of these clichés. And that is my most sincere wish for anyone reading this work. Thank you for putting up with my rants.

Index

Index

Index

334

www.ingramcontent.com/pod-product-compliance
Lightning Source LLC
Chambersburg PA
CBHW031234090426
42742CB00007B/191